Inherent Rights, the Written Constitution, and Popular Sovereignty

**Recent Titles in
Contributions in Legal Studies**

Judicial Entrepreneurship: The Role of the Judge in the Marketplace of Ideas
Wayne V. McIntosh and Cynthia L. Cates

Solving the Puzzle of Interest Group Litigation
Andrew Jay Koshner

Presidential Defiance of "Unconstitutional" Laws: Reviving the Royal
Prerogative
Christopher N. May

Promises on Prior Obligations at Common Law
Kevin M. Teeven

Litigating Federalism: The States Before the U.S. Supreme Court
Eric N. Waltenburg and Bill Swinford

Law and the Arts
Susan Tiefenbrun, editor

Contract Law and Morality
Henry Mather

The Appearance of Equality: Racial Gerrymandering, Redistricting,
and the Supreme Court
Christopher M. Burke

Religion, Law, and the Land
Brian Edward Brown

The Supreme Court's Retreat from Reconstruction: A Distortion of
Constitutional Jurisprudence
Frank J. Scaturro

Respecting State Courts: The Inevitability of Judicial Federalism
Michael E. Solimine and James L. Walker

Basic Principles of Property Law: A Comparative Legal and Economic
Introduction
Ugo Mattei

Inherent Rights, the Written Constitution, and Popular Sovereignty

The Founders' Understanding

THOMAS B. MCAFFEE

Contributions in Legal Studies, Number 95

GREENWOOD PRESS
Westport, Connecticut • London

Library of Congress Cataloging-in-Publication Data

McAffee, Thomas B., 1952–
    Inherent rights, the written constitution, and popular sovereignty : the founders'
understanding / Thomas B. McAffee.
        p.   cm.—(Contributions in legal studies, ISSN 0147–1074 ; no. 95)
    Includes bibliographical references and index.
    ISBN 0–313–31507–8 (alk. paper)
    1. Civil rights—United States.   2. Constitutional history—United States.
I. Title.   II. Series.
KF4749.M39   2000
342.73′085—dc21   00–021049

British Library Cataloguing in Publication Data is available.

Library of Congress Catalog Card Number: 00–021049
ISBN: 0–313–31507–8
ISSN: 0147–1074

First published in 2000

Greenwood Press, 88 Post Road West, Westport, CT 06881
An imprint of Greenwood Publishing Group, Inc.
www.greenwood.com

Printed in the United States of America

The paper used in this book complies with the
Permanent Paper Standard issued by the National
Information Standards Organization (Z39.48–1984).

10 9 8 7 6 5 4 3 2 1

The author and publisher gratefully acknowledge permission to reprint the following material:

Chapter 4 based on the article "The Federal System as Bill of Rights: Original Understandings, Modern
Misreadings," by Thomas B. McAffee. Reprinted with permission from Villanova Law Review. Volume
43, pp. 17–154 © Copyright 1998 by Villanova University.

To Lynda, who has accepted it all well.

Contents

1. The Modern Debate over Inherent Constitutional Rights:
   What Is at Stake?   1

2. State Constitutions in the Early American Republic: The
   Experiment with Republican Government   9

3. Constitutional Practice in the Confederation Period: The
   Search for Effective Limits on Legislative Power   45

4. The Decision at the Philadelphia Convention: The Federal
   System as Bill of Rights   83

5. The Ratification-Era Debate over the Omission of a Bill of
   Rights: The Constitution as Fundamental Positive Law   119

6. The Ninth Amendment and Modern Constitutional Theory   169

Bibliography   175

Index   185

I

The Modern Debate over
Inherent Constitutional Rights:
What Is at Stake?

This book confronts an important trend in thinking about our constitutional order. We have gotten into the habit of looking for constitutional rights that are difficult, if not impossible, to justify based on the text of the Constitution.[1] For some, the gap between enumerated and unenumerated rights simply does not exist; the difficulty is not in justifying looking beyond the text, but in recognizing that the distinction between enumerated and unenumerated rights makes no sense.[2] Another view looks at rights with little foundation in the Constitution's text as having a shaky foundation in a system based on a theory of popular sovereignty. There is room for both sorts of views in our constitutional history. The so-called Chase/Iredell debate of 1798 suggests that, early in the nation's history, there were those who looked to the constitutional text to find limits on government power, but there were also those who looked beyond any constitutional text.[3]

There are, to be sure, those who conceive of our constitutional order as subject to a kind of general trump card in the form of a moral reality which provides a measure of the validity of all legislation. This idea that there is a moral trump card, or substantive measure of the legality of all acts (or omissions) of government, might be viewed as a requirement of an appropriate theory of jurisprudence;[4] as implicit in the social contract of which the written Constitution is a partial integration, as reflected in the terms of the Ninth Amendment;[5] or as a reflection of the general purpose of the Constitution, as indicated by the Preamble's statement that the Constitution was to "establish justice."[6] In particular, this book will examine the views of those who claim that the drafters and ratifiers of the Constitution believed that it supplied this moral trump card as to laws that impacted on fundamental rights.[7]

One thing is clear: the view that we have rights so fundamental that it becomes a measure of the legal system whether we have adequate tools to secure them, since the written Constitution should not be viewed as an adequate safeguard, has become an increasingly popular position to defend. This was dramatically illustrated when the Senate had to decide whether to confirm the nomination of Judge Robert Bork to the Supreme Court. At least one of his scholarly critics, and this reflected a candor that may not have carried the day outside the academy, said that Judge Bork should have been rejected for his positivism alone because it precluded him from judging correctly in the "cases that come before the Supreme Court in which it is not *unconstitutionality,* but *injustice*—the violation of human rights and liberties—that calls for rectification and redress."[8] Even among the less candid it became common to charge Judge Bork with ignoring the clear implications of the text and history of the Ninth Amendment.[9] Indeed, the Senate Judiciary Committee noted with great favor Judge Kennedy's testimony "that the first eight amendments were not an exhaustive catalogue of all human rights," and his further conclusion that the Ninth Amendment is a "reserve clause" for use when other constitutional provisions seem inadequate.[10] The candor disappeared, for this same scholarly critic reassured his readers that the founders intended the Supreme Court to vindicate basic human rights and were committed to equating natural rights with constitutional rights.[11]

THE NINTH AMENDMENT

Many today contend that, under our constitutional system, a law's conflict with the norms of moral reality invalidates that law, even if other proffered criteria are met. The framers of our constitution, according to this view, rejected legal positivism's claim that there is another way to examine a law's validity than to examine the moral claims that the law sustains.[12] In some hands, the claim is advanced that the founders gave priority to this moral reality even over popular sovereignty: "By their own understanding, [the American people] had every right to which [the laws of nature and nature's God] entitled them, but no right to anything to which those self-same laws did *not* entitle them."[13] Perhaps the most common argument in support of a constitutionalism that is subject to the dictates of natural law is one that relies on the text and history of the Ninth Amendment to the federal Constitution.[14] In many hands, even though there is acknowledgement of a lack of evidence to apply natural rights, based on the Ninth Amendment, to the states, there is a willingness to apply these rights even against state governments.[15]

For those who have adopted this reading of the Ninth Amendment, it not only equates natural and "inalienable" rights with constitutional rights, but also calls into question any view of the Constitution that roots the status of human rights in their being an expression of popular will.[16] On this view, the Ninth Amendment text states a simple truism that our natural rights cannot be fully and finally identified inasmuch as our unfolding comprehension might reveal new rights from time to time.[17] Nor, for that matter, given this general theory, could any of the rights properly identified as natural rights be restricted or cabined by a mere text, no matter the specific intent of the drafters of the text. This is merely a matter of putting first things first: the Bill of Rights is, after all, a mere "adjunct to natural law," for the written Constitution which contains the Bill of Rights, "cannot limit those rights and should not purport to."[18]

There are, of course, advocates of an expansive reading of the Ninth Amendment who are not natural law constitutionalists. They are those who see the amendment as an attempt to call our attention to rights that go beyond the constitutional text, but who believe that we are searching for what was considered fundamental in 1787 (or perhaps what is considered fundamental today). As an example, Professor Thomas Grey has argued that the written constitution embraced slavery and that the Ninth Amendment was not intended to unleash the issue to be scrutinized again.[19] He has thus suggested that the founders spoke both ways; what we have faced "was in fact not a choice of one over the other, but a confusing attempt to have it both ways, an ambivalence within our constitutional tradition that has lasted to our own day."[20]

THE CONSTITUTION'S FOUNDATION

What is ultimately at stake in this debate is the appropriate foundational account of our constitutional order. One may conclude that the founding generation believed in higher law and saw the principle limiting government power as inherent in the social contract, which the written constitution only partially embodies.[21] There is also scholarly authority for the view that interpreters are limited to enforcing the terms of the written Constitution.[22]

One thing is clear. History did not supply a clear path to follow at the time of the founding. Three of the thinkers who most influenced the framers of the Constitution, John Locke, Edward Coke, and William Blackstone, do not supply us with definitive answers to the questions we would ask. Locke was committed to republican government and legislative supremacy that went hand in hand with his commitment to limited government and natural rights enforceable by the people's inherent right of revolution.[23] Coke described as void any Act of Parliament that is "against common right and reason, or repugnant, or impossible to be performed."[24] Yet Coke's famous utterance "seems to have enjoyed only a brief usefulness in pre-Revolutionary polemics,"[25] for citations to Coke ceased after Blackstone construed the statement as a mere rule of construction.[26] Blackstone was committed to the common law and natural law, but he also believed in Parliamentary sovereignty (and the related idea of legislative supremacy).[27]

Gordon Wood was undoubtedly correct in his general assessment that "[t]here was ... no logical or necessary reason why the notion of fundamental law ... should lead to the American invocation of it in the ordinary courts of law."[28] For one thing, the American experience included the revolution against England and the development of the uniquely American doctrine of popular sovereignty. This was all bound to impact on American thinking about fundamental law as it existed in 1776.[29] The written Constitution was the result, and there have always been those willing to defend the decisions embodied in the writing above the dictates of those who think they have received better answers than are found in any writing.

NOTES

1. The connection between this political view and the Constitution is significant because Americans see our founding document as "the outgrowth of a racial tradition, of an ancient struggle for liberty." Edward S. Corwin, *The Worship of the Constitution,* in 1 Corwin on the Constitution 47, 50 (Richard Loss, ed., 1981).

2. Ronald Dworkin, Freedom's Law: The Moral Reading of the American Constitution (1996); Michael S. Moore, *Do We Have an Unwritten Constitution?,* 63 S. Cal. L. Rev. 107 (1989).

3. *Calder v. Bull,* 3 U.S. (3 Dall.) 386 (1798). For some expression of doubt whether even this example illustrates textualism versus nontextualism, see Thomas B. McAffee, *Prolegomena to a Meaningful Debate of the "Unwritten Constitution" Thesis,* 61 U. Cin. L. Rev. 107, 130 n. 73 (1993). *See generally* David P. Currie, The Constitution in the Supreme Court: The First Hundred Years 1789–1888, at 41–49 (1985).

4. Charles E. Rice, *Some Reasons for a Restoration of Natural Law Jurisprudence,* 24 Wake Forest L. Rev. 539 (1989).

5. The Ninth Amendment provides that "[t]he enumeration in the Constitution, of certain rights, shall not be construed to deny or disparage others retained

by the people." U.S. Const. Amendment IX. *See generally* Harry V. Jaffa, Original Intent and the Framers of the Constitution: A Disputed Question 13–50 (1994); David A.J. Richards, Foundations of American Constitutionalism 80–91, 220–23 (1989); Randy E. Barnett, *Introduction: James Madison's Ninth Amendment*, in The Rights Retained by the People: The History and Meaning of the Ninth Amendment 1 (Randy E. Barnett, ed., 1989) [hereinafter The Rights Retained by the People].

6. *E.g.*, Sotirious A. Barber, *The Ninth Amendment: Inkblot or Another Hard Nut to Crack?*, 64 Chi.-Kent L. Rev. 67, 78–81 (1988); Stephen Macedo, *Morality and the Constitution: Toward a Synthesis for "Earthbound" Interpreters*, 61 U. Cin. L. Rev. 29, 37 (1992); Edwin Vieira, Jr., *Rights and the United States Constitution: The Declension from Natural Law to Legal Positivism*, 12 Geo. L. Rev. 1447, 1459 (1979).

7. *See* the sources cited *supra* notes 4, 5, and 6. *See, e.g.*, Suzanna Sherry, *The Founders' Unwritten Constitution*, 54 U. Chi. L. Rev. 1127, 1161 n. 143 (1987); Thomas C. Grey, *The Original Understanding and the Unwritten Constitution*, in Toward a More Perfect Union: Six Essays on the Constitution 145 (Neil L. York, ed., 1988). *See generally* Douglas W. Kmiec & Stephen B. Presser, The American Constitutional Order: History, Cases, and Philosophy 137–71 (1998). For a general critique of this sort of vision of our constitutional order, see Thomas B. McAffee, *Substance Above All: The Utopian Vision of Modern Natural Law Constitutionalists*, 4 So. Cal. Interdisciplinary L.J. 501 (1996).

8. *E.g.*, Mortimer Adler, *Robert Bork: The Lessons to Be Learned*, 84 Nw. U. L. Rev. 1121, 1124 (1990).

9. Sanford Levinson, *Constitutional Rhetoric and the Ninth Amendment*, 64 Chi.-Kent L. Rev. 131, 134–35 (1988).

10. *Id.* at 135 n. 19 (citing Senate Comm. on the Judiciary, Nomination of Anthony M. Kennedy to be an Associate Justice of the United States Supreme Court, S. Exec. Rep. No. 113, 100th Cong., 2d Sess. 20–21 (1988)). For elaboration of the charge that candor did not characterize the work of Judge Bork's scholarly critics who testified before the Senate Judiciary Committee, see Thomas B. McAffee, *The Role of Legal Scholars in the Confirmation Hearings for Supreme Court Nominees—Some Reflections*, 1 St. John's J. Legal Comm. 211 (1991).

11. Adler, *supra* note 8, at 1124.

12. *See, e.g.*, Vieira, *supra* note 6, at 1478. *See generally* McAffee, *supra* note 3, at 113.

13. Terry Brennan, *Natural Rights and the Constitution: The Original "Original Intent,"* 15 Harv. J.L. & Pub. Pol'y 988; H. Jaffa, *supra* note 5, at 95. For a different understanding of the people's authority under the framers' thinking about popular sovereignty, see Akhil Reed Amar, The Bill of Rights: Creation and Reconstruction 119–123 (1998).

14. *E.g.*, Brennan, *supra* note 13, at 998–99; Sherry *supra* note 7; Grey, *supra* note 7; Randy E. Barnett, *Unenumerated Constitutional Rights and the Rule of Law*, 14 Harv. J.L. & Pub. Pol'y 615, 626 (1991).

6 Inherent Rights

15. *E.g.,* Calvin R. Massey, *Federalism and Fundamental Rights: The Ninth Amendment, in* The Rights Retained by the People, *supra* note 5, at 291, 335 (contending that the Ninth Amendment should be applied to the states, despite the lack of evidence of an original intent to do so, "because the theoretical understanding of the ninth amendment reservation" is to "vest these rights in the people, rather than in any government"); Norman G. Redlich, *Are There "Certain Rights . . . Retained by the People?,"* 37 N.Y.U. L. Rev. 787, 806 (1962); Charles Black, Jr., *"One Nation Indivisible": Unnamed Human Rights in the States,* 66 St. John's L. Rev. 17, 29 (1991).

16. *See* Lawrence G. Sager, *You Can Raise the First, Hide Behind the Fourth, and Plead the Fifth. But What on Earth Can You Do with the Ninth Amendment?,* 64 Chi.-Kent L. Rev. 239, 254–55, 258–59 (Ninth Amendment calls into question "majoritarianism" as a foundational account for the individual rights project of the Constitution; it shows that the provisions of the Bill of Rights must be seen as part of a larger project in political morality rather than as "disembodied acts of capricious will that somehow gained widespread support").

17. A concern about the Bill of Rights which has been linked to the Ninth Amendment is Edmund Pendleton's objection that "in the progress of things, [we may] discover some great and important [right], which we don't now think of." Edmund Pendleton to Richard Henry Lee (June 14, 1788), in 2 The Letters and Papers of Edmund Pendleton 1734–1803 at 532–33 (1967). *But see* Thomas B. McAffee, *The Original Meaning of the Ninth Amendment,* 90 Colum. L. Rev. 1215, 1276 n. 232 (1990) (alternative reading of Pendleton's argument).

18. Mark Levison & Charles Kramer, *The Bill of Rights as Adjunct to Natural Law,* Det. C.L. Rev. 1267, 1285 (1991).

19. Grey, *supra* note 7, at 164.

20. *Id.* at 157.

21. D. Richards, *supra* note 5, at 220; Macedo, *supra* note 6, at 29; Grey, *supra* note 7; Sherry, *supra* note 7.

22. Philip A. Hamburger, *Natural Rights, Natural Law, and American Constitutions,* 102 Yale L.J. 907, 909 (1993); Thomas B. McAffee, *The Bill of Rights, Social Contract Theory, and the Rights "Retained" by the People,* 16 S. Ill. U. L.J. 267, 276–89 (1992).

23. *See* Walter Berns, Taking the Constitution Seriously 27–28, 187–88 (1987); Edward S. Corwin, Liberty Against Government 45–51, 57 (1948); Garson, The Intellectual Reference of the American Constitution, Reflections on the Constitution 1, 7–9, 19 (1989).

24. Dr. Bonham's Case, 8 Coke Rep. 107, 118a (1610), *quoted in,* Julius Goebel, Jr., History of the Supreme Court of the United States: Antecedents and Beginnings to 1801, at 92 (1971).

25. J. Goebel, *supra* note 24, at 93.

26. *Id.* at 94. While Coke was cited for a broad notion of the power of courts to set aside legislation, there is room for doubt whether he intended the power of courts to be as broad as some of his interpreters have taken him as advocating. *See*

James R. Stoner, Common Law and Liberal Theory 59–62 (1992). For the opinion that Coke's views "never took root in England," and that even in this country they were replaced by the doctrine of judicial review of the *written* Constitution, see D. Kmiec & S. Presser, The American Constitutional Order, *supra* note 7, at 168–71 & n. 56 (reviewing views expressed on modern Supreme Court by Justices Rehnquist and Souter); Helen K. Michael, *The Role of Natural Law in Early American Constitutionalism: Did the Founders Contemplate Judicial Enforcement of "Unwritten" Individual Rights?*, 69 N.C.L. Rev. 421, 425–27, 443, 453, 490 (1991). For a different view of Coke's role in developing American thinking concerning fundamental law, see Calvin R. Massey, Silent Rights: The Ninth Amendment and the Constitution's Unenumerated Rights 27–35, 44–45 (1995).

27. Grey, *supra* note 7, at 152; Sylvia Snowiss, Judicial Review and the Law of the Constitution 13–16, 114–17, 128, 203–4 (1990); J.W. Gough, Fundamental Law in English Constitutional History 192 (2d ed. 1961). *See generally* D. Kmiec & S. Presser, The American Constitutional Order, *supra* note 7, at 122–28.

28. Gordon S. Wood, The Creation of the American Republic, 1776–87, 292 (1969).

29. *See id.* at 528–32. A key development was the shift to the popular constitutional convention that established a document that bound all branches of government (including the executive). *See, e.g.,* Thomas G. West, *The Rule of Law in the Federalist,* in Saving the Revolution 150, 155 (C. Kesler ed., 1987); Herman Belz, *Constitutionalism and the American Founding,* in The Framing and Ratification of the Constitution 333, 339 (Leonard W. Levy & Dennis T. Mahoney, eds., 1987).

2

State Constitutions in the Early American Republic: The Experiment with Republican Government

Among the first items on the agenda of the new republic was the effort to put the political ideals of the Revolution into effect through the drafting of new forms of government for the various states.[1] These new state constitutions almost invariably included a written document that was entitled a "frame"or "form" of government, which established the government and distributed its various powers. In addition, a number of these state constitutions included a separate declaration of rights that stated fundamental political principles and set forth the fundamental rights retained by the people. The state constitutions that lacked a declaration of rights typically included at least some "rights" provisions in the frame of government. The assumptions embodied in these state constitutions, as well as the practice that developed under them and the reaction to that practice, illuminate the development of thinking about the relationship between natural law and positive law in fundamental law theory in the early American republic.

The revolutionary state constitutions included among their leading features: (1) the embodiment of the American commitment to written constitutions; (2) the implementation of the doctrine of popular sovereignty and a corresponding reliance on representative government as the chief means of preventing arbitrary government; (3) the securing of liberty and limited government through the adoption of the principles of government revealed by reason and nature, which included both the declaration of basic rights of the people (typically in a separate constitutional document) and the concept of separation of powers; (4) reliance on the doctrine of separation of powers as a critical key to restraining government and preventing the arbitrary exercise of power. The sections that follow will explicate these leading features as they relate to the status of inherent individual rights norms—including their interrelationships and the tensions that existed among them.

THE WRITTEN CONSTITUTION

The American colonial experience had been characterized by reliance on written instruments of various types—crown charters and their supplemental agreements, organic acts, ordinances, combinations, and frames of government characterized the governments of some colonies, while the "mutual pledging and association under civil-religious covenants" had characterized the governments of others.[2] Either way, the historical experience made written instruments seem like second nature. But there was an even more immediate reason that it seemed not only natural but essential to adopt written constitutions. If the colonists' struggle with Great Britain taught the Americans anything, it was that constitutionalism is concerned not only with identifying rational principles of government, including the rights of man, but also with realizing them in practice.

During the struggle leading to independence, the colonists had set forth the arguments of reason, based on English constitutionalism and natural law, and these had gone unheeded. In the end, the unwritten English constitution failed them; and though they justified revolution by the same resort to reason and nature, revolt supplied an extralegal remedy for the perceived tyranny visited upon them. The Americans came to believe that if the pattern of tyranny and revolution were to be avoided, it was crucial that the principles of liberty and republican government be set in a form not easily disputed.[3] As James Cannon, a framer of the Pennsylvania Constitution, put it: "To deduce our rights from the principles of equity and justice and the Constitution, is very well; but equity and justice are no defense against power."[4]

Whereas the British relied on "an unstipulated, imprecise constitution," the Americans "insisted in contrast that the principles and rules essential to organizing power and preserving liberty be separated from the government and objectively fixed in positive form."[5] The Americans had learned that the British constitution had existed only in their minds and was premised on the idea that "thinking makes it so."[6] Therefore, they now embraced a constitutionalism that "rested on the idea that 'saying makes it so,' or at least the hope that putting something in writing so it can be authoritatively consulted makes it easier to achieve specified ends."[7]

Unwritten Principles of Law

This commitment to written constitutions of itself suggests that the legal significance of unwritten principles of law would be a matter to be read-dressed in the new legal and political environment. At the very least, in underscoring the uncertainties now perceived in the tradition of unwritten fundamental law, written constitutions would immediately raise the question whether time-honored principles would continue to bind without being reduced to writing. Unsurprisingly, in the early American republic thoughtful Americans essentially concluded that the English lacked a meaningful constitution both because of the lack of specific written law and because of the doctrine of Parliamentary sovereignty.[8]

A central justifying mechanism of English legal theory was the idea that unwritten principles of the English constitution were part of an "original contract" between the government and the governed.[9] The new American states, however, were forming their own political compacts, and this suggested the possibility that all former contracts and understandings were done away and subsumed within the written constitutions adopted within the various states.[10] As we shall see, this sort of view would necessarily gain greater force as the doctrine of popular sovereignty took a larger hold in the American states, and particularly as constitutions increasingly came to be viewed as the enactment of a sovereign people.

The Importance of the Writing Grows

Notwithstanding the revolutionaries' commitment to Lockean natural rights theory, it seems equally clear that the act of putting the principles of reason and nature into written form of itself presents an important sort of qualification of a natural law methodology. The written constitution underscores that the most serious commitment is not to natural law as an open-ended methodology,[11] but to the particular vision of natural law that is embodied in the writing.[12] Thus at least to the extent that the written constitution addresses a particular question, the text serves as the primary, if not exclusive, reference point for constitutional analysis rather than the background principle that informed (or arguably should have informed) the text.[13] The attempt to embody natural law principles in an instrument of government, moreover, necessarily requires individuals to face the reality that reasonable people differ as to the existence and scope of particular natural rights as well as on questions of how the principles can best be realized in practice.[14] This immediately raises the question whether the written constitution is designed to embody a mediation of such competing views, ultimately the judgment of the sovereign people on precisely such questions. Thus even a written constitution explicitly grounded on principles of natural law and natural right might be viewed with dissatisfaction by (at least some) natural rights thinkers to the extent that it limited (or even omitted) those rights favored by particular adherents.

One encounters disagreement even as to whether particular ideas about government embody natural law, or are at least essential to its realization in practice, or are instead merely contingent judgments about which reasonable people might differ as to which varying circumstances may call for varying responses—and hence are unworthy of receiving constitutional status.[15] Facing this sort of experience with disagreement, even proponents of the view that natural law is binding law, in some sense, will see that omission of a cherished principle from the written instrument is at least ambiguous in the world of practice: the principle may have been omitted because the notion of natural law embodied in the instrument deemed the principle as non-fundamental, or it may have been omitted because it was thought to be so well understood and established as not to require inclusion.

Given the reality that the written constitution thus necessarily serves to some extent as arbiter of the natural law for the society it governs, it is almost inevitable that the written constitution will loom larger over time in a society characterized by fundamental disagreements as to the content and practical implications of natural law. And the importance of the content of the writing will only grow to the extent that the written constitution is effective in yielding compliance to the principles it embodies. Moreover, the difficulty of the process by which consensus is reached as to the principles deemed sufficiently fundamental to be given the special status of inclusion in the written constitution—a status that contemplates the overriding of popular will and limiting ordinary legislative flexibility over time—will necessarily mean that the attempt to claim that same fundamental status for contested unwritten principles of natural law almost inevitably will be confronted with particularly strong objections from those who disagree as to the status or application of the principle. For all these reasons, even though a written constitution does not logically entail the legal positivist emphasis on laws established authoritatively, or necessarily imply that constitutional rights are limited to those inferable from the constitution's text, its tendency is to push constitutionalism in that direction.

POPULAR SOVEREIGNTY AND LEGISLATIVE POWER

It has been asserted that "[t]he principle enunciated in the Declaration of Independence that governments derive their just powers from the 'consent of the governed' lies at the foundation of the American republic."[16] While the idea had referred most centrally to the notion that the people held the ultimate power to create, alter, or destroy (when appropriate) the form of government under which they lived,[17] during the revolutionary and confederation periods the concept became associated for many with the more immediate power of the people to govern through their representatives.[18] The identification of the legislature as the voice of the people during the revolutionary era is reflected in the fact that most of the constitutions adopted in the early period were enacted by the legislatures in the same manner as an ordinary statute, rather than by the institution of a constitutional convention that has come to characterize our constitutional practice.[19]

It is also true that from the earliest moment the view that ordinary legislators could adopt a constitution had its critics. Willi Adams observes that in May of 1776 a Pennsylvania newspaper argued that only the people could form a new constitution, and that since "[b]odies of men have the same selfish attachments as individuals," a legislative body would inevitably claim "powers and prerogatives inconsistent with the liberties of the people."[20] Even so, as Herman Belz observes, the legislative origin of the state constitutions, as well as the legislative power to alter or abolish the constitutions that was recognized in most states, meant in practice that these constitutions ordained a framework of government but failed to provide effective control of legislative power.[21] Consequently the developing view of constitutionalism, that it restrains as well as establishes government, especially including the power of the people's representative assemblies, could not fully emerge until the power of the legislature was disassociated from the power of the people.[22]

The Power of the People

Political liberty during the confederation period was thus associated, first and foremost, with representative government; and the states' declarations of rights were accordingly filled with communal rights, including provisions for popular sovereignty,[23] officials' responsibility to the people,[24] and provision for the authority of the people to regulate the internal government and police of the state.[25] The underlying philosophy of the early state constitutions was summed up in the following provision in the Delaware constititution's declaration of rights: "That the right of the people to participate in the Legislature, is the best security of liberty."[26] The tension inherent in the potentially competing ideas that the people exercised their sovereignty in constituting government, and thus may limit legislative (and ultimately their own) power, and the notion that the people were entitled to govern through their representatives was seldom acknowledged, let alone resolved.[27] As Adams states, the "full implications of the principle of popular sovereignty were left to be developed through future political action."[28]

The Key Assumption

The crucial assumption for reconciling this emphasis on the liberty of the people to govern themselves with the potentially competing principles of limited government and protection of individual rights is the idea that the people are not the source from which to fear tyranny or arbitrary government.[29] Given this assumption, the most important security for the liberty of the people was the creation of a dominant legislature and provision for adequate representation, along with frequent elections, so as to ensure that government was responsive to the people who were the source of its authority.[30]

Thus the 1776 Pennsylvania state constitution included a single-house legislature that was elected annually, which was in turn empowered to effectively control the other two branches. Other states followed a similar pattern of giving practical sovereign power to the legislature, while seeking to ensure that its power would be directed by a vigilant public through frequent elections.[31] As Robert C. Palmer has observed, the state constitutions created "governments dedicated to popular sovereignty and structured so as to retain an identity between the people and their representatives in assembly. As in Britain, the fight for liberty had taken the form of empowering elected representatives at the expense of the executive."[32]

The People as All-Powerful

The assumption of the people's basic commitment to freedom, which supported the idea that the power of the people to govern was the primary freedom, is what explains the frequent equation of the people's constitutive power with the traditional definition of sovereignty as entailing absolute and uncontrollable power. Thus in 1776, the Massachusetts General Court proclaimed: "It is a maxim that, in every Government, there must exist a Supreme, Sovereign, absolute, and uncontroulable Power; but this Power resides, always in the body of the People, and it never was, or can be delegated, to one Man or a few."[33] A provision in the Pennsylvania Declaration of Rights asserted the community's "unalienable and indefeasible" right to reform or alter government "in such a manner as shall be by that *community* judged most conducive to the public weal."[34] Given that the people's right to constitute government was conceived as essentially limitless and as based on inalienable right (we may assume, once again, that the presumption was that the people would not choose arbitrary government), legislative power quite naturally acquired a derivative legitimacy so long as it was identified with the will of the people by virtue of effective representation.

The thought underlying such formulations of popular sovereignty was less the notion that the people could constitute oppressive government as that the people were the only proper judge of the appropriate balance between order and liberty. Many agreed that "[t]he community, however represented, ought to remain the supreme authority and ultimate judicature."[35] As this view developed, moreover, it went beyond the idea of consent to the establishment of a government, or the right to alter the powers of government once established. The "one supreme, absolute, and rightful judge over the whole [of society]," identified as "no other than the majority of whole," held "a right at all times to order, direct, and dispose of the persons, actions and properties of the individuals of the community, so far as the good of the community shall require it."[36] Reliance on the people to preserve liberty and prevent oppression through republican involvement and public virtue was sufficiently strong that skepticism about the very need for bills of rights and other sorts of constitutional limitations on government became a theme in political dialogues from the confederation era through the debate over ratification of the federal Constitution.[37]

THE DECLARATIONS OF RIGHTS

The state declarations of rights reflect at once America's fundamental law heritage, including the commitment to natural rights and government based on principles of reason, and the drive to reduce the governing principles to written law. The goal was to establish constitutional rights "on a foundation never more to be shaken,"[38] and this would be accomplished only if they were "specified and written down in immutable documents."[39] While it is not inaccurate to emphasize that the framers of these documents perceived themselves as "declaring" fundamental principles rather than "creating" new legal rights,[40] the step of putting them in writing was not viewed as a superfluous act—and the perceived importance of reducing natural law to positive law would grow even larger over time.[41]

Popular Power to Establish Rights

There is, of course, nothing logically inconsistent in demanding a written stipulation to secure natural and fundamental rights while still insisting that their status as fundamental legal rights does not depend on such a stipulation. And having so recently relied upon colonial charters guaranteeing fundamental norms derived from the unwritten British constitution, the revolutionary generation as an entirety did not immediately shift to a legal positivist stance toward the rights they embodied in their declarations. Articulate spokesmen continued to insist that the rights they cherished did not depend on their being written down and promulgated.[42]

Even so, the move toward reducing rights to positive form undoubtedly contributed to the tendency to equate constitutionalism with written limitations on government, particularly as Americans pondered the consequences of failing to have needed limitations put into writing. This point is illustrated by the tendency of Americans, now that they had decided in favor of revolution, to see the British constitution through new eyes and in decidedly realistic terms. Accordingly, thoughtful Americans saw the British constitution's flexibility and mutability (the qualities they had so recently insisted that it lacked) as embodying the very antithesis of a true constitution—one that fixes basically immutable limitations on government power.[43] If the absence of effective checks on power could yield a system of positive law that violated the norms of tradition and natural law with impunity, including norms deemed fundamental by the political order itself, it was a short step to conclude that unwritten natural and fundamental law provides a standard for judging positive law but does not have the status of positive law in a given legal system.

Given the pull between seeing fundamental and natural law norms as binding and the recognition that systems of positive law in fact violated them, Gordon Wood concluded that as often as advocates reaffirmed the view that putting rights on parchment reaffirmed, but did not create, rights, the significance of such statements "was not fully appreciated, and a pervasive confusion about law remained."[44] It is possible to go further: if the significance of such statements was unappreciated, it would have been because they were ambiguous, inasmuch as they failed to clarify the precise status of such preexisting rights in legal theory. It is entirely possible, as we have seen in the case of William Blackstone, to be firmly committed to the idea of preexisting natural rights, and to assert the superiority of the (moral) obligation they raise to mere positive law, but to nevertheless recognize a sovereign power as having authority to establish or fix the content of the law so as to bind all citizens.

It is also possible that much of the confusion here belongs to the modern mind. In modern courses on jurisprudence, natural law theory is treated as a theory of legal obligation and as a method for identifying "law." This way of thinking tends us toward presuming a dichotomy between natural law and legal positivist views of the nature of law; this, in turn, obscures the reality that even a legal system purportedly grounded on natural law norms must confront challenging institutional questions about implementing those norms in political and legal practice. American constitutional thinkers were engaged in this very sort of process; and, based on a careful analysis of the founding-era materials, Professor Philip Hamburger has concluded that "Americans who discussed natural liberty and constitutions typically assumed that only such natural liberty as reserved by a constitution would be a constitutional right."[45] To understand how this could be so, we must briefly consider the relationship between the declarations or bills of rights and the way in which Americans conceived the power given to the state legislatures by the revolutionary-era state constitutions.

Bills of Rights and Republican Government

We have already noted a minority view that perceived bills of rights as unnecessary in republican governments. For some, the theory of popular control was deemed a sufficent safeguard of the natural rights, and a bill of rights was deemed superfluous.[46] A related point was that bills of rights had been employed to limit the prerogatives of the crown, and indeed many English limitations were not viewed as binding on Parliament.[47] In America there would be no king. But many insisted that constitutions were the appropriate vehicle to set forth the rights that the people reserved to themselves as they entered into the social compact. They contended further that these rights are in their nature held as against all government, and even the sentiment of a majority of the people, and not simply against a specific source of tyranny (like the crown).[48]

The necessity of a bill of rights was powerfully reinforced, moreover, by the general understanding of the significance of the people's grant of power to the government in their constitutions. The written constitution was viewed as the memorialization of the contract between the government and the governed, and the powers held by government were viewed as grants from the people. Given that these were to be governments with general legislative powers, the presumption was that the people parted with all the power they did not expressly reserve. The drafters of these constitutions "assumed that government had all power except for specific prohibitions contained in a bill of rights."[49] Under this view of the matter, notwithstanding that there exist "inherent rights pertaining to all mankind in a state of natural liberty" and that government is instituted to provide greater security to these rights, it nevertheless follows from the universal nature of the grant of powers to a general legislature that such legislative powers will, in the absence of express reservations, "include every power of acting, and every claim of possessing or obtaining any thing."[50] Consequently there is a strict necessity to have "an express stipulation for all such rights as are intended to be exempted from the civil authority."[51]

These assumptions about the need to limit legislative authority in the written constitution are reflected, moreover, in the debate surrounding particular provisions of state declarations of rights. In Virginia, for example, Patrick Henry successfully opposed the inclusion of a ban on legislative criminal trials, in the form of bills of attainder, in the declaration of rights. According to one account, Henry presented "a terrifying picture of some towering public offender, against whom ordinary laws would be impotent."[52] This victory was won notwithstanding that the practice of legislative trials for criminal conduct quite obviously undermined traditional common law guarantees relating to due process and fair trials, most especially the right to trial by jury. In addition, to the extent that traditional due process guarantees, especially the fundamentals of notice and hearing, were also viewed as civil guarantees of natural rights, given that they secured the most fundamental rights of life, liberty, and property, a bill of attainder could be called an invasion of an individual's natural rights.[53] Considering that bills of attainder had been employed in English practice, however, it was assumed by those considering the proposed guarantee that the Virginia assembly would hold such a power in the absence of the guarantee.[54] And subsequently Virginia actually enacted a bill of attainder against an unpopular Tory at the instigation of Governor Patrick Henry.[55]

Similarly, the "natural equality" principle declared in the 1776 Virginia Declaration of Rights was amended by the convention that considered it because of the fear that under such a governing declaration, slavery would be viewed as an unconstitutional infringement of the stated principle.[56] With the critical change italicized, the amended provision stated that all men are "by nature free and independent, and have certain inherent rights, of which, *when they enter into society,* they cannot, by any compact, deprive or divest their posterity."[57] As Warren Billings observes, the language inserted into the provision under consideration was included precisely in order to clarify that the fundamental rights that people retain as they enter civil society did not apply to the Black race because the slaves had never entered into a state of civil society in Virginia.[58] This Virginia example is especially compelling inasmuch as it first, assuredly dealt with a quintessential natural right and second, presumed that constitution-makers were empowered to determine the scope of constitutional limits on legislative powers—including limits rooted in principles of natural right. As we will see, this assumption pervaded the debate over the federal Constitution that would occur eleven years later.[59]

A Special Category of Norms?

Suzanna Sherry has suggested that the state declarations of rights embody a special category of norms which, unlike the provisions of the separate forms of government, are both inherent and inalienable. On this view, although the frames of government described governmental structure and allocated power within that structure—and thus constituted a law of the government—they were nevertheless seen as a system of "evolving fundamental law" that would change in accordance with advances in the science of government.[60] By contrast, the declarations stated "the inherent natural rights which formed an integral and unalterable part of the broader fundamental law."[61] Accordingly, says Sherry, three of the state constitutions expressly prohibited amendment or violation of their declarations of rights.[62] For Sherry, this dichotomy supports seeing the written Constitution as definitive, but alterable, with respect to issues of governmental structure and allocation of authority, but as stating absolute limits on government on behalf of individual rights.[63]

While the state declarations were undoubtedly conceived as stating important first principles,[64] the claim that the frames of government and declarations of rights embodied a dichotomy between a mutable governmental structure and immutable principles of individual liberty does not seem warranted by the evidence. For one thing, although several declarations contained "inalienable rights" clauses,[65] referring to the traditional idea of inalienable natural rights, none of the declarations claimed that every principle set forth should be regarded as a natural and inalienable right.[66] While all the rights set forth were obviously deemed sufficiently fundamental to warrant inclusion as a protection of liberty against oppression, thoughtful analysis of the constitution-making period distinguished between the inalienable natural rights and other sorts of rights that warranted being secured in fundamental laws.[67]

A related point is that many of the rights found in the declarations are in no sense Lockean-type natural rights that individuals bring with them to the social contract. As we have noted, the declarations contain numerous provisions that secure collective rights of the people as a whole (including the right to govern and regulate the internal police of the state[68])—rights that the republican theory of the day saw as equally fundamental as the rights which individuals bring to the social contract.[69] Even if the declarations were thought to state more fundamental principles than the frames of government, these provisions undercut any purported dichotomy that recognizes individual rights as inherent and natural (and hence more fundamental) while seeing the power of the community to realize collective needs of soci-

ety as related to a more transitory realm of government structure and authority. Individual liberty and collective rights were placed on the same footing.

Along similar lines, a number of provisions in the declarations can only
be described as structural in nature, including the Virginia declaration's
provision requiring a complete separation of powers.[70] This declaration
thus sees the confining of the branches of government to their proper functions as itself constituting a fundamental right of the people. Many thoughtful Americans would also have conceived of the separation of government
powers as every bit as much a requirement of natural law as the natural
rights of individuals.[71] Just as separation of powers was considered to be
fundamental to securing liberty, there is every reason to think that provisions in the frames of government designed to ensure the maintenance of
representative government would have been deemed equally fundamental
as many of the provisions found in the declarations.[72] This inference is
strengthened inasmuch as the central issues of government structure and
authority were viewed by many during this period as controlled by natural
law principles just as much as issues of individual rights, partly because
they were viewed as essential prerequisites for preserving liberty.[73]

While the declarations were undoubtedly thought to state fundamental
principles of government that ought to be honored perpetually, nothing in
them reflects a founding-era consensus limiting the power of the people to
decide the fundamental questions about government by altering their constitutions. As we have noted, the people's power to alter and reform their
governments was among the fundamentals set forth in a number of declarations of rights.[74] While the idea of perpetual constitutions dominated the
framing of both the declarations and the frames of government, so that, for
example, most of the early state constitutions created no mechanism for
amendment,[75] there is no reason to think that in general this implied any
limitation on the power of the people to alter and reform their government
according to their will.[76]

The Power to Amend Declarations of Rights

As one would expect where the power to alter governments is considered
fundamental, and even inalienable, Sherry's claim that specific state constitutional provisions made the declarations of rights unalterable is not
borne out by a careful examination of the provisions upon which she relies. The Pennsylvania and North Carolina provisions establish the declarations of rights as part of their constitutions, and both state that the
declarations "ought never to be violated on any pretence whatever."[77] These
statements seem designed to clarify the constitutional status of the declara-

tions, and to enjoin their violation, rather than to foreclose any possibility of amendment.[78]

In Delaware, the other state with a similar provision, article 30 of the "constitution of government" combines this injunction against violating the separately enacted declaration of rights, as well as specified articles of the constitution, with a specific provision for legislative amendment of the balance of the constitution by the legislature.[79] While the provision as a whole does read as an implicit prohibition on amending the declaration and the other named articles, given the legislature's role in the amending process it is properly read as a legal limitation on the people's representatives.[80] Moreover, two of the state constitutions that provided for constitutional amendment by the legislature did not draw any distinction between different sorts of provisions, such as those dealing with government structure and those securing individual rights.[81] Both no doubt presumed the people's sovereign power, acting through their legislature, to alter their government to better meet their collective needs and to secure their fundamental rights. Similarly, Pennsylvania and Maryland recognized the right of the people to alter, reform, or abolish their governments within the very declarations of rights that, according to their constitutions, should not be "violated."[82] It therefore seems unlikely that the provisions under discussion would have been conceived as legal and constitutional limitations on the sovereign power of the people to make and amend constitutions in the future.

The alternative understanding of these provisions offered here is lent additional support by a little-noted trend in constitutional drafting that commenced during the confederation period. Sherry reads great meaning into the very fact of the division of the state constitutions into separable declarations (or bills) of rights and frames of government.[83] Other commentators, such as Donald Lutz, have underscored that this demarcation recapitulated a pattern of the drafting of "compacts" in America's colonial experience— the declarations, as well as the preambles, embodied the foundational covenant that established (or reestablished) a political community, while the frames of governments were "organic acts" that stated the rules for government and related to the agreement between the people and their government.[84] Lutz even suggests that it is really the frame of government that is "more properly called a constitution,"[85] given that historically that term had been associated more with the document describing and regulating institutions of government than with the foundational document setting forth the basis of the political society establishing the government.[86] Lutz's analysis explains why it was that in Virginia in 1776 that government-oriented document was called "The Constitution or Form of Government " while the state's declaration of rights is denominated as "Bill of Rights."[87]

As Lutz acknowledges, however, the institutional description grew so that in 1780 the people of Massachusetts would "establish the following declaration of rights and frame of government as the constitution of the commonwealth of Massachusetts."[88] By this process of inclusive usage, Lutz concludes, "essentially compacts and constitutions became linguistically indistinguishable."[89] Equally important, constitutions employing the inclusive language recognized that both elements—the declarations or bills of rights as well as the frames of government—are designed "to remain in force" forever, "unaltered, except in such articles as shall herafter on experience be found to require improvement, and which shall by the same authority of the people . . . be amended."[90]

Whatever the precise reason, history shows that any idea that bills of rights could not be amended, if it ever existed at all, never took hold. Article V of the federal Constitution includes no limitations on the amending power in favor of fundamental rights guarantees, despite the inclusion of some fundamental rights in the body of the Constitution. The Constitution's opponents objected to the failure to supply a more comprehensive statement of rights, but no one asserted that the rights included were diminished by virtue of their being placed within the body of a single constitutional document and thereby subjected to the amendment process.[91] Moreover, despite all the controversy surrounding ratification, none of the state proposals for amendments included a prohibition on amending the Bill of Rights that was to be added to the original Constitution.[92] Similarly, when Delaware adopted a new constitution in 1792, the provision for amendment was not restricted to any portion of the constitution.[93] The basic statements of rights and principles had been assimilated into a single article of a fully developed document described as the "constitution of government for the State of Delaware,"[94] and the provision enjoining violations of the declaration of rights was omitted.[95]

There is, moreover, a compelling body of research showing that the founders of the federal Constitution, as well as their counterparts during the confederation period, believed that constitutional law in general (and not simply bills of rights) should be permanent and unchanging.[96] Constitutions were contrasted with "temporary laws,"[97] and those charged with drafting constitutions were asked to remember "that they are *painting for eternity*."[98] In an important recent treatment, Philip Hamburger has shown that a good deal of constitutional debate during the drafting and ratification of the federal Constitution centered on the problem of reconciling the need to accomodate inevitable social change with this governing assumption that constitutions should be comprised of immutable provisions. The basic solution to the problem was the idea that the Constitution should exclude all provisions that were likely to become obsolete and that provision should be made for amendment so that unanticipated changes could be accomodated while preserving the notion of a permanent Constitution.[99]

Qualifying Inalienable Rights

The temptation to think that the natural and inalienable rights of individuals held a uniquely special status in revolutionary constitutional thought reflects in part the tendency over the years to ascribe a liberal foundation to the American commitment to natural rights. But the state constitutions reflect the predominance of republican thought during the period. In republican social contract theory, some natural rights were given up as the "price" for obtaining the advantages of civil government, while others were deemed instead to be "inalienable."[100] While some formulations of the concept of inalienable rights suggested that they were entirely beyond the control of the community,[101] the more standard view was that even the inalienable rights were subject to regulation for the general good of the community, so that they were qualified (rather than absolute) rights, even though not subject to alienation.[102] Thoughtful Americans would largely have concurred in Blackstone's view that civil liberty "is no other than natural liberty so far restrained by human laws (and no farther) as is necessary and expedient for the general advantage of the publick."[103]

When individual liberty is thus linked to, and limited by, the good of society as a whole, it becomes clear how the framers of these constitutions reconciled natural rights with the doctrine of popular sovereignty. As the "supreme authority and ultimate judicature,"[104] the people would be the best judges of the public good by which the natural rights would be qualified. Given the predominance of the republican ideals, including the premise that government existed in large part to protect the citizenry against the harms that might be inflicted by individuals, it is not surprising that the collective power to regulate the police of the state would receive equal billing with the basic statements of individual rights.[105] Indeed, if the claim that these declarations state immutable principles of fundamental law (and cannot be amended, as with the frames of government) were taken completely seriously—so that the political philosophy thus embodied in them were actually taken as binding on us—the case for the modern double-standard of judicial review in individual rights cases would be undercut rather than strengthened, and the entire apparatus of modern fundamental rights adjudication would be called into doubt. Taken as a whole, the early state constitutions, as well as the declarations of rights that a number of them included, reflected a philosophy of state power versus individual liberty that most Americans would find difficult to accept.

The individual rights provisions of the state declarations of rights reflect these assumptions of republican social contract theory. While the qualified nature of the individual rights guarantees was often presumed,[106] various provisions of the founding era conveyed the idea by express language.[107] Most often, however, the qualified nature of the individual rights enumerated in the state declarations of rights is suggested by the drafters' reliance on language of obligation and of statement of principle—language that itself suggests something other than a hard legal rule—rather than the language of direct command and prohibition.[108]

The declarations' individual rights provisions were framed in terms of "ought" or "ought not" rather than "shall" or "shall not,"[109] or occasionally as statements of political ideals.[110] These formulations were clearly not inadvertant. As Palmer points out, the declarations were drafted by sophisticated draftsmen, and the frames of government consistently use the language of direct command and prohibition.[111] This wording very probably reflects in part the idea of restating the fundamental principles, which inherently bind government, as opposed to promulgating new sovereign commands. In a sense, this language conveys their greater importance; but in another sense, it also reflects the recognition of the drafters that such principles are to be honored rather than enforced. The language of the declarations conveys the idea that the enumerated liberties were "serious principles by which the government was to abide,"[112] but were nevertheless subject in general to qualification as essential for the public good.[113]

Palmer goes so far as to conclude that the declarations were thus only statements of "governmental principles" rather than constitutional or legal "guarantees" or exceptions to powers.[114] These statements of principle were, moreover, "directed at the legislative assemblies, stating fundamental principles by which that assembly should have felt bound," and "in that sense also, they were not guarantees."[115] While one might quarrel as to the claim that these were not "constitutional guarantees,"[116] the wording of the declarations points up that the declarations' role of stating first principles was a weakness as well as a strength.[117] The declarations stated some of the fundamental principles that were thought to underlie the socal contract which the constitutions embodied, but that very choice of language fit the democratic climate of the times and made it likely that the provisions would be treated by many as less than binding as well as non-absolute and qualified.[118]

SEPARATION OF POWERS AND GOVERNMENT STRUCTURE

As has been noted, Virginia and Massachussetts both provided for separation of powers within their declarations of rights, a fact which reflects their framers' recognition of the connection between governmental structure and the preservation of liberty.[119] Even so, the revolutionary era of constitution-making was dominated more by the identification of liberty with popular (and hence legislative) power than with the recognition of the need to divide and limit power.[120] Despite the example of Virginia and Massachusetts, only six state constitutions adopted prior to 1787 explicitly required separation of powers.[121] Even when separation of powers was established, by explicit provision or as an implicit understanding of the structual division of the form of government, the concept was occasionally formulated merely as "little more than a caution against plurality of offices,"[122] and the definition of the legislative power was readily understood as including any power which the legislature might choose to exercise by parliamentary forms.[123]

This early preference for legislative predominance was reflected in the lodging of specific powers as well. In the first wave of state constitutions, adopted in 1776 and 1777,[124] the executive was typically chosen by the legislature and was hardly an independent branch of government.[125] The distrust of executive power embodied in these forms of government reflected the colonial experience in which the people so identified with the legislature, and against the executive, that colonial references to "the government" typically referred to the executive alone.[126] In this move to strengthen the legislature and weaken the executive, the judiciary "came off with little more than an honorable mention."[127] Whereas the courts were under the executive during colonial times, the state constitutions placed them under the legislature.[128]

Some of the states took account of colonial experience with a dependent judiciary and attempted to provide for judicial independence through stipulations regarding tenure and salary.[129] What they did not sufficiently appreciate, however, was that the national mood in favor of popular sovereignty and legislative predominance meant that legislative interference with the judicial function would not be understood as undercutting the independence of the judiciary.[130] Thus even Jefferson, no advocate of an unlimited legislature, observed in his *Notes on Virginia* that, under Virginia's 1776 constitution, the legislative exercise of judicial powers was unlikely to produce opposition, and that, even if it did, the legislature could obligate the other branches simply by putting their quasi-judicial proceedings "into the form of an assembly."[131] Even if some thinkers would have viewed legisla-

tive interference in judicial decision-making as a violation of the provisions
for judicial independence, or of separation of powers more generally, the judicial independence provisions were clearly inadequate as safeguards for
securing a strong coordinate branch of government.[132]

Indeed, the lack of safeguards against the abuse of legislative power is the
single most striking characteristic of the early state constitutions. Not a single constitution of the pre-1787 era made explicit provision for judicial review.[133] Their framers had failed to learn from their colonial experience
"the profound truth of the old maxim 'no writ, no right'—that without implementation a right remains a mere abstraction."[134] But this very lack of
perspicacity as to the need for more meaningful safeguards is itself evidence that most Americans at this time placed the greatest trust in the popular branch of government.[135] They truly believed that representation was
the most effective safeguard of liberty.

The Omission of Rights

It is against the backdrop of this early commitment to popular government (and the corresponding lack of effective safeguards for securing the
limitations contained in the declarations of rights) that we can meaningfully
analyze the significance of the state constitutions that omitted a declaration
of rights from their constitutional frameworks. Sherry contends that, considering the universal commitment to natural rights and the declarations'
function of declaring rights that existed inherently, the omission of declarations from state constitutions that included a few rights in their frames of
government simply underscored "that the vast majority of rights were something apart from the frame of government."[136] This conclusion is buttressed,
she argues, because "no evidence exist that the drafters of these . . . constitutions intended to cede the unlisted rights."[137]

Sherry is almost certainly correct that the omission of declarations of
rights did not imply a repudiation of the moral and political claims of natural rights. But her further claim that their omission lacked legal significance
because of a tacit assumption that the right would serve as an implied limitation, whether or not placed in positive form, is at best a more doubtful point.
The lack of an expressed intent to "cede" the rights can hardly be dispositive
of that question. Given the state constitutions' clear orientation toward legislative predominance, it seems more plausible to think that the omission of
declarations of rights proceeded from the assumption that liberty would be
adequately protected by popular control of government rather than from the
view that the rights would be legally enforceable as unwritten fundamental
law. The adopters of these constitutions may have shared the attitude of

Noah Webster, who argued near the end of this era that "[l]iberty is never secured by such paper declarations; nor lost for want of them."[138] Bills of rights were on this view simply "Don Quixotes fighting windmills."[139]

This at least was the sort of view taken of the omission of a bill of rights in New York by at least one advocate of a bill of rights during the debate over ratification of the federal Constitution.[140] Defenders of the omission of a bill of rights from the proposed federal Constitution occasionally relied upon the omission of a declaration or bill of rights in some of the state constitutions.[141] The author of *Address by Sydney*, widely believed to be either Robert or Abraham Yates,[142] states that there had been three main arguments used to oppose inclusion of a bill of rights in the original New York constitution. First, doubts were expressed about "the propriety of the measure" because of "the peculiar situation in which the country then was," when "all the powers of government [were] avowedly temporary, and solely calculated for defence."[143] Second, by contrast to the "implied constitution" under which the colonists had lived, it was believed that the state's express constitution, formed under the authority of the people and setting forth the basic principles and forms of government, "would operate as a bill of rights."[144] Finally, the frequency of electing legislators rendered them "liable to be displaced in case of malconduct."[145]

The clear implication of Sydney's first argument is that a bill of rights might state legal barriers to government action that would be unduly limiting during the revolutionary struggle with Great Britain.[146] The underlying assumptions are both that provisions in a declaration of rights state limits to legislative power that would otherwise not exist (at least in the same sense) and that such limits must be carefully considered in light of the important role that government plays (especially in time of war). The other arguments advanced by New York's opponents of a state bill of rights indicate that the commitment to civil and political liberty among the founders did not in all cases refer to legal limitations on the exercise of the powers granted to government; security for freedom might stem from constitutional limitations, but also from constitutional structure and an involved electorate. Indeed, as we have seen, reliance on republican government is the predominant theme of the early constitution-making period.

NOTES

1. In fact, late in 1775 the Continental Congress instructed the states to establish independent governments by drafting constitutions. Donald S. Lutz, The Origins of American Constitutionalism 100 (1980). Consequently, in the first two years following independence eleven states drafted new constitutions, and one of

these states, South Carolina, drafted two. Daniel Farber & Suzanna Sherry, A History of the American Constitution 15 (1990).

2. Herman Belz, *Constitutionalism and the American Founding, in* The Framing and Ratification of the Constitution 333, 336 (Leonard Levy & Dennis Mahoney, eds., 1987). As to the importance of this colonial experience with written instruments in shaping the revolutionary insistence on a written constitution, *see also* Julius Goebel, Jr., 1 History of the Supreme Court of the United States: Antecedents and Beginnings to 1801, at 96 (1971).

3. As Stanley Katz has observed, "the impetus for a written constitution was that the imperial crisis of 1775–1776 and the decision for Independence required popular agreement upon and identification of the fundamental law (as well as the creation of a mechanism for enforcing that law against government)." Stanley Katz, *The American Constitution: A Revolutionary Interpretation, in* Beyond Confederation 23, 30 (R. Beeman, S. Botein, & E. Carter, eds., 1987); *see* Goebel, *supra* note 2, at 96 (need for a written constitution "was a conviction afforced by the controversies which had led to revolt").

4. Gordon S. Wood, The Creation of the American Republic 1776–1787, at 293 n.56 (1969). *The Essex Result* (1778), an important revolutionary-era tract, stated "the class of unalienable rights . . . ought to be clearly defined and ascertained in a BILL OF RIGHTS previous to the ratification of any constitution. The bill of rights should also contain the equivalent every man receives, as consideration for the rights he has surrendered." (1 American Political Writing During the Founding Era 1760–1805 [hereafter American Political Writing], at 480, 488–89 [Charles Hyneman & Donald Lutz, eds., 1983]).

5. Belz, *supra* note 2, at 337.

6. *Id.* at 337, *quoting* Benjamin Fletcher Wright, Consensus and Continuity, 1776–1787, at 54 (1966).

7. *Id.*

8. Thus Thomas Paine complained of "the want of a Constitution in England to restrain the wild impulse of power," Thomas Paine, *Rights of Man, in* The Selected Work of Tom Paine 218 (H. Fast, ed., 1945), and Madison characterized the English constitution as merely "a law established by the government," in contrast to America's constitutions that were "unalterable by the government." James Madison, The Federalist No. 53, at 360–61 (Jacob Cooke, ed., 1961). *See infra* note 43.

9. *See, e.g.,* John Philip Reid, Constitutional History of the American Revolution: The Authority of Rights 137 (1986). On the original contract generally, see *id.* at 132–38. It is also true that English rights were described as rooted in a "changeless time" and as "inherent" or "indefeasible." Thomas B. McAffee, *Prolegomena to a Meaningful Debate of the Unwritten Constitution Thesis,* 61 U. Cinc. 107, 147 (1992). While these formulations were intended to underscore that these rights were more than mere grants from King or Parliament, they do not preclude the possibility of the people themselves choosing to cede a particular traditional right; nor, for that matter, do they suggest that such rights will invariably be

"carried over" and found implicit in a new constitutional order, especially one involving a written constitution adopted by a sovereign people.

10. In fact, a standard critical view was that wherever the constitution was incompatible with "the ancient customs, rights, the laws or constitutions heretofore established," the current constitution would prevail. *Letters from a Federal Farmer*, 2 The Complete Anti-Federalist 246 (Oct. 12, 1787) (Herbert J. Storing, ed., 1981).

11. It has been observed, accurately it seems, that what most characterizes a jurisprudence of natural law is not its "particular content at any given time or place," but its general commitment to the search for answers to "the problems of politics." Benjamin F. Wright, American Interpretations of Natural Law: A Study in the History of Political Thought 345 (1931).

12. *See, e.g.,* William Van Alstyne, *Notes on a Bicentennial Constitution: Antinomial Choices and the Role of the Supreme Court (Part 2),* 72 Iowa L. Rev. 1281, 1289 (1987) (suggesting the probability that the Constitution "may have its own theory of justice," and further suggesting that, given the premises underlying a written Constitution, it is *that* theory "which is to govern" rather than the system of ideal justice apprehended by the Constitution's interpreter).

13. This is illustrated by Madison's reservation about a written bill of rights that "there is great reason to fear that a positive declaration of some of the most essential rights could not be obtained with the requisite latitude." James Madison to Thomas Jefferson, Oct 17, 1788, *in* 5 Writings of James Madison 271–72 (Gaillard Hunt, ed., 1904). Madison's concern reflected his assumption that the positively enacted formulation of the right would be the one that would be constitutionally binding over and against the underlying principle he perceived as rooted in natural law.

14. *See* Belz, *supra* note 2, at 334 (noting that "[t]he meaning of liberty, especially the relation between the individual and the community that was central to any practical definition of it, was a deeply controversial issue that divided Americans in state and national constitution-making").

15. Consider Ralph Lerner's observation about the modern tendency to simply presume an obvious consensus around the principles we purport to discover in the thinking of the founding era: "It is almost natural that people today should take principles for granted and find it hard to envision an earlier world when many minds were filled with a sense of fundamentals contending as real alternatives and inviting reasoned choice." Ralph Lerner, *The Constitution of the Thinking Revolutionary, in* Beyond Confederation, *supra* note 3, at 36, 67.

16. Merrill Peterson, *Thomas Jefferson, the Founders, and Constitutional Change,* in The American Founding: Essays on the Formation of the Constitution 276 (J. Barlow, L. Levy, & K. Masugi, eds., 1988) [hereinafter The American Founding].

17. *See id.,* G. Wood, *supra* note 4, at 306–10.

18. Leslie Friedman Goldstein, *In Defense of the Text: Democracy and Constitutional Theory* 75 (1991) (noting that "legislative power over constitutions

stemmed from the prevailing assumption in 1776 that the legislature represented the people"); Willi Paul Adams, The First Constitutions: Republican Ideology and the Making of the State Constitutions in the Revolutionary Era 142–43 (1980) (observing that Americans had concluded that popular sovereignty as limited to the power to constitute government "was not enough to avoid a cycle of oppression and revolution" and that what was required was the insistence "on a permanent role" for the people in the form of frequent elections and timely constitutional reforms); G. Wood, *supra* note 4, at 362.

19. L. Goldstein, *supra* note 18, at 74 (observing that the first six state constitutions were adopted by the state legislatures); *see also* Belz, *supra* note 2, at 339; Suzanna Sherry, *The Founders' Unwritten Constitution*, 54 U. Chi. L. Rev. 1127, 1131 (1987); Thomas G. West, *The Rule of Law in the Federalist*, in Saving the Revolution 150, 155 (Charles Kesler, ed., 1987).

20. W. Adams, *supra* note 18, at 63 (*quoting* Penn. J., May 22, 1776).

21. Belz, *supra* note 2, at 339.

22. *Id.*

23. The Virginia Declaration of Rights, which was drafted a month prior to adoption of the Declaration of Independence, asserted "[t]hat all power is vested in, and consequently derived from, the people." Va. Const. of 1776, Bill of Rts. § 2 (1776), *reprinted in* 7 Francis N. Thorpe, The Federal and State Constitutions, Colonial Charters, and Other Organic Laws of the State, Territories, and Colonies Now or Heretofore Forming the United States of America (1909) [hereinafter State Constitutions], at 3813; N.C. Const. of 1776, Decl. of Rts. art. I (1776), *reprinted in* 5 State Constitutions, *supra,* at 2787.

24. *E.g.,* Va. Const. of 1776, Bill of Rts. § 2 (1776), *reprinted in* 7 State Constitutions, *supra* note 23, at 3813 (providing that "magistrates are [the people's] trustees and servants, and at all times amenable to them"); Pa. Const. of 1776, Decl. of Rts. art. IV (1776), 5 State Constitutions, *supra* note 23, at 3082 (similar formulation).

25. *E.g.,* Pa. Const. of 1776, Decl. of Rts. art. III (1776), 5 State Constitutions, *supra* note 23, at 3082; N.C. Const. of 1776, Decl. of Rts. art. III (1776), 5 State Constitutions, *supra* note 23, at 2787.

26. Del. Const., Decl. of Rts. art. V, *cited in* Robert C. Palmer, *Liberties as Constitutional Provisions* 1776–1791, in Constitution and Rights in the Early American Republic 69 n.80 (1987).

27. At least one author early in this period clarified that the principle was that all power was *derived* from the people, while stressing that "it has never yet been said, that all power is *seated* in the people." *Ludlow*, Penn. J., June 4, 1777, *quoted in* W. Adams, *supra* note 18, at 129. The author concluded that government "supposes and requires a delegation of power" and could not exist without it. *Id.* But this sort of thinking cut against the emphasis on popular control and republican government that many were coming to derive from the premises underlying the popular sovereignty principle.

28. W. Adams, *supra* note 18, at 137.

29. *See* Michael Kammen, Sovereignty and Liberty 14 (1988) (from 1765 to 1785 "popular sovereignty appeared utterly compatible with individual liberty because the power of the people as a collective force would shield free individuals from governmental tyranny"). A key element of the assumption, however, as Forrest McDonald observes, was "the tendency, shared by most Americans who embraced the revolutionary cause, to confuse popular power with popular liberty." Forrest McDonald, Norvus Ordo Seclorum: The Intellectual Origins of the Constitution 157 (1985). In 1774, for example, Hamilton wrote that the only distinction between freedom and slavery is that under freedom "a man is governed by the laws to which he has given his consent, either in person or by his representative," whereas under slavery "he is governed by the will of another." Alexander Hamilton, 1 The Papers of Alexander Hamilton 47 (1961–1979), *quoted in* F. McDonald, *supra,* at 160 n. 33.

30. *See* West, *The Classical Spirit of the Founding*, in The American Founding, *supra* note 16, at 30.

31. McDonald observes that "[t]he slogan, 'Where annual elections ends, slavery begins' was on thousands of lips." F. McDonald, *supra* note 29, at 160.

32. Palmer, *supra* note 23, at 83.

33. Massachusetts General Court, Proclamation of the General Court, Jan 23, 1776, *cited in* G. Wood, *supra* note 4, at 362. Similarly, in 1783 it was asserted that it was in the people alone "that plenary power rests and abides which all agree should rest somewhere." Hartford Conn. Courant, Aug. 12, 1783, *quoted in,* G. Wood, *supra* note 4, at 382. In 1788, the federal Constitution was described as "[a] WHOLE PEOPLE exercising its first and greatest power—performing an act of SOVEREIGNTY, ORIGINAL, and UNLIMITED." F. Hopkinson, Account of the Grand Federal Procession 14 (1788), *quoted in* Kammen, *supra* note 29, at 23.

34. Pa. Const., Decl. of Rts. art. V (1776), 5 State Constitutions, *supra* note 23, at 3082. Lawrence Leder observed that this political theory, emphasizing popular authority, had roots in the colonial period and predated the revolutionary struggle. Lawrence J. Leder, Liberty and Authority: Early American Political Ideology, 1689–1763, at 82 (1968) (observing that the colonists believed that if government failed to attain the ends for which it was created, "the compact is void," as one spokesman put it, *"frustratione finis,"* inasmuch as the people always reserve a right to alter the contract as warranted). For a useful review of the founding period's emphasis on the authority of the people, see Akhil Reed Amar, *Of Sovereignty and Federalism*, 96 Yale L.J. 1425, 1436–39 (1987).

35. G. Wood, *supra* note 4, at 382; L. Leder, *supra* note 31, at 57 (quoting 1750's letter to the Boston Weekly newsletter asserting that the people "have an undoubted right to judge for themselves whether that power is improved to good purposes or not").

36. Whiting, *An Address to the Inhabitants of Berkshire County, Mass.* (1779), in 1 American Political Writing During the Founding Era, *supra* note 4, at 461, 466. A related implication is the assumption that only the people can be "the

constitutional judges of legislative or public oppressions." William Paca, *quoted in* G. Wood, *supra* note 4, at 371.

37. *Compare* Noah Webster, *Government*, in 1 American Magazine 141, 142, *quoted in* G. Wood, *supra* note 4, at 377–78 (expressing skepticism as to whether bills of rights and written constitutions were really necessary or effective), *with* Samuel Holden Parsons to William Cushing (Jan. 11, 1788), *reprinted in* 14 The Documentary History of the Ratification of the Constitution 569, 569 (Merrill Jensen, ed., 1976) [hereinafter Ratification of the Constitution] (arguing that since the proposed Constitution "is grounded on the idea that the people are the fountain of all power, that no dominion can rightfully be exercised over them but by their consent, and that every officer of government is amenable to them in the exercise of the authorities granted," it follows that "it is the ruler who must receive a bill of rights from the people and not they from him"). Though hardly the standard defense of the omission of a bill of rights, Parsons' argument, as we will discover, was a theme often invoked in the defense of the proposed Constitution.

38. G. Wood, *supra* note 4, at 293, *quoting*, [James Cannon] *Cassandra*, April 1776, American Archives, 4th serv., V, 1094 (Force, ed.).

39. G. Wood, *supra* note 4, at 293; *see* J. Goebel, *supra* note 2, at 100 (resort to written declarations to limit government reflected "a general determination that the principle of the controlling effect of the constitution upon law-making should be put on as solid a footing as the frame of government itself"). As we shall see, however, the declarations of rights achieved only a partial success, given that they remained mainly restatements of fundamental principles and of government's obligations rather than legal commands and prohibitions.

40. *See, e.g.,* Sherry, *supra* note 19, at 1133; David N. Mayer, *The Natural Rights Basis of the Ninth Amendment: A Reply to Professor McAffee*, 16 S. Ill. U. L.J. 313, 322 (1992).

41. As Benjamin Barber states, "[e]ven the most zealous naturalists acknowledge that rights need to be secured or recognized or enforced in order to acquire operational force in the real world." Barber, *The Rights of We the People Are All the Rights There Are, in* To Secure the Blessings of Liberty 189, 201 (S. Thurow, ed., 1988). This recognition would increasingly prompt dedicated naturalists during the founding era to insist on the absolute necessity of reducing natural law to positive law.

42. *See, e.g.,* G. Wood, *supra* note 4, at 293–96.

43. Belz, *supra* note 2, at 337; Gordon S. Wood, *The Political Ideology of the Founders,* in Toward a More Perfect Union 7, 23 (Neill York, ed., 1988). The revolutionary, Tom Paine, would write: "From the want of a Constitution in England to restrain and regulate the wild impulse of power, many of the laws are irrational and tyrannical, and the administration of them vague and problematical." Thomas Paine, *Rights of Man,* in The Selected Work of Tom Paine 218 (H. Fast, ed., 1945). *See also* James Madison, The Federalist No. 53, *supra* note 8, at 359, 360–61 (noting that the distinction "between a constitution established by the people, and unalterable by the government" and "a law established by the govern-

ment," has not been understood elsewhere, and that Parliament is viewed as "uncontrollable" even by the constitution); Philodemus (Thomas Tucker), *Conciliatory Hints, Attempting, by a Fair State of Matters, to Remove Party Prejudice*, in American Political Writing During the Founding Era, *supra* note 4, at 606, 610 (describing the British system as granting Parliament "undefinable privileges, transcendent power, and political omnipotence"). As we will see, such distinctions between American constitutions and the English constitution became important themes for Madison and other key players in the drafting and ratifying of the 1787 Constitution.

44. G. Wood, *supra* note 4, at 294.

45. Philip A. Hamburger, *Natural Rights, Natural Law, and American Constitutions*, 102 Yale L.J. 907, 932 (1991). *See also id.* at 932–35. Perhaps Hamburger's most striking example of a statement adhering to this view, from the period prior to the drafting of the federal Constitution, is one proffered by Thomas Jefferson. In his famous work reflecting on the state of affairs in Virginia around 1784, Jefferson referred to the inalienable natural rights and offered that "our rulers can have no authority over such natural rights, *only as we have submitted to them.*" Thomas Jefferson, Notes on the State of Virginia (1784), *reprinted in* The Life and Selected Writings of Thomas Jefferson 274–75 (Adrienne Koch & William Peden eds., 1944).

46. Alexander Hamilton, The Federalist No. 84, *supra* note 8, at 580.

47. A compelling example is that limits on the power to fight wars were viewed as directed at the crown; they were simply not viewed as limiting the power of Parliament the way our Second Amendment purports to limit Congress. Alexander Hamilton, The Federalist No. 26, *supra* note 8, at 166–67 (arguing that state provisions that limited authority to legislatures to call up the military were superfluous because the authority had always resided there).

48. *See generally* W. Adams, *supra* note 18, at 145–46.

49. Donald S. Lutz, Popular Consent and Popular Control 60 (1980). Even an advocate of the unenumerated rights reading of the Ninth Amendment has acknowledged "that state governments have universally been regarded as possessing all powers except those explicitly denied them in their constitutive documents." Calvin R. Massey, Silent Rights: The Ninth Amendment and the Constitution's Unenumerated Rights 87 (1995). Indeed, Massey acknowledges that, under the state constitutions the grant of powers was "presumptively unlimited" because it rested on the "presumption that state governments possess all powers except those explicitly denied to them." *Id.*

50. *The Impartial Examiner*, 5 The Complete Anti-Federalist, *supra* note 10, at 177 (Feb. 20, 1788).

51. *Id.* The prescription became clear. The people must insist upon a bill of rights, and then they "ought to give up no greater share [of the mass of natural rights] than what is understood to be absolutely necessary." *Id.* at 176.

52. Edmund Randolph, *Essay on the Revolutionary History of Virginia, reprinted in* 1 B. Schwartz, The Bill of Rights: A Documentary History 249 (1971).

53. Thus Sherry contends that the founding generation perceived at least the prohibition on *ex post facto* laws as a guarantee protecting a natural right that would have been deemed implicit in the state constitutions if the limitation were not stated explicitly in a state's declaration of rights. Sherry, *supra* note 19, at 1157. She contends that this is the reason some at the Philadelphia Convention opposed inclusion of such a prohibition in the proposed federal Constitution as unnecessary. *Id.*

54. Sherry contends that the prohibition on bills of attainder was viewed as a positive right, rather than a natural right; thus a written guarantee was required so as to exclude legislative trials as a weapon that constitutionally could be employed. *Id. See infra* Chapter 5, notes 30–34 and accompanying text.

55. Thomas B. McAffee, *The Bill of Rights, Social Contract Theory, and the Rights "Retained" by the People*, 16 S. Ill. U.L.J. 267, 294 (1992).

56. *See generally* Warren M. Billings, *"That All Men are Born Equally Free and Independent": Virginians and the Origins of the Bill of Rights, in* The Bill of Rights and the States 335, 339–40 (Patrick J. Conley & John P. Kaminski, eds. 1992).

57. Va. Const., Decl. of Rts. Sect. 1, *reprinted in* 7 State Constitutions, *supra* note 23, at 3813 (emphasis added).

58. Billings, *supra* note 56, at 339–40.

59. Here the doctrine of popular sovereignty worked as a key to limiting the powers granted to government. Constitutional conventions, which gradually became the norm, "gave institutional reality to the theoretical ideal that governmental authority should rest on a constitution that proceeded directly from the people and that took precedence over ordinary legislation." Thomas C. Grey, *The Original Understanding and the Unwritten Constitution, in* Toward a More Perfect Union: Six Essays on the Constitution 145, 155 (1988).

60. Sherry, *supra* note 19, at 1134.

61. *Id.*

62. *Id.* at 1133 & n. 32. The relevant provisions include: Pa. Const. Sect. 46 (1776), *reprinted in* 5 State Constitutions, *supra* note 23, at 3091; N.C. Const. art. XLIV (1776), *reprinted in* 5 State Constitutions, *supra* note 23, at 2794; Del. Const. art. 30 (1776), *reprinted in* 1 State Constitutions, *supra* note 23, at 568. For contrasting analysis of these constitutional provisions, see *infra* notes 74–92 and accompanying text .

63. *Id.* at 1132–34, 1135, 1145–46, 1158 n. 137.

64. The spirit of the declarations is well expressed in the 1790 Pennsylvania constitution's statement that the article declaring the people's rights was included so that the "essential principles of liberty and free government may be recognized and unalterably established." Pa. Const., Decl. of Rts. art. IX (1790), *reprinted in* 5 State Constitutions, *supra* note 23, at 3099.

65. Sherry, *supra* note 19, at 1133.

66. Gordon Wood accurately describes the declarations as generally involving "a jarring but exciting combination of ringing declarations of universal princi-

ples with a motley collection of common law procedures in order to fence them off from the rulers' power." G. Wood, *supra* note 4, at 271.

67. *E.g., Letters From a Federal Farmer,* in 2 The Complete Anti-Federalist, *supra* note 10, at 261 (Dec. 25, 1787) (stating the conventional view that some rights are "natural and inalienable" while others "are constitutional or fundamental"; the latter are rights that "individuals claim under the solemn compacts of the people, as constitutions"; finally, listing a third sort of right that "are common or mere legal rights," the sort that "individuals claim under laws which the ordinary legislature may alter or abolish at pleasure"); Rep. James Madison (speech presenting proposed federal Bill of Rights to Congress explaining that such bills of rights include "retained natural rights" and also "specify positive rights, which may seem to result from the nature of the compact"), 1 Annals of Congress col. 454 (June 8, 1789). *See generally* Hamburger, *supra* note 45, at 920–22. Gerald Stourzh observes that the process of "constitutionalizing" rights went in two directions: natural rights were "reduced" to written law, and what had been procedural protections alterable by ordinary legislation were frequently "raised" to the status of constitutional rights. Stourzh, *Fundamental Laws and Individual Rights,* in The American Founding, *supra* note 16, at 159, 172.

68. *See supra* note 24. *See generally* Palmer, *supra* note 26, at 64 n. 41 (citing and discussing several such state constitutional provisions).

69. As Robert C. Palmer observes, individual liberties were set alongside provisions to secure "communal well-being." Palmer, *supra* note 26, at 66, precisely because their framers "considered the communal right to qualify liberties as important as the individual's right to be free from governmental interference." *Id.* at 64. Thus the inclusion of the people's police power in the declarations reflected the belief that the "liberty of republican government was primary," *id.* at 66, and was itself considered to be a liberty "because the aggregate of individuals could thereby assert the essential rights of safety, morality and well-being against the licentious." *Id.*

70. Va. Const., Bill of Rts. § 5 (1776), *reprinted in* 7 State Constitutions, *supra* note 23, at 3813. *See also* Mass. Const., Decl. of Rts. art. XXX (1780) (requiring separation of powers "to the end it may be a government of laws and not of men"), *reprinted in* 3 State Constitutions, *supra* note 23, at 1893.

71. Thus John Adams claimed that the "three branches of power have an unalterable foundation in nature; that they exist in every society natural and artificial; and that if they are not acknowledged in any constitution of government, it will be found to be imperfect, unstable, and soon enslaved." John Adams, 4 The Works of John Adams, 292 (Charles Adams ed., 1851).

72. A potent symbol of this reality is that the Virginia constitution included a separation of powers provision within its frame of government and its declaration of rights. Similarly, the Pennsylvania frame of government guaranteed seemingly individual rights provisions, including a provision that "[t]he printing presses *shall* be free to every person who undertakes to examine the proceedings of the legislature, or any part of government." Pa. Const. of 1776 § 35, *reprinted in* 5

State Constitutions, *supra* note 23, at 3090. Palmer suggests that what most distinguishes this and similar provisions within the Pennsylvania frame of government is the use of mandatory language, reflecting that such provisions were deemed less qualifiable than the statements of principle found in the declaration of rights: they represented "structural necessities for the basic liberty of republicanism." Palmer, *supra* note 26, at 67.

73. As Goebel observes, in general the declarations involved a combining of basic principles of government with a statement of individual rights, for which there was precedent in the English bill of rights. J. Goebel, *supra* note 2, at 101.

74. Professor Amar observes that American thinking about this authority of the people "built on the language of the Declaration of Independence's assertion that it is the *Right of the People* to alter or abolish [their government], and to institute new Government." Akhil Reed Amar, The Bill of Rights: Creation and Reconstruction 122 (1998). Goldstein states that eight of the fourteen state constitutions adopted between 1776 and 1780 included paraphrases of the notion of the people's right to "alter or abolish" their "form" of government. L. Goldstein, *supra* note 18, at 73–74.

75. *See, e.g.,* D. Lutz, *supra* note 1, at 105 (observing that only four of the first eleven state constitutions made explicit provision for amendment). For the relevance of the goal of drafting perpetual constitutions, see *infra* notes 93–96 and accompanying text.

76. Andrew McLaughlin long ago argued that the failure to provide for amendment probably reflected haste and the failure to pause to consider that there would be such a need. Andrew McLaughlin, The Courts, the Constitution, and Parties 115 (1912); *see also* A. Amar, *supra* note 34, at 122 (observing that in The Federalist No. 78, Alexander Hamilton relied upon "that fundamental principle of republican government which admits *the right of the people* to alter or abolish the established Consitution whenever they find it inconsistent with their happiness. . . ."). McLaughlin's insight seems confirmed by the provision for amendment in most of the second wave of constitutions, enacted from 1777 to 1786. D. Lutz, *supra* note 1, at 105. I have seen no evidence of fundamental objections being raised to any of these constitutions providing for amendment nor any evidence that the power of amendment was conceived to be limited only to the frame of government.

77. Pa. Const. § 46 (1776), *reprinted in* 5 State Constitutions, *supra* note 23, at 3091; N.C. Const. Pt. XLIV (1776), *reprinted in* 5 State Constitutions, *supra* note 23, at 2794 (slightly different punctuation from Pennsylvania provision).

78. Given that these provisions appear to reflect the need to remove potential doubt as to the constitutional status of the declarations, they suggest that the framers of these constitutions recognized that constitutions were increasingly viewed as devices for *limiting,* and not merely *constituting,* government. It may also be that the widespread use of the language of principle and obligation in the declarations, rather than of command and prohibition, helps explain the perceived need for a provision confirming the constitutional status of the provisions.

79. Del. Const. art. 30 (1776), *reprinted in* 1 State Constitutions, *supra* note 23, at 568. The provisions in the constitution to which this language was applied included the articles clarifying the name of the state, requiring the legislature to meet at least annually, and providing for the self-regulation of the legislature. *Id.* at 562–63 (art. 1, 2, and 5). Once again, the division between provisions that may or may not be amended does not break down purely along lines of individual rights and organizational provisions.

80. This conclusion is reinforced by the requirement that a super-majority vote of the legislature was required even when amendment of the constitution was allowed. This reflects the movement to dissociate the sovereign power of the people from the legislative branch's power as well as an inclination to inform the legislature that it is bound by the constitution. But even this prohibition on amending a few matters would not limit the authority of the people to adopt a new constitution or to alter or reform the existing one.

81. Md. Const. art. LIX (1776), *reprinted in* 3 State Constitutions, *supra* note 23, at 1701 (providing for amendment of both the "Form of Government" and the "Declaration of Rights" by a bill passed after publication prior to an election for the legislative assembly); S.C. Const. art. XLIV (1778), *reprinted in* 6 State Constitutions, *supra* note 23, at 3257 (generally worded amendment provision requiring ninety days of notice and passage by state's two-house legislature). Of the two, only Maryland's constitution included a declaration of rights, but South Carolina's constitution included several individual rights provisions within the body of the form of government.

82. Pa. Const., Decl. of Rts. art. V (1776), *reprinted in* 5 State Constitutions, *supra* note 23, at 3083; Del. Const., Decl. of Rts. § 5 (1776), *reprinted in* 1 Bill of Rights: A Documentary History 277 (Bernard Schwartz, ed., 1971). Considering that the Pennsylvania provision describes this sovereign authority as "unalienable," it seems especially implausible that the prohibition on violating the declaration of rights would be construed as an implied limitation on the power of the community to amend the Constitution or any part of it.

83. Sherry, *supra* note 19, at 1131–34.

84. D. Lutz, *supra* note 1, at 18–19, 32–34, 98–99, 151–52. In fact, Lutz contends that the Declaration of Independence served the foundational, covenant-establishing role that created the social compact at a national level, just as the declarations and preambles served this historical function in the state constitutions. *Id.* at 114–15, 124.

85. *Id.* at 98.

86. *Id* at 33.

87. *See* Va. Const. (1776), 7 State Constitutions, *supra* note 23, at 3812, 3814. *Compare* Md. Const. (1776), 3 State Constitutions, *supra* note 23, at 1691 (denominating the second part as "The Constitution, or Form of Government, & C."); N.C. Const. (1776), 5 State Constitutions, *supra* note 23, at 2789 (same). Lutz thus concludes that the early state constitutions are "really compacts in which the constitution [or frame of government] became predominant," D. Lutz, *supra* note 1,

at 344. And it is this distinction that created the basis for (or perhaps the confusion underlying) James Wilson's 1787 argument defending the omission of a bill of rights from the proposed federal Constitution on the ground that the Virginia constitution did not include a bill of rights. Defined narrowly enough, the Virginia constitution did not contain a bill of rights.

88. D. Lutz, *supra* note 1, at 34, *quoting* Mass. Const. preamble (1780), *reprinted in* 3 State Constitutions, *supra* note 23, at 1889. *Compare* Pa. Const. preamble (1776), *reprinted in* 5 State Constitutions, *supra* note 23, at 3082 (establishing "the following *Declaration of Rights* and *Frame of Government,* to be the Constitution of this commonwealth"); Vt. Const. preamble (1777), *reprinted in* 6 State Constitutions, *supra* note 23, at 3739 (basically same as Pa.).

89. D. Lutz, *supra* note 1, at 34.

90. Pa. Const. preamble (1776), *reprinted in* 5 State Constitutions, *supra* note 23, at 3082; *accord* Vt. Const. preamble (1777), reprinted in 6 State Constitutions, *supra* note 23, at 3739. *Compare* Mass. Const. ch. VI, art. X (1780), *reprinted in* 3 State Constitutions, *supra* note 23, at 1911 (providing for procedure by which "such alterations as from experience shall be found necessary" might be adopted—without distinguishing between the different parts of the constitution as denominated in the preamble).

91. It would have contradicted the often cited Antifederalist position to have proffered such an argument, inasmuch as the Antifederalists' contention was precisely that "a constitution does not imply any more than a declaration of the relation which the different parts of the government have to each other, but does not imply security to the rights of individuals." Letters of Agrippa (Jan. 9, 1788), 4 The Complete Anti-Federalist, *supra* note 10, at 108.

The author of *Letters from a Federal Farmer,* perhaps the leading work against ratification, stated the standard view:

We often find, these [limiting] articles and stipulations placed in bills of rights, but they may as well be incorporated in the body of the constitution, as selected and placed by themselves. The constitution, or whole social compact, is but one instrument, no more or less, than a certain number of articles or stipulations agreed to by the people, whether it consists of articles, sections, chapters, bills of rights, or parts of any other denomination, cannot be material. (Letters from a Federal Farmer, *in* 2 The Complete Anti-Federalist, *supra* note 10, at 323.)

92. While the focal point of discussion concerning the need for amendments to the Constitution was its failure to supply a comprehensive "bill" of rights, the amending process by and large did not proceed as though there were an intent to give a unique status to a separate body of liberty-bearing, as opposed to structurally oriented, norms. In fact, the amendments considered in the Congress ranged from individual rights guarantees to proposals reflecting opposition to the allocation of power to the national government, and no one suggested that these various amendments would hold any different status from any other. In truth, the traditional description of the first ten amendments as the "Bill of Rights" probably reflects that Madison by and large succeeded in limiting the amendments mainly to essential guarantees of liberty while avoiding wholesale structural changes. *See*

generally Paul Finkelman, *The First Ten Amendments as a Declaration of Rights,* 16 S.Ill.U. L.J. 351, 352, 368–78 (1992).

Notice also that Madison did not follow the state constitutional pattern by proposing that the amendments be placed in a separate document as a declaration of rights that would precede the Constitution as the frame of government. Rather, he proposed to insert the amendments in the body of the Constitution, thus reinforcing the conclusion that the amendments were to hold the same status as every other constitutional guarantee. *See Madison Resolution, in* Creating the Bill of Rights 11–14 (Helen E. Veit, Kenneth R. Bowling, Charlene Bangs Bickford, eds., 1991). Even the decision to append the amendments reflected a decision that they would enjoy the same status as the provisions included in the text.

93. Del. Const. art. X (1792), *reprinted in* 1 State Constitutions, *supra* note 23, at 580. *See also* N.C. Const. art. XIII (1868), *reprinted in* 5 State Constitutions, *supra* note 23, at 2821 (constitution next adopted after 1776 constitution provides for amendment and creates no restriction on amendment to any portions of the constitution).

94. Del. Const. preamble (1792), *supra* note 23, at 568. In this constitution, the organization scheme is continuous and incorporates both a declaration of rights and a frame of government. This contrasts with early constitutions, such as those of Pennsylvania and Massachusetts, that explicitly refer to both documents as "Parts," but which numbered the sections of each of these elements separately.

95. Likewise, there is no similar provision in the constitution that succeeded North Carolina's 1776 constitution. Pennsylvania's 1790 constitution does not include that same provision enjoining violations of the declaration of rights, but article IX does state that everything contained therein is "excepted out of the general powers of government, and shall forever remain inviolate." Pa. Const. art. IX, sect. 26 (1790), *reprinted in* 5 State Constitutions, *supra* note 23, at 3101 (subsequent constitution includes an article denoted as a "Declaration of Rights," but fully incorporated in the body of a single, continuously flowing constitution, as its first article).

96. *E.g.,* Philip A. Hamburger, *The Constitution's Accomodation of Social Change,* 88 Mich. L. Rev. 239 (1989).

97. *Id.* at 265–325. *Id.* at 263, *quoting* Four Letters on Important Subjects 16 (1776).

98. *Id.* at 263, *quoting* The Genuine Principles of the Ancient Saxon or English Constitution (1776).

99. *Id., quoting,* The Genuine Principles of the Ancient Saxon or English Constitution (1776). *See also id.* at 267–71, 275–300, 300–01, 325–27. Because of the agreement as to the principle that the Constitution should include only provisions for perpetuity, the main areas of debate over proposed amendments during the struggle for ratification turned on the question whether the particular safeguards demanded by the Constitution's opponents were essential perpetual safeguards to liberty or provisions likely to become obsolete over time and thus better omitted from the Constitution. *Id.* at 298–99.

100. *See* D. Lutz, *supra* note 1, at 99, 105; Palmer, *supra* note 26, at 65.

101. In *The Essex Result,* for example, the "supreme power of the State" is viewed as residing in society as a whole, but inasmuch as no individual "parts with his unalienable rights, the supreme power therefore cannot controul them." Theophilus Parsons, *The Essex Result* (1778), *in* 1 American Political Writing, *supra* note 4, at 480, 487. Moreover, the individual surrenders "the power of controlling his natural alienable rights, ONLY WHEN THE GOOD OF THE WHOLE REQUIRES IT." *Id.*

102. Palmer asserts that while some rights were not to be surrendered completely, "[e]very right was qualified by entry into society; no right was absolute in the modern sense, that is, unqualifiable." Palmer, *supra* note 26, at 65–66. The state declarations seem to bear out his claim. There is little question, for example, that the natural right of property was understood as being subject to regulation by the community for the public good. In Massachusetts, for example, although the "unalienable" rights clause included property rights, a later provision acknowledges the power of the legislature to take property for public use so long as it pays just compensation. Mass. Const., Decl. of Rights art. I, X (1780), *reprinted in* 3 State Constitutions, *supra* note 23, at 1889, 1891. More generally, for a treatment of the highly qualified nature of property rights as they were understood in America and Great Britain during the founding era, see F. McDonald, *supra* note 26, at 13–36.

103. William Blackstone, 1 Commentaries on the Laws of England 121 (Chi. 1979 reprint of 1765–69 ed.). *See* Palmer, *supra* note 26, at 65–66 & n.51. Even the author of *The Essex Result* would not differ markedly from Blackstone's formulation, given that his concept of inalienable rights was narrow. *See* Theophilus Parsons, *The Essex Result* (1778), *in* 1 American Political Writing, *supra* note 4, at 492 (stating the view that each individual "surrendered his right of controul over his person and property, (with an exception to the rights of conscience) to the supreme legislative power, to be exercised by the power, *when the good of the whole demanded it").* *See also* D. Lutz, *supra* note 1, at 105 (suggesting that most rights were viewed as "alienable," with the "right to free exercise of religion" and the "right to trial by jury" as the only "consistent exceptions").

104. G. Wood, *supra* note 4, at 382. For the articulation of similar views, see *supra* notes 3–4, 8–10, 17–20, 27–35 and accompanying text. Even those who argued that the inalienable rights could not be subjected to control believed that, in determining the public good by which the alienable natural rights might be controlled, "there can be but one absolute judge in the State*"*—the majority of the people. Theophilus Parsons, *The Essex Result* (1778), *in* 1 American Political Writing, *supra* note 4, at 488. As a practical matter, Parsons might have acknowledged, as many others did, that the people were necessarily the supreme judge of the scope of the rights that were to be considered inalienable as well. His only institutional suggestion, after all, is that "these unalienable rights" should be "clearly defined and ascertained in a Bill of Rights, previous to the ratification of any constitution." *Id.* at 495. Since Parsons took it as a given that it was "[t]he freemen inhabiting the territory of the Massachusetts-Bay" who were "forming a po-

litical society for themselves," *id.* at 486, it would seem to follow that those same freemen would be charged with the task of defining and ascertaining the inalienable rights in adopting a constitution and bill of rights. Moreover, if it would be inappropriate for a minority of the community to dictate the answer to questions of qualifing the alienable rights, it would be even less fitting for a minority (such as a court, for example) to hold the authority of identifying the inalienable rights and establishing their boundaries against the judgment and will of the sovereign people.

105. For many republicans, liberty was primary because a widely held view was that "men acting privately were not to be trusted and that they needed to be protected from one another by governments which were based upon popular consent." F. McDonald, *supra* note 29, at 160. In fact, as Professor Hamburger observes, the moral constraints on private rights were viewed as injunctions of natural law, so that legislative limits on the exercise of personal freedom, even of inalienable rights, were viewed as dictated by natural law and as quite consistent with the securing of legitimate exercises of the natural rights. Hamburger, *supra* note 45, at 927–30.

106. Thus "Americans frequently said or assumed that certain types of speech or press—including blasphemous, obscene, fraudalent, or defamatory statements—lacked or should have lacked constitutional protection." Hamburger, *supra* note 45, at 935. Even so, guarantees of "freedom of speech" often failed to include language stating explicit limits on free speech rights. *See, e.g.,* Va. Const., Bill of Rts. § 12 (1776), *reprinted in* 7 State Constitutions, *supra* note 23, at 3814 (calling "the freedom of the press" one of "the great bulwarks of liberty," and stating further that it "can never be restrained but by despotic governments"); Mass. Const., Decl. of Rts. art. XVI (1780), *reprinted in* 3 State Constitutions, *supra* note 23, at 1892 (similar wording).

107. A typical example of a limiting principle reflecting the interests of the community is the New Hampshire Bill of Rights' provision for free exercise of religion "provided he doth not disturb the public peace, or disturb others, in their religious worship." N.H. Const., Bill of Rts. art. V (1784), *reprinted in* 4 State Constitutions, *supra* note 23, at 2454. For other examples from eighteenth century state constitutions, see Hamburger, *supra* note 45, at 936 & n. 83.

108. For a treatment of the relationship between the nature of the language employed and the qualified nature of the rights in question, see Palmer, *supra* note 26, at 64–65.

109. Typical of this pattern is New Hampshire's statement that "[a]ll penalties ought to be proportioned to the nature of the offence." N.H. Const., Bill of Rts. art. XVIII, *quoted in* Palmer, *supra* note 26, at 68 n. 77. But this sort of construction is pervasive. *See* Palmer, *supra* note 26, at 64–65.

110. *E.g.,* Va. Const., Bill of Rts. § 4 (1776), *reprinted in* 7 State Constitutions, *supra* note 23, at 3813 (stating the principle "[t]hat no man, or set of men, are entitled to exclusive or separate emoluments or privileges from the community, but in consideration of public services"); *id.* § 12, quoted *supra* note 106 at

3814 (stating free press principle). Sometimes the two methods were combined. *See id.* § 11 (stating that "in controversies respecting property, and in suits between man and man, the ancient trial by jury is preferable to any other, and ought to be held sacred").

111. New Hampshire's proportionality provision continued: "No wise legislature will affix the same punishment to the crimes of theft, forgery, and the like, which they do to those of murder and treason. . . ." N.H. Const., Bill of Rts. art. XVIII. Similarly, Virginia provided that freedom of the press "can never be restrained but by despotic governments." Va. Decl. of Rts. § 12, *quoted in* Palmer, *supra* note 26, at 68.

112. Palmer, *supra* note 26, at 65, 75. Donald Lutz adds that such formulations reflected the earlier history of the declarations of rights as "a public elaboration, almost a celebration, of a people's fundamental values," that served mainly to remind that "action contrary to these commitments should not be undertaken lightly." D. Lutz, *supra* note 1, at 32–33.

113. Palmer, *supra* note 26, at 69. It is this assumption that the rights could be qualified for the public good that explains why various guarantees, such as free speech and press provisions, were often stated without qualifying language even though no one during this era would have questioned that traditional limitations, such as the provision for liability for libels, would continue to have force and effect.

114. *Id.* at 61. The provisions stated "values that had to be taken into consideration when the individual and collectivity confronted each other." *Id.* at 82.

115. *Id.* at 83.

116. Clearly, these were intended as statements of fundamental law, and the idea that a constitution was binding on government was a basic tenant of the colonists in their struggle with Great Britain. Indeed, as Palmer acknowledges, one contemporary formulation was that by virtue of the declarations, rights "should be *guaranteed*, not *granted*." G. Wood, *supra* note 4, at 271. Moreover, Goebel points out (and we have seen) that several of the state constitutions included provisions forbidding enactments in violation of, or repugnant to, the declarations of rights, or occasionally of the entire constitution. J. Goebel, *supra* note 2, at 102.

117. At the very least, Leonard Levy correctly describes the formulations as "flabby" and "namby-pamby." *See* Palmer, *supra* note 26, at 64 n.44; Bernard Schwartz, The Great Rights of Mankind 169–70 (1977) (referring to state declarations as "simple admonitions, rudimentary efforts to restrain the legislatures" and calling them important largely because of how they came to be used at a later time); Belz, *supra* note 2, at 339 (more than "language of urging and admonition" found in the state constitutions "was needed to transform them into effective restraints on the actual exercise of power").

118. It is no coincidence, as Belz observes, that state declarations of rights had little effect on legislative power "because they were treated as hortatory rather than legally binding." Belz, *supra* note 2, at 338–39. As we will see, the lack of forcefulness in the language employed was reinforced by the general failure in the

state constitutions to provide a meaningful mechanism for enforcing the limits stated by the constitution.

119. *See supra* notes 67–69 and accompanying text.

120. *See* West, *supra* note 19, at 30 (initially Americans had difficulty reconciling the principle of government by consent, and the implication of purely republican government, with the idea of separating government powers).

121. McLaughlin, *supra* note 73, at 116 n. 23, *citing* W. Bondy, The Separation of Governmental Powers.

122. Edward S. Corwin, *The Progress of Constitutional Theory Between the Declaration of Independence and the Meeting of the Philadelphia Convention, in* I Corwin on the Constitution 56, 60 (R. Loss ed. 1981). *But see* G. Wood, *supra* note 4, at 156–59 (arguing that separation of powers, even in the earliest days of the republic, went beyond prohibition of plural officeholding, but nevertheless focused on preventing encroachment by the executive on the popular branch).

123. Corwin, *supra* note 122, at 61.

124. Lutz describes three waves of adoptions of state constitutions, each of which reflects trends of thinking about constitutionalism. *See* D. Lutz, *supra* note 1, at 104; 104–08 (describing first wave); *id.* at 108–110 (describing some of the salient differences between the first two waves of state constitutions).

125. *Id.* at 105.

126. *Id.*

127. J. Goebel, *supra* note 2, at 97.

128. D. Lutz, *supra* note 1, at 105.

129. J. Goebel, *supra* note 2, at 98. Gordon Wood points out, however, that some constitutions granted tenure during good behavior while giving the legislature control over salaries and fees, providing for fixed terms of office, and nonetheless providing fairly liberal procedures for removal. G. Wood, *supra* note 4, at 161.

130. While these state constitutions improved upon the colonial period by giving the judiciary independence from the executive (which many equated with "the government"), Wood observes that "most of the early constitution-makers had little sense that judicial independence meant independence from the people." Wood, *supra* note 4, at 161.

131. Thomas Jefferson, *Notes on Virginia,* 2 Writings 163–64 (Memorial ed. 1903), *quoted in* Corwin, *supra* note 122, at 61. Jefferson offers this commonplace analysis of the legislative power notwithstanding that he is writing as a critic of the revolutionary constitution of Virginia as lacking sufficient controls of legislative power. *See, e.g., id. See also* J. Goebel, *supra* note 2, at 98–100.

132. J. Goebel, *supra* note 2, at 102.

133. The omission of any textual provision for judicial review reflects the confidence reposed in the revolutionary-era legislatures; there is little reason to think that the framers of the early state constitutions intended the exercise of judicial review. Indeed, Goebel's review of the few non-judicial devices relied upon to secure compliance with the state constitutions reflects a basic confidence in the

power of the people as the best corrective of the abusive exercise of power. *See id.* at 102–05. New Hampshire and Pennsylvania provided for consideration of the state of their constitutions after seven years—by means of a provision for amendment to preserve "effectual adherance" to the constitution in New Hampshire, *id.* at 192, *quoting* 4 State Constitutions, *supra* note 23, at 2470, and by a Council of Censors to pass censors, order impeachment, and recommend legislative repeal of laws "enacted contrary to the principles of the constitution" in Pennsylvania. J. Goebel, *supra* note 2, at 103. Even New York's Council of Revision, to which the legislature was to present all bills before they became law, was only empowered to provide the legislature with a statement of objections to a law that appeared "improper" on constitutional or other grounds, and its role was thus advisory only. J. Goebel, *supra* note 2, at 103–04.

134. J. Goebel, *supra* note 2, at 102.

135. As Goebel observes, "[t]he tenor of the petitions which poured in at the commencement of [the legislative] sessions indicates a widespread belief in [the legislatures'] omnipotence." *Id.* at 100.

136. Sherry, *supra* note 19, at 1133; *see id.* at 1132–33.

137. *Id.* at 1133.

138. Noah Webster, *Government*, in 1 American Magazine 141, *quoted at* G. Wood, *supra* note 4, at 377. Webster contended that written constitutions, bills of rights, and perpetual constitutions made no sense in a republican form of government, where there was no need to articulate limits to the prerogatives of a royal sovereign. *Id.*

139. *Id.* at 13, *quoted at* G. Wood, *supra* note 4, at 378.

140. *Address by Sydney*, 6 The Complete Anti-Federalist, *supra* note 10, at 107, 109–110.

141. Alexander Hamilton, The Federalist No. 84, *supra* note 8, at 578. As we have seen, Wilson made a similar argument, only partially correctly, with respect to the Virginia state constitution. *See supra* note 87.

142. "Sydney" is widely believed to have been either Robert or Abraham Yates, both prominent New York Antifederalists.

143. *Address by Sydney*, 6 The Complete Anti-Federalist, *supra* note 10, at 109.

144. *Id.*

145. *Id.*

146. Belz observes that the revolutionary struggle impacted as well on thinking about liberty even where there were declarations of rights. Although the revolutionaries had justified independence based on universal natural rights, it seemed apparent that "[w]artime exigencies required decisive political action," which was justified theoretically "based on the right of local communities to control individuals for the sake of the common good." Belz, *supra* note 2, at 344. The Revolutionary War thus delayed the day of reckoning when the Americans would have to reconcile their competing ideas of liberty as political freedom and liberty as individual rights. *Id.*

3

Constitutional Practice in the Confederation Period: The Search for Effective Limits on Legislative Power

The confederation period, 1776–1787, was characterized by a continuing dialogue over how to resolve the tension between government by consent and the idea of limited government that preserved liberty.[1] On the one hand, the period after 1776 was easily the most democratic of any period prior to that time, and the idea of popular sovereignty became more concrete and intensely real than during any prior time in the history of these states.[2] Representation was enlarged,[3] checks on the popularly-elected legislative branch were fewer than during the colonial period, and many offered theories of representation that underscored the idea of popular control of the legislators.[4]

On the other hand, there rather quickly emerged a recognition by many that legislative sovereignty, even as buttressed by the idea of popular control, ran against the grain of revoutionary-era thought that emphasized the need for effectively limiting and checking the power of all government, and this view held whether the government was monarchical or republican.[5] As we will see, although the differences of viewpoint about the extent of the need to check republican government emerged early, so that the devices for control were developed and debated throughout the confederation period, there was by 1787 a growing sense of urgency about the need to provide checks against arbitrary power.

THE PROBLEM OF LEGISLATIVE EXCESS

It did not take long before critics of the early state constitutions began complaining of the abuse of power by the legislatures, which they saw as aided and abetted by the design of the state constitutions (and, in many instances, by the overemphasis of particular themes of the revolutionary struggle as well).[6] The complaints went primarily to two interrelated claims: that the legislatures were overstepping the proper boundaries of legislative power in violation of the principle of separation of powers,[7] and that they were infringing on the rights of individuals.[8] While both claims could be simply supported, the charges of legislative abuse did not go uncontested, and even when there was agreement that there had been abuse, there remained disagreement as to what remedies and reforms were available or required.[9]

By modern standards, among the most startling departures from separation of powers was the tendency of the state legislatures to invade the judicial function in a variety of ways. Several state legislatures had vacated proceedings, suspended judicial actions, annulled or modified judgments, canceled executions, reopened controversies, authorized appeals, expounded the law of pending cases, and passed bills determining the merits of particular disputes.[10] This sort of legislative practice did not clearly violate accepted or well-established principles as to the nature of legislative action,[11] and undoubtedly reflected at least in part the chaotic situation facing the American legal system in the wake of independence.[12] However, in the midst of growing concern about the extent of unchecked legislative power Jefferson complained in 1782 that the Virginia legislature had "decided rights which should have been left to judiciary controversy."[13]

Beyond the danger to liberty perceived when the law-maker also applies the law, some of these legislative exercises of the judicial function were viewed as especially serious invasions of individual rights. In particular, the passage of bills of attainder and *ex post facto* laws by state legislatures effectively denied fair trials, including the element of trial by jury, to affected individuals.[14] Legislative bodies would also interfere directly with procedural rights by, for example, suspending trial by jury for disfavored classes of defendants.

But the invasion of individual rights did not stop at the denial of procedural guarantees. Among the abuses cited by critics of the state constitutions and legislatures were confiscation of property, banishments, the defrauding of creditors by the issuance of paper money tender laws that required acceptance of paper money, and various laws designed to suspend the legal processes for the recovery of debts. These perceived excesses caused great alarm among many of the nation's most prominent leaders. In

1786, for example, Washington wrote to John Jay that the legislature's unwillingness to do justice was "the origin of the evils we now feel."[15] The experience in the states almost certainly prompted Gouverneur Morris' comment at the Philadelphia Convention that "the public liberty is in greater danger from Legislative usurpations than from any other source."[16] A number of modern commentators thus appear to concur with Madison's 1787 assertion that the frequency and flagrancy of the legislative abuses, as perceived by leading statesmen, "contributed more to the uneasiness which produced the Convention, and prepared the public mind for a general reform, than those which accrued to our national character and interest from inadequacy of the Confederation to the immediate objects."[17]

Remedies and Reforms

It has become a standard practice in American constitutional law to recur to fundamental principles, and one task of the state legislatures' critics was to argue against absolute legislative power from the principles of natural right and limited government that were as foundational as popular sovereignty in the ideology of the revolutionary struggle with Great Britain.[18] Thus Thomas Jefferson pointed to the effective concentration of power in the Virginia legislature, observing that "173 despots would surely be oppressive as one," and concluded with the reminder that "[a]n elective despotism was not the government we fought for."[19] But the critics believed that more than argument was required; there was also the need for constitutional reform.

From the 1770s through the adoption of the federal Constitution and beyond, reformers advocated constitutional change by contending against the degree of power granted to the legislative branches and the failure to provide satisfactory mechanisms for checking and limiting that power. Despite the reliance on natural rights theory to support the need for reform, however, in most cases the reformers criticized existing law, or charged that express constraints were being ignored, rather than claiming that implicit legal norms were being violated.[20] Despite the claim that first principles were being ignored, one does not encounter the stark claim that state constitutions, or one of their provisions, was itself "unconstitutional" or illegal because it violated, or granted the power to violate, the individual's natural rights.[21]

To move beyond the mere paper declarations of separated powers, reformers offered proposals to strengthen the nonlegislative branches of government and in general to supplement separation of powers theory with a renewed emphasis on concepts of checks and balances and (to a lesser extent) mixed government.[22] Related ideas that were proposed and adopted included a stronger executive with the power to veto legislation as a check on legislative abuse,[23] reform of the states' bicameral legislatures to more effectively attract the most qualified individuals to the state senate to promote deliberation and to check the popular branch of the legislature,[24] and various measures to strengthen the judiciary, including the substitution of appointment, election, tenure during good behavior, and fixed salaries.[25] In each case, the proposed reforms qualified the initial commitment to democratic government, but to the ends of realizing competing revolutionary ideals; and the rationale for such reforms was more often than not cast in terms of realizing the ends of government that the people themselves had chosen in their written frames of government and declarations of rights.[26]

Given that the perceived legislative excesses came to many as a revelation of the danger of popular tyranny,[27] we might expect a corresponding qualification of the commitment to the doctrine of popular sovereignty or to republican forms of government.[28] For the most part, however, the arguments for reform were advanced in the name of vindicating popular sovereignty rather than overturning it.[29] In encroaching on the tasks of other branches and in violating individual rights as contained in the declaration of rights, the legislatures were exceeding the limited trust vested in them by the people. In the words of James Wilson in Pennsylvania, "[w]ith how much contempt we have seen the authority of the people treated by the legislature of the state."[30] The reforms were thus presented as the means of vindicating the power of the people rather than the attempt to move away from the republican forms of government. In Madison's phrasing, they were republican cures for the diseases of republicanism.[31]

Beyond the specific reforms aimed at restoring the balance of power among the branches of state governments, at the most general level critics of the state constitutions began to recognize that the written constitutions could not be effective as fundamental unless they were more completely disassociated from ordinary positive law and the legislative power that enacted it.[32] If legitimate power flowed from the people's consent, as asserted in important revolutionary documents, only a fixed and unalterable constitution enacted by a popular convention could be truly legitimate.[33] A related reform was the development of special procedures for amendment that distinguished that process from ordinary lawmaking processes.[34]

Refining Popular Sovereignty

These reforms both promoted and required a refining of the concept of popular sovereignty to reemphasize the idea of the people as the "fountain" of power rather than the more democratic conception of the people ruling immediately through their representatives.[35] For example, Thomas Young of Pennsylvania distinguished between "constituent" powers and "delegated" powers, a distinction which separated the people's sovereign power to constitute government from the legislative powers that were merely delegated by the constitution.[36] To the extent that this sort of shift embodied a recognition of the lack of identity between the legislature and the people, it comported with the more radical Whigs' fear that the will of the people might be thwarted by their representation.[37]

Many supporters of the revolutionary-era state constitutions, however, perceived this effort to limit the people's sovereign power to that of constituting government and delegating authority as an antidemocratic assault on their immediate power to rule and to judge the value and validity of proposed laws.[38] Similarly, attempts to restrict the powers of the representatives of the people were also perceived by many in the same terms, so that the reform efforts were often perceived as both antidemocratic and elitist.[39] The continued widespread support commanded by this preference for popular control explains why reformers argued more in terms of vindicating the people's sovereign power than in terms of recognizing its limitations, but always with the aim of inducing the people to adopt more effective limits on legislative power.

The National Government

In the final analysis, however, Madison and others became persuaded that only a more powerful federal government could effectively check the excesses of the state legislatures. Madison in particular hoped that a stronger federal system might thwart legislative excess both by including a national power to veto state legislation and by the creation of a diverse, extended republic that would thwart the tendency to produce unwise and abusive legislation.[40] The state constitutional reform movement thus culminated in the adoption of the federal Constitution, which relied upon federalism and a number of the devices developed within the states to avoid legislative abuses at the national level.

Madison, of course, lost the battle for a national veto on state legislation, and was forced to settle for the Supremacy Clause.[41] Ironically, however, it was the Supremacy Clause, more than any other constitutional text, that established the federal Constitution as a form of binding and enforceable fundamental law created by the authority of the people.[42] This was the development that, perhaps more than any other, solidified the theoretical case for the doctrine of judicial review, the final check on legislative power that emerged during the confederation period. Given the centrality of this development of judicial review to understanding the constitutional jurisprudence of the founders, it is to that development that we next turn.

The Doctrine of Judicial Review and the Sources of Constitutional Decision Making

Despite the revolutionary-era reliance on Lord Coke for the notion that courts might invoke the strictures of higher law to limit the power of the legislature, it seems reasonably clear that most Americans in 1776 would not have viewed favorably the prospect of judicial reliance on fundamental law to invalidate duly enacted laws of their own popularly elected legislatures. Americans at that time by and large shared a wariness of judicial discretion that almost matched their enthusiasm for popular government.[43] The previously noted lack of explicit provision for judicial review, as well as the language of the states' declarations of rights, almost certainly reflected in part this preference for popular control of government and suspicion of judicial power.[44]

Moreover, corresponding to the idea that the people would be the ultimate judges of the laws was the notion that the lodging of such a power in the judges would amount to oligarchy. In a republican government, it was thought that the constitution itself required judges to strictly follow the enacted law so that the people did not become slaves to the magistrates.[45] Courts were thus to follow the law "without any pretense to judge its right or wrong."[46] While there has been a tendency to debate whether this sort of view was truly predominant in terms of whether most thoughtful Americans had embraced the doctrine of legislative sovereignty,[47] Gordon Wood points out that a number of English Whigs who had influenced American thought, including Locke, saw Parliament as limited by an overriding natural law while believing that the only remedy for abuse was the people's ultimate right of revolution.[48] Given the prevalence of these sorts of views, the doctrine of judicial review would be unlikely to take hold until fears generated by legislative excesses began to swallow up concerns about the dangers of judicial discretion.[49]

As those fears grew, however, the perceived threat to liberty and property by unrestrained legislatures helped to foster attention on the conception of popular sovereignty as constituent power and opened the door to reconsideration of whether judicial review might actually serve to vindicate the written constitution and to revitalize the expressed will of the people, rather than constituting a repudiation of republican government.[50] Moreover, as people sought the same sorts of limitations on their state legislatures as they had earlier contended for against Parliament, it was inevitable that they would employ arguments from the broader fundamental law tradition in addition to relying on the written constitution.[51]

Nevertheless, it is no mere coincidence, nor a reflection of a lack of potential for litigation, that judicial review was exercised on only a handful of occasions during the confederation period and in every case generated considerable controversy.[52] Historically the debate over the significance of these confederation-era cases revolved around whether the courts actually exercised the power of judicial review as well as whether the framers of the federal Constitution understood them to have exercised such a power.[53] More recently, however, they have been reconsidered for the light they shed on the issue as to whether it was thought that judges might go beyond the written constitution in exercising the power of judicial review.[54]

For modern exponents of the unwritten constitution, the state cases confirm both the repudiation of Blackstone's doctrine of legislative supremacy and a commitment extending back to the revolutionary attempt to invoke Lord Coke's doctrine that the courts might enforce all of the fundamental law, written and unwritten, against the legislature.[55] In the most complete treatment, Suzanna Sherry contends that the confederation-era cases also lend important support to the dichotomy, described above, between the natural rights that are binding and enforceable whether or not embodied in text and issues of constitutional structure in which the court's focus is restricted to the written constitution.[56] They confirm that the "constitution" of an American state consisted both of the written document and the natural and inherent rights, whether or not embodied in the writing.[57]

In the section that follows we consider these early cases in their historical settings to evaluate what they reveal about the relative acceptance of the doctrine of judicial review and for the light they shed on the conception of the "constitution" in the early American republic. The basic conclusion is that the cases reveal no consensus about judicial review, let alone one that defines constitutionalism in terms of a commitment to judicially enforceable unwritten norms. After considering the early cases discussing judicial review, we turn to a consideration of the justifications offered for the doctrine of judicial review during the confederation period to determine whether it seems most likely that those who accepted judicial review spurned Blackstone for Coke or, instead, put together some kind of synthesis of the views each has come to symbolize.

THE CONFEDERATION-ERA CASES

Although several of the cases to be considered confirm that the notion of binding and enforceable general principles of law remained available for legal argument in the 1780s, they in fact establish controversy rather than consensus as to whether such principles could be enforced against a conflicting enactment of a state legislature or were properly considered to be an implicit part of the constitution of the states. Moreover, as we shall see, the courts were less than clear as to the relationship between reason and precedent in even the judicial elaboration of such principles in ordinary legal cases. Nor did they do much to clarify the nature of the relationship between such general law, the written constitutions, and legislative power.

Rutgers v. Waddington

Rutgers v. Waddington,[58] a New York case decided in 1784, provides the most compelling example of a controversy resolved through the exercise of judicial review, as well as reliance on general principles of law in judicial decision making. Rutgers brought a trespass action under a 1783 New York statute against Waddington, an agent for British merchants who had occupied property abandoned by Rutgers during the war. On its face, the statute prohibited justifying occupation by reliance on the authorization of the British military in direct contradiction of the law of nations and the Treaty of Peace between Great Britain and the United States. As counsel for the defendant, Alexander Hamilton faced the formidable challenge of persuading the court that the strictures of the law of nations and a national treaty constituted fundamental law that the court should recognize as superior to the enacted law of the state.[59]

Sherry observes that Hamilton relied primarily on the law of nations, arguing that the application of the statute contrary to international law principles would work "injustice and violation of the law of Universal Society."[60] Moreover, in responding to the argument that "the state of New York has no common law of nations,"[61] Hamilton first argued that "it results from the relations of Universal Society" and only secondly that the state constitution had expressly adopted the common law of which the law of nations was a part.[62] As Sherry observes, implicit in Hamilton's argument is the assumption that fundamental principles of common law may be binding as law and enforceable in court even as against a conflicting act of legislation.[63] As an alternative avenue of relief, however, Hamilton also set forth an elaborate argument, complete with numerous authorities, to warrant strict construction of the statute's general language so as to harmonize it with both the treaty and the law of nations in its application to the case at hand.[64]

Although the court decided in favor of Hamilton's client in spite of the language of the statute, and thereby engendered the same controversy that invalidating the statute would have produced, the court's decision failed to embrace the largest number of Hamilton's arguments, including his implicit reliance on the doctrine of judicial review. Rather than taking the statute head on, the court accepted Hamilton's invitation to rely upon canons of strict construction of generally worded statutes that derogate from common law principles of justice.[65]

Thus although the court asserted that the precepts of the law of nations, being based on the law of nature, "are as obligatory on nations in their mutual intercourse, as they are on individuals in their conduct towards each other,"[66] the opinion remained equivocal as to whether this natural law was inherently binding as municipal law within a given nation-state. On the one hand, the court accepted Hamilton's contention that "no state can by its separate ordinance, prejudice any part of such a law," given that it is "immutable" because it rests on "moral obligation."[67] At the same time, in responding to the objection that New York was not bound as matter of municipal law "any further than" it had "adopted" or "engrafted" the law of nations, the court relied exclusively on the state constitution's adoption of the common law, omitting Hamilton's argument from the inherent obligation imposed by natural law.[68]

If the court was equivocal with respect to the precise nature of the legal status of the law of nations, it was quite unequivocal in embracing Blackstone's doctrine of legislative supremacy and in rejecting the doctrine of judicial review. The court stated: "[t]he supremacy of the Legislature need not be called into question; if they think fit *positively* to enact a law, there is no power which can controul them. When the main object of such a law is clearly expressed, and the intention manifest, the Judges are not at liberty, altho' it appears to be *unreasonable*, to reject it: for this were to set the *judicial* above the legislature, which would be subversive of all government."[69] The decision in *Rutgers*, then, clarifies that the commitment to natural law thinking during the founding period was not necessarily irreconcilable with the idea of legislative supremacy; and the doctrine of legislative supremacy is closely associated historically with the rise of positivist jurisprudence.

It is also true that the court in *Rutgers* managed to construe the statute to avoid giving effect to the most straightforward reading of an obnoxious provision because such a reading was deemed contrary to natural justice and established principles of customary law. As Gordon Wood has observed, the court's decision can be viewed as being in the spirit of Lord Coke's statements giving priority to principles of law.[70]

At the same time, the court's application of Blackstone's formulation of Coke's *Dr. Bonham's* dictum as a rule of construction hardly amounts to a move "worthy of John Marshall."[71] In *Marbury v. Madison*[72] Justice Marshall skillfully used debatable arguments to invalidate a relatively unimportant statutory provision and thereby avoided an immediate confrontation over the exercise of judicial power while establishing the more fundamental matter of judicial review. In *Rutgers* the court exercised power to confront the immediate problem of an inequitable statute, but nevertheless acknowledged ultimate legislative sovereignty. Far from establishing the power of judicial review, *Rutgers* called any such doctrine into serious doubt.[73] The court's approach was thus as much a demonstration of the powerful influence of views in opposition to a judicial power to invalidate legislation as it was a reflection of a growing recognition of the need to check legislative power.[74]

Trevett v. Weeden

The other decision that has been treated as based on unwritten principles of law was *Trevett v. Weeden*.[75] The case grew out of a statute requiring merchants to accept paper money, which also provided for trial by special courts to prevent jury nullification of the statute. The defendant, Weeden, objected to the prosecution, and the superior court unanimously ruled that the case was not cognizable before the court.[76] While extrinsic evidence suggests that at least several of the judges based their ruling on a finding that the statute was unconstitutional,[77] the judges themselves refused to explain their actions when called before the legislature during the controversy engendered by the decision.[78]

Weeden's counsel, James Varnum, argued that the statute had expired by its own terms, in addition to advancing the constitutional claims that the special court lacked jurisdiction both because the statute made that court independent of the state's highest court and because the statute was void in denying defendants the right to trial by jury.[79] For Varnum, at least, the jury trial issue was the most central.[80] Sherry observes that Rhode Island's written fundamental law, the Rhode Island Charter of 1663, lacked a provision guaranteeing jury trials and that Varnum relied on a variety of sources to establish the right to jury trial.[81] She concludes that Varnum's argument, at least, embraces the unwritten constitution idea and "is representative of legal analysis of the day."[82] Grey goes somewhat further, concluding that Varnum's argument "was framed in terms of the pure Cokean unwritten constitutionalism" and that the court's ruling was "apparently on the basis of the constitutional argument."[83]

While *Weeden* is an important example of confederation-era judicial review, and reflects a growing view as to one implication of viewing constitutions as binding fundamental law, the decision does not address or resolve the status of unwritten principles under a written constitution ratified by the people. Given that Rhode Island had continued under its colonial charter after the Revolution, *Weeden* is mainly suggestive of revolutionary constitutional theory under such charters and the unwritten British constitution.[84] Resort to the established principles of British contitutionalism, as they had been understood in the colonies, was essential if Rhode Island was to operate under any meaningful constitutional constraints.

Varnum thus based his constitutional argument in part on the colonial era claim that Americans held the rights common to all Englishmen by virtue of having come to America as English settlers.[85] The argument that these rights of Englishmen would be unaffected when Rhode Island elected to continue under its colonial charter is of much greater force than a similar argument that such unwritten rights would continue after the adoption of whole new frame of government (perhaps especially if it included a declaration of rights).[86] Moreover, Varnum was able to point to the specific charter provision that stated that its subjects "shall have and enjoy all liberties and immunities of free and natural subjects . . . as if they, and every one of them, were born within the realm of England."[87] Given the colonists' frequent assertion that such charter provisions gave legal protection to basic liberties such as the right to trial by jury, Varnum can properly be understood as contending that the state's written constitution secured his client's rights.

Seen in this light, Varnum's arguments relying on unwritten sources of law to demonstrate that the right to trial by jury was a time-honored fundamental right would nevertheless constitute an explication and application of the written charter that continued in effect in Rhode Island.[88] The court in *Weeden* could thus have based its judgment on the charter's effective adoption of the well-established right to trial by jury, especially since the jury trial right had been expressly affirmed by a 1663 act of the assembly "declaring the rights and privileges of the Majority's subjects within this colony."[89] Though the court would be drawing on the tradition of British constitutionalism as understood by the colonists, a ruling based on the charter need not have embodied any open-ended version of Cokean unwritten constitutionalism. The right to trial by jury, moreover, would have been viewed as so fundamental as to be a given for virtually all Americans, whether or not they had embraced a full-blown natural law jurisprudence based either on eighteenth century natural law theory or a particular view of British constitutional tradition.[90]

Varnum's argument to the court also reasoned from broader social contract theory and the idea that the people retain as well as grant a portion of their natural rights when they form governments.[91] Relying on Locke, Varnum asserted that it would be improper to presume that it was the will of society that the legislature would have power to destroy the rights which men enter into civil society to secure.[92] Even so, Varnum's argument does not establish that a natural law jurisprudence of judicially enforceable natural rights was the standard legal analysis of the day.[93]

Varnum's own social contract argument gave priority, however, to the people's authority to alter the constitution.[94] Varnum therefore does not present a pure natural law jurisprudence. And while Varnum also appeared to argue for a presumption that a constitutional system secures men's natural rights,[95] he equally stresses that the constitution consists of "the fundamental rules of the community."[96] Given Varnum's reliance on charter provisions to buttress his social contract analysis and his emphasis on the consensual foundation of law, it becomes difficult to predict how he would apply his theories in the context of a popularly adopted written constitution that included, for example, a supremacy clause and a bill of rights.[97]

It is, moreover, a doubtful practice in general to assume that a court embraced the full range of an advocate's argument, let alone that an advocate's argument reflected the predominant view within the legal culture. Varnum could have included his broader social contract arguments mainly to buttress his more positive oriented legal arguments not because he believed a court would have accepted the more open-ended argument standing alone. As to legal culture generally, even if *Weeden* provides an example of a confederation-era case in which a court relied upon social contract theory for decision, this possibility does not tell us much about the prevalence of natural law jurisprudence in general. Even if *Weeden* reflects the rejection of legislative supremacy and the embracing of enforceable fundamental law, it does not tell us much of the general current of thought about unwritten fundamental law. It especially does not speak to the situation in which the people themselves have reduced the principles of fundamental law to a written constitution.[98]

The *Symsbury Case*

The same can be said with respect to the *Symsbury Case*,[99] a 1785 Connecticut case arising from a property dispute. The court there ruled in favor of the earlier of two grantees claiming under separate legislative grants, concluding that the later enactment "could not legally operate to curtail the land before granted" to the original grantee.[100] While the dissenting opinion found that the later enactment had fairly resolved ambiguities in the initial grant, and thus rested on "principles consonant to law and equity,"[101] it also acknowledged that the legislature was not empowered simply to take property it had granted to the original grantee without consent.[102] Since the colonial charter in force in Connecticut included no provision specifically protecting property rights, it is arguable that both opinions assumed that general principles of law (and perhaps the idea of due process of law) prohibited the legislature from enacting a naked transfer of private property.[103]

As with *Weeden, Symsbury* reflects the renewal of concern for effectively limiting legislative power that developed during the confederation period, and it supplies another early example of the growing presumption in favor of judicial review on behalf of fundamental law. In light of the conventional revolutionary-era arguments that the colonial charters guaranteed the rights of Englishmen—including the fundamental law guarantee of due process of law—*Symsbury* can also be read as a legal construction of norms implicit in the charter rather than as an application of general principles of law that would continue to have force even under a popularly ratified written constitution (and particularly one that included a bill of rights). Considering, moreover, that legislatures had during this same period regularly acted with impunity to affect private rights by intervention in particular disputes, it is difficult to conclude that *Symsbury* says anything in particular, either about unwritten rights or even in favor of judicial review. Indeed, the case refers to the lack of legislative power to take away vested property rights, but does not speak of unwritten rights more generally.

Holmes v. Walton

Nor can we conclude much from *Holmes v. Walton*.[104] There the state supreme court in New Jersey invalidated a statute that permitted conviction for trading with the enemy by a jury of only six people. The New Jersey constitution provided for trial by jury but did not define its essential elements.[105] Lacking an opinion by the court, Sherry points to court minutes indicating that counsel had argued that a six-person jury was "contrary to law," "contrary to the constitution of New Jersey," and "contrary to the constitution, practices, and laws of the land."[106] Sherry suggests, in turn, that the reference to the "laws of the land" probably referred "to various charters and legislative enactments."[107] She then concludes that, when read in light of the other cases, *Holmes* "suggests that in New Jersey, as in other states, fundamental law was derived from more than the written constitution."[108]

But the cited statutes and charters, which were supplied by Professor Austin Scott in support of the claims of counsel in the case,[109] were all historical enactments that had been passed within the boundaries of what became New Jersey. Since these enactments were almost certainly superseded by the 1776 state constitution, they could have been used to shed light on the contemporary understanding of the jury right guarantee of the state constitution at least as readily as to illuminate the established principles of an unwritten constitution. Moreover, considering that we do not have the supporting arguments and authorities on behalf of the reasons offered for reversal of the lower court judgment,[110] it is virtually impossible to determine whether counsel's varying formulations of the jury right claim provided independent bases for the defendant's claim or were simply examples of the redundancy in drafting for which lawyers are famous.[111]

In any event, counsel's argument, as we have noted, does not tell us the ground of the court's judgment or the predominant views within the legal culture. What little historical evidence we have raises doubt whether the idea of an unwritten constitution was in the minds of contemporaries who understood the case as providing precedent for judicial review. For example, in 1785 Gouverneur Morris of Pennsylvania alluded to *Holmes* in an address to the Pennsylvania legislature while discussing the idea of judicial review.[112] Citing *Holmes* as invalidating a law as "unconstitutional," Morris acknowledged that "[s]uch power in judges is dangerous," but insisted that "unless it somewhere exists, the time employed in framing a bill of rights and form of government was merely thrown away."[113] Morris, at least, seemed to equate the idea of a ruling of unconstitutionality with a decision based upon the written constitution.[114]

Bayard and *Caton*

Two early cases of judicial review, *Bayard v. Singleton*[115] and *Commonwealth v. Caton*,[116] concerned issues arising under written constitutions. In *Bayard*, the court justified its invalidation of a statute denying a jury trial on the ground that no act of legislation "could by any means repeal or alter the constitution."[117] While it is probably accurate to assert that reliance on a provision of the written constitution does not necessarily "indicate the appropriate grounds of decision when the written document contains no such provision,"[118] the court's choice of language, as well as its argument from the lack of power to "repeal" the constitution, reflects the growing tendency among thinkers of this period to equate the term "constitution" with the written constitution. Similarly, the court's rationale for judicial review seems to focus on the collective decision to establish an unalterable and nonrepealable fundamental law rather than on the roots of jury trial in securing fundamental natural rights or the right's status as long-established fundamental law. While the court could have been writing as broadly as the occasion demanded, it remains true that the court was speaking to a question of individual rights and, according to Sherry's theory, should not have relied upon the written constitution.

In *Caton*, Virginia's highest court upheld a statute empowering the legislature to grant pardons in certain cases and rejected the claim that under the state constitution the statute would be valid only if it provided for pardon by the lower branch of the state assembly.[119] Sherry suggests that the case lends support to her proposed distinction between individual rights issues, as to which unwritten principles of law bind courts and legislatures, and issues of government structure and powers that are governed exclusively by the written constitution.[120] Thus, according to Sherry, one of the two opinions that dwelt with the constitutional issue at length, Judge Wythe's, clearly limited itself to deciding the issue of division of powers between the branches of government and offers no indication that the written constitution would remain paramount in an individual rights dispute.[121] Sherry also finds it significant that Judge Pendleton, the other judge who wrote at length, framed the issue in terms of whether the statute conformed to the "constitution of government," which she takes as referring specifically to the frame of government rather than to the declaration of rights.[122]

Caton, however, does not appear to lend substantial support to the proposed distinction between issues of government structure and individual rights. For one thing, even though counsel for the prisoners relied on constitutional text, they also contended that "the construction ought, in favour of life, to incline to the side of mercy,"[123] suggesting that they viewed the case as concerned with the relation between individuals and the state and ultimately the natural right to life, as well as with issues of division of governmental competence. Not surprisingly, then, Judge Wythe introduces his opinion with the observation that human knowledge is concerned with resolving "the respective rights of the sovereign and the subject"as well as "the powers which the different branches of government may exercise."[124] He, in turn, suggests that it is by meaningful engagement with both types of questions that "tyranny has been sapped, the departments kept within their own spheres, the citizens protected, and general liberty promoted."[125]

That Wythe sees these ends of constitutionalism is confirmed by his further observation that such ends are promoted by judicial review when the branches "who hold the purse and the sword" differ "as to the power which each may exercise."[126] Thus in arguing for the importance of thwarting the attempt of one branch of the legislature to claim undue power, Wythe generalizes to the case of the "whole legislature" attempting "to overleap the bounds, prescribed to them by the people," and the judicial duty in such cases to point "to the constitution" to affirm that "here is the limit of your authority."[127] While Wythe does not unequivocally speak to the question of the enforceability of unwritten individual rights, he justifies judicial power by equating the constitution with something prescribed by the people that could be pointed to in resolving issues of the reach of government power; this emphasis on the written constitution cuts against rather than in favor of the distinction proposed by Sherry.[128]

As to Judge Pendleton, his reference to the "constitution of government" appears in context to be inclusive of both the frame of government and the Virginia declaration of rights. In the statement following this allusion to both, Pendleton makes this clear:

The *constitution of other governments* in Europe or elsewhere, seem to throw little light upon this question, since we have a written record of that which the citizens of this state have adopted as their social compact; and beyond which we need not extend our researches. It has been very properly said, on all sides, that this act [the constitution], *declaring the rights of the citizens, and forming their government*, divided it into three great branches, the legislative, executive, and judiciary, assigning to each its proper powers, and directing that each shall be kept separate and distinct, must be considered as a rule obligatory upon every department, not to be departed from on any occasion.[129]

Pendleton refers to the constitution as the "act" that both declares rights and divides power, and nothing in his opinion supports a unique status for individual rights.

While affirming the supremacy of the written constitution, Pendleton nevertheless expressed the period's concerns about the propriety of judicial review. According to Pendleton, the question whether courts could exercise judicial review "without exercising the power of [the legislative] branch, contrary to the plain terms of that constitution, is indeed a deep, important, and I will add, a tremendous question, the decision of which might involve consequences to which gentlemen may not have extended their ideas."[130] He was thus relieved that the instant case gave the court no occasion to consider invalidating the challenged statute.[131]

THE DEBATE OVER JUDICIAL POWER

Apart from the reasoning and holdings of these early state decisions, the unsettled status of the doctrine of judicial review in the early American republic is reflected in the popular reaction to the decisions we have reviewed. The decision strictly construing the New York trespass statute in *Rutgers v. Waddington* was condemned in public gatherings and in petitions to the legislature, and the legislature adopted a resolution denouncing the decision.[132] Forrest McDonald observes that "[t]herafter the legislature did as it pleased, and judges dared not interfere."[133] The legislature in Rhode Island called in the judges who decided *Trevett v. Weeden* and demanded an explanation of their ruling of unconstitutionality. Not being satisfied with the explanations offered, the legislature passed a resolution of opposition to the decision, and the following spring all of the judges except one who had remained silent were not reappointed to their offices.[134]

As reflected in the opinion of the court in *Rutgers* and Judge Pendleton's opinion in *Commonwealth v. Caton*, reactions of doubt and concern about the prospect of a power of judicial review were not limited to the popular masses and their elected representatives. After the decision in *Bayard v. Singleton*, Richard Spaight, a delegate from North Carolina to the federal convention, wrote a strongly worded objection to judicial review in a letter to James Iredell, who argued the case to the court.[135] Spaight objected both that there was not "any thing in the Constitution, either directly or impliedly, that will support [judicial review]," and that such a provision "would have been absurd," inasmuch as it "would have operated as an absolute negative on the proceedings of the Legislature, which no judiciary ought ever to possess."[136] In short, the relatively occasional exercise of ultimate judicial power and the strong and persistent charges of usurpation evoked by such decisions reflected both the centrality of legislative power during the confederation era and the pervasive fear of granting such potentially enormous power to unelected government officials. If the enthusiasm for legislative power waned as the confederation period drew to a close, the reservations about the propriety of judicial review have dogged the exercise of judicial power down to the present.

Competing Theories of Judicial Review

Edward Corwin long ago pointed out that two competing theories of judicial review have characterized American legal thought from the earliest days of the republic.[137] The first theory, which can be traced to Lord Coke's descriptions of the superiority of unwritten principles of law to the ordinary enactments of legislatures, posited the power of courts to give effect to the higher law of natural justice.[138] As we have seen, in American hands Coke's statements suggesting the juridical status of higher law concepts were sometimes combined with Locke's more universal natural law to justify judicial enforcement of natural law. Thus, for example, in 1772, George Mason argued against a 1682 act of the Virginia assembly, which had purported to sell certain Indian women into slavery, that it was "void of itself, because contrary to natural right."[139] But it is not clear that reliance on Coke in support of judicial review on behalf of unwritten principles of law entailed a commitment to an open-ended judicial power to implement natural law.

The competing conception of judicial review, which historically grew up as a response to Blackstone's doctrine of legislative supremacy, justifies judicial power based on the written constitution and the sovereign power of the people to adopt written law that is superior to ordinary enactments of legislatures.[140] On this view, courts are cast in their ordinary role of determining the law which binds them, and they are viewed as obligated to prefer the act of the people themselves to the enactments of the agents of the people whose power is granted and limited by the constitution.[141] This sort of rationale was employed by the court in *Bayard v. Singleton,* as well as by Judges Wythe and Pendleton in *Commonwealth v. Caton.*[142]

The Lack of a Clear Consensus during the Confederation Period

A difficult and important issue of constitutional history concerns the extent to which the founding generation chose between these conceptions or viewed them as reconcilable. While the unwritten principles of natural law were frequently equated with the governing principles of British constitutionalism in the revolutionary-era arguments of the colonists, the argument could also be cast in terms of a jurisprudence of pure natural law (which presumably would control even the written constitution).[143] Mason, for example, contended in 1772 that the laws of nature are binding because they are the law of God and asserted that courts of justice had ruled that "[a]ll human *constitutions* which contradict [God's] laws, we are in conscience bound to disobey."[144] Arguably under Mason's 1772 formulation even the written constitution would be binding on courts only to the extent that it actually embodied principles of natural right, and courts might invalidate even provisions of a popularly adopted written constitution.

Alternatively, the unwritten principles of higher law might be viewed as implicit in the legal order, and perhaps cast as part of the constitution, supplementing (or perhaps supplemented by) the written constitution. On this view, the people are considered capable of implementing the principles of natural right by a written constitution, but are presumed to have intended that the constitution be treated as embodying the correct principles of justice, whether or not embodied in any text. Whereas under the pure natural law view the written constitution could be the true source of binding fundamental law only where the natural law was indifferent with respect to the question at hand, the legal positivist formulation might well have included the assumption that the written constitution is binding where it clearly applies, whatever arguments from natural justice might be advanced.[145]

Whether the unwritten principles are described as imminent within the "constitution" or as an independent source of binding fundamental law, an important question is whether most founding era thinkers would have expected courts to give priority to the fundamental law established by the people or to the unwritten principles discerned by the judges. To the extent that the doctrine of popular sovereignty was predominant during this era, the people's fundamental law would be viewed as having priority. The people, of course, would hold power to limit government consistently with perceived natural principles of liberty and justice, but they would equally have power to enable government to act, subject only to the limits inherent in the powers granted or to the limitations specified in the written constitution. If such were the case, most of the courts and advocates that apparently relied on unwritten principles would have reason to remain silent on the status of those principles under a written constitution, let alone whether such unwritten principles would be treated as more fundamental than a conflicting provision of the written instrument.

James Iredell—Did He Resolve the Issue?

A classic example of the uncertainties attending arguments for judicial power is provided by the defense of judicial review in 1787 by James Iredell. In an August 26 letter to Richard Spaight, responding to Spaight's letter attacking the exercise of judicial review in *Bayard v. Singleton*, Iredell relied most prominently on the argument from the written constitution but then appeared to leave room (in some settings at least) for judicial review on behalf of unwritten principles. Since the constitution was "a real, original contract between the people and their future government,"[146] it was "*a fundamental law*, and a law *in writing*" which the courts "must take notice of . . . as the groundwork of [the judicial power] as well as of all other authority."[147] For Iredell, it followed that "the exercise of judicial power is unavoidable, the Constitution not being a mere imaginary thing, about which ten thousand different opinions may be formed, but a written document to which all may have recourse, and to which, therefore, the judges cannot wilfully blind themselves."[148]

Prior to this discussion of the written constitution, Iredell had asserted "Without an express Constitution the powers of the Legislature would undoubtedly have been absolute (as the Parliament in Great Britain is held to be), and any act passed, *not inconsistent with natural justice* (for that curb is avowed by the judges even in England), would have been binding on the people."[149] Sherry concludes from this statement that at this time Iredell "clearly viewed the written constitution as supplementing natural law rather than as replacing it with a single instrument."[150] But Iredell's statement is equivocal in a number of respects, especially when placed in the context of the entire letter.

For one thing, although Iredell makes it clear that there would be some curb to the otherwise absolute legislative power in the absence of a written constitution, he does not clearly indicate that this curb is considered essential *after* the adoption of a formal, written constitution.[151] The sentence following this statement, which indicates that written constitutions were prompted by "[t]he experience of evils which the American war fully disclosed, attending an absolute power in a legislative body," suggests that the "original contract" between the people and their government was conceived as replacing the system characterized by an absolute (if a somewhat qualified absolute) legislature.[152] Indeed, Iredell provides a sharp contrast between the written constitution and the system that would exist without it when he emphasizes that it is not "a mere imaginary thing, about which ten thousand different opinions may be formed."[153]

A related point is that Iredell does not seem to equate the "natural justice" that qualified absolute legislative power in England with a perfect scheme of liberty and justice. For example, he specifically suggests that without the adoption of written constitutions, bills of attainder would have been within the absolute power of the legislature, as they had been in England.[154] His reference to the "evils" that "suggested the propriety"of adopting written constitutions further indicates that the qualification alluded to was conceived by Iredell as being of exceedingly narrow dimensions.[155] Despite the reference to natural justice, then, Iredell does not appear to embrace anything like a full-blown natural law jurisprudence.

Finally, while Iredell does not really elaborate on the relationship, if any, between the natural justice limitation, the written constitution, and the idea of constitutionalism, it does seem quite clear that every reference to the constitution found throughout his letter to Spaight is a reference to the written constitution. If Iredell believed that some kind of natural justice curb on legislative power survived the adoption of a written constitution, there is nothing in his letter to suggest that he viewed it as a *constitutional* limitation. Considering this, it may well be significant that at one point Iredell relies upon a state statute requiring an oath of allegience "to the powers and authorities which are or may be established for the government [of North Carolina], *not inconsistent with the Constitution*."[156] This again suggests that Iredell may have viewed the "natural justice" limitation, with its roots in Coke's notion of a judicially enforceable common law limitation on legislative power, as inapplicable under such a written constitution.

The possibility that Iredell saw the written constitution as the exclusive source of limitations on government in North Carolina seems the most consistent with what we know about Iredell himself. He is famous, of course, for a 1798 opinion rejecting natural law jurisprudence in response to an opinion advocating reliance on natural law by Justice Chase in *Calder v. Bull.*[157] But that was not a recently adopted view, given that less than a year after his letter to Spaight, Iredell stated his view before the North Carolina ratifying convention that all rights not reserved in a bill of rights are thereby included within the powers granted to a legislature of general legislative powers (such as the North Carolina legislature).[158] At least by the time of the debate over ratification of the federal Constitution, Iredell appeared to be committed to the view that the written constitution represented in effect the complete and integrated agreement between the people and their government.[159] It seems more reasonable to interpret Iredell's letter to Spaight in light of this well-considered position rather than to perceive it as a fairly dramatic change in position.

The Centrality of the Written Constitution

At the same time, of course, some spokesmen harked back to conceptions of law as associated with Coke and the ideas of natural right and reason as justification for an expanded judicial role.[160] An important issue is whether one of these rationales for an increased judicial role had come to predominate by the time of the federal convention. It is relevant in this regard that modern scholarship has recognized that it was during the American founding era that this nation's fundamental law made a transition from being a general norm for judging ordinary law to itself being a part of the enforceable law of the legal system.[161] As Gerald Stourzh has contended, the functioning eighteenth-century British constitution had come to recognize "certain imperatives or prohibitions as fundamental elements of the laws of the land *without* thereby creating a special category of legal norms."[162] For example, the right to habeas corpus was considered "fundamental" within the British constitutional system, and yet Parliament could by a simple majority change or suspend it and had done so several times.[163] Although England's doctrine of Parliamentary sovereignty should not be confused with the view that such fundamental principles have no significance in their political and constitutional order,[164] it is the special category of "constitutional" norms which bind even the legislature that most clearly distinguishes American from British constitutionalism.

According to Stourzh, an important contribution of American constitutional law was its effective establishment of a higher law "in the technical

sense that it cannot be abrogated or changed by normal legislative procedure."[165] This creation of a special category of legal norms that the British
constitution lacked was accomplished by giving the higher law roots in a
document that proceeded from the people, the fountain of all political
power. In thus reducing the higher law to positive constitutional law—what
German authors call "Positiviering des Naturrechts" ("transforming natural
law into positive law")—America put into political practice what had been
only a dissenting theory and revolutionary doctrine as to British constitutionalism. If Stourzh's basic analysis is correct, the state declarations of
rights represent a critical step in the direction of creating meaningful positive constitutional law limitations on government, but they arguably embody a middle ground between unwritten higher law and the positive
guarantees that presented themselves as the supreme law of the land and
constituted our federal Bill of Rights.[166]

NOTES

1. *See* Gordon S. Wood, The Creation of the American Republic
1776–1787, at 362 (1969).
2. *See* Donald S. Lutz, The Origins of American Constitutionalism 104
(1980) (enfranchisement of white adult males at a rate eight to ten times above
what it was in England). Even so, of course, the state governments remained only
relatively democratic by modern standards. Although property ownership was
sufficiently widespread to make America the broadest-based electorate in the
world, only about one in six Americans were eligible to vote. Forrest McDonald,
Norvus Ordo Seclorum: The Intellectual Origins of the Constitution 162 (1986).
3. Lutz observes that the new state legislatures were not only more representative than their colonial counterparts—and were thus less dominated by a
highly educated elite that had tended to operate as a check on the factionalism that
can characterize democratic legislatures—but now faced an enfeebled executive
instead of crown-appointed governors who had acted as a barrier to unbridled ma-
joritariansm. Lutz, *supra* note 2, at 107–08.
4. Americans were divided between traditional Whigs, who saw legislators
as men of superior virtue who were to calmly deliberate on how to promote the
good of the community, and radical Whigs, who insisted that representatives
should be made of the "same stuff" as their constituents so that the legislature
would be the equivalent of the entire population. Lutz, *supra* note 2, at 89–90.
5. For treatments of the evolution from the tendency toward populism and
legislative sovereignty in the period immediately following independence toward
renewed emphasis on the need to provide meaningful checks on government over
the course of years leading to the federal convention, *see,e.g.,* F. McDonald, *supra* note 2, at 154–79; G. Wood, *supra* note 1, at 393–467; Leslie Friedman Goldstein, In Defense of the Text: Democracy and Constitutional Theory 76–83

(1991); Edward S. Corwin, *The Progress of Constitutional Theory Between the Declaration of Independence and the Meeting of the Philadelphia Convention,* in 1 Corwin on the Constitution 56, 62–64 (R. Loss, ed., 1981); Gordon S. Wood, *Interests and Disinterestedness, in* Beyond Confederation 69, 69–81, 57–78 (R. Loss ed. 1981); Gerald Stourzh, *Fundamental Laws and Individual Rights in the 18th Century Constitution, in* The American Founding—Essays on the Formation of the Constitution 159, 176–93 (J. Barlow, Leonard Levy, & K. Masugi, eds., 1988) [hereinafter cited as The American Founding]; Martin S. Flaherty, *The Most Dangerous Branch,* 105 Yale L.J. 1725, 1756–1774 (1996).

6. For excellent overviews of these themes, see F. McDonald, *supra* note 2, at 155–57; G. Wood, *supra* note 1, at 403–13; Corwin, *supra* note 5, at 58–64. For original sources, see James Madison, The Federalist No. 47, at 331 (Jacob E. Cooke, ed., 1961) (citing instances of "too great a mixture" or "even an actual consolidation of the different powers," reflecting the lack of "competent provision . . . for maintaining in practice the separation delineated on paper"); James Madison, The Federalist No. 48, *supra,* at 335–38; Thomas Jefferson, *Notes on the State of Virginia* 120–25 (William Peden, ed., 1955).

7. G. Wood, *supra* note 1, at 403–09; McDonald, *supra* note 2, at 156–57, 175–76; Raoul Berger, Congress v. The Supreme Court 10–11 (1969).

8. Corwin, *supra* note 5, at 59–64. *See also* Julius Goebel, 1 History of the Supreme Court: Antecedents and Beginnings to 1801, 99–100 (1871); Goldstein, *supra* note 5, at 76; G. Wood, *supra* note 1, at 83–85, 161, 396–413; Herman Belz, *Constitutionalism and the American Founding, in* The Framing and Ratification of the Constitution 338–39, 345 (Leonard & Dennis Mahoney, eds., 1987) (bills of rights treated as hortatory by state legislatures, which resulted in encroachments on liberty and property); Stourzh, *supra* note 5, at 177 (period of legislative supremacy followed by "counterarguments and countermeasures" drawing on natural law doctrine and the lessons of experience). For original sources, see Philodemus (Thomas Tucker), *Conciliatory Hints, Attempting, by a Fair State of Matters, to Remove Party Prejudice,* in 1 American Political Writing During the Founding Era 1760–1805, at 606, 610 (Charles Hyneman & Donald Lutz, eds., 1983) (1784 criticism of South Carolina constitution as giving the legislature "every power formerly exercised or claimed under a monarchical government"); James Madison, *Vices of the Political System of the United States, in* 2 The Writings of James Madison 365–66 (Gaillard Hunt, ed., 1901).

9. The various remedies and reforms offered for the perceived problems are taken up *infra* notes 19–42 and accompanying text.

10. The single largest target of such laws, of course, were the former loyalists. New York's Trespass Act of 1783, for example, manipulated traditional principles of jurisdiction to favor plaintiffs, prohibited certain defenses contrary to customary international law and the provisions of the treaty of peace, and denied loyalist defendants any right of appeal. McDonald, *supra* note 2, at 155–56.

11. *See* G. Wood, *supra* note 1, at 154–59; F. McDonald, *supra* note 2, at 156–57.

12. *See* G. Wood, *supra* note 1, at 154–55; J. Goebel, *supra* note 8, at 100; Corwin, *supra* note 5, at 59–60.

13. Jefferson, *supra* note 6, at 21.

14. *See* G. Wood, *supra* note 1, at 403–07; F. McDonald, *supra* note 2, at 156–57; R. Berger, *supra* note 7, at 10–11.

15. George Washington to John Jay, May 18, 1786, *quoted in* Wood, *supra* note 1, at 73. Julius Goebel has observed that The Federalist was particularly effective in its "references to the structure of state governments and of experience there." Goebel, *supra* note 8, at 307.

16. 2 Max Farrand, The Records of the Federal Convention of 1787, at 76 (1911), *quoted in* Berger, *supra* note 7, at 11.

17. Madison to Jefferson, Oct. 24, 1787, *in* 12 Papers of Jefferson 276 (Julian P. Boyd, ed., 1950). For commentators who seem to concur that the perceived excesses of the state legislatures were a central motivation for the adoption of a new federal Constitution, see G. Wood, *supra* note 1, at 467; F. McDonald, *supra* note 2, at 144, 162–66, 175–79, 182–83; Corwin, *supra* note 5, at 62–64, 76.

18. In Pennsylvania, for example, Benjamin Rush complained that "the supreme, absolute, and uncontrolled power of the State is lodged in the hands of *one body* of men." *Quoted in* G. Wood, *supra* note 1, at 441.

19. Jefferson, *supra* note 6, at 120. *See also* Corwin, *supra* note 5, at 63.

20. As Corwin observed, "[t]he sharp edge of 'legislative omnipotence' did not pause with the Tories who, as enemies of the state, were perhaps beyond the pale of the Constitution," but legislatures "were led to attempt results which . . . we should today regard as requiring constitutional amendments." Corwin, *supra* note 5, at 62. Scholars generally acknowledge that legislative assemblies acted within their constitutional powers when they acted in ways that "early affixed to the state legislature a stigma of which as an institution it has never even quite ridded itself." *Id.* at 62–63.

21. For example, I have found little evidence to support Thomas C. Grey's undocumented claim that "it was common to invoke the fundamental law-natural rights tradition to urge that there were implied limitations on legislative power in addition to the express ones enacted in the new constitutions." Thomas Grey, *The Original Understanding and the Unwritten Constitution, in* Toward a More Perfect Union: Six Essays on the Constitution 145, 156 (Neil L. York, ed., 1988).

22. For useful commentary on the American fits and starts with "mixed" and "balanced" government, see G. Wood, *supra* note 1, at 197–255. The need to check popular power related, in many minds, to the need to restore the claims of creditors and those of other unpopular minorities. L. Goldstein, *supra* note 5, at 76–77; Corwin, *supra* note 5, at 62–63; 76–78. That these remained important themes through the convention and beyond is clear. Paul Eidelberg, The Philosophy of the American Constitution 52–60 (1968).

23. Corwin states that the "executive veto" became central to the constitutional reform advocated by John Adams, and that it was "to so good purpose that it is today in nearly every constitution in the country." Corwin, *supra* note 5, at

65. *See also* Flaherty, *supra* note 5, at 1769. For comments on an emerging awareness of the possibilities for "democratic despotism," see G. Wood, *supra* note 1, at 409–13, 430–53.

24. It has been observed that "drafters of state constitutions, realizing that the legislature did have the power of rulers and that such power could usefully be checked, moved toward strengthening the executive and judicial branches." S. Goldstein, *supra* note 5, at 76.

25. *See* G. Wood, *supra* note 1, at 446–63. The Virginia constitution required that judges be paid a fixed salary, James Madison, The Federalist No. 48, *supra* note 6, at 337, but the courts did not possess much real independence in the early state constitutions. G. Wood, *supra* note 1, at 161. Efforts were made to reform the judiciary to make it more independent than it had been, and they continued to the Philadelphia Convention. *See* F. McDonald, *supra* note 2, at 253–54.

26. For a remarkable summary of the process by which Americans in turn showed commitment to republican forms of government while developing a complete devotion to a constitution as a means of protecting rights, see Gerald Stourzh, *Fundamental Laws and Individual Rights in the 18th Century Constitution*, in The American Founding, *supra* note 5, at 159.

27. G. Wood, *supra* note 1, at 430–33; *see also* F. McDonald, *supra* note 2, at 164–65; Grey, *supra* note 21, at 156–59.

28. The perception of abuse prompted more second thoughts about popular sovereignty, and even republican government, than some modern thinkers imagine. Forrest McDonald documents that a number of prominent Americans held serious doubts about the future of republican government as the federal convention approached and that some delegates even pondered the possibility of a limited monarchy. F. McDonald, *supra* note 2, at 179–83. Such thoughts were never offered as serious proposals, however, inasmuch as there was a general recognition at the convention that the American people would never accept anything other than a republican form of government. *Id.* at 182–83.

29. *See* G. Wood, *supra* note 1, at 411–13.

30. 2 The Documentary History of the Ratification of the Constitution 450 (Merrill Jensen, ed., 1976) (Pennsylvania Ratifying Convention, Dec. 1, 1787). Wood observes that state constitution reformers consistently relied on the theme that the legislatures were abusing the people by violating the terms of the written constitutions. G. Wood, *supra* note 1, at 443–43.

31. James Madison, The Federalist No. 51, *supra* note 6, at 349–52. Recently, Professor Amar has done us the service of showing us how the federal Bill of Rights was partly designed to reinforce these "republican cures." The framers counted on the state governments to alert them to federal intrusions, relied upon state militias protected by the Second Amendment to thwart tyrannical standing armies, and in general conquered government power in part "by dividing it between two rival governments." Akhil Reed Amar, The Bill of Rights: Creation and Reconstruction 123 (1998). In general, Amar seems on the mark in asserting

that in the minds of the framers, "populism and federalism—liberty and local-ism—work together." *Id.*

32. There is no question that the adoption of written constitutions of itself "helped, if they did not require, the founders to enforce the distinction, unknown in England, between the constitution-making authority and the lawmaking authority." Merrill Peterson, *Thomas Jefferson, the Founders, and Constitutional Change, in* The American Founding, *supra* note 5, at 276, 279. Peterson acknowl-edges, however, that this significance of written constitutions was imperfectly grasped for a period of time and that it was reinforced by the development of "America's basic institution," the popular convention. *Id.* at 275, 277. For a treat-ment of the rise of the popular convention as a device for separating fundamental law from ordinary law, see Herman Belz, *Constitutionalism and the American Founding, in* The Framing and Ratification of the Constitution, 333, 339–40 (Leonard Levy & Dennis Mahoney, eds., 1987).

Thus in South Carolina, Thomas Tucker linked his concern that the legislature had been effectively granted unlimited powers by the state constitution with the need to call for a convention to the end of "fixing it on the firm and proper foun-dation of the express consent of the people, unalterable by the legislative, or any other authority but that by which it is to be framed." Philodemus (Thomas Tucker), *supra* note 8, at 620.

33. *See* Stourzh, *supra* note 5, at 179.

34. For treatments of the rise of the popular convention as a device for sepa-rating fundamental law from ordinary law, see Belz, *supra* note 8, at 339–40; Thomas West, *The Classical Spirit of the Founding, in* The American Founding, *supra* note 5, at 32 (conventions were developed to fit the theory that "a constitu-tion was to be supreme over the government").

35. Stourzh, *supra* note 5, at 177–78.

36. *Id.* at 178. Similarly, Benjamin Rush, observing that "the people of America have mistaken the meaning of the word sovereignty," distinguished be-tween the people's true sovereign power, by which all power is derived *from* the people, and that false notion that all power is vested immediately *in* the people. Rush, *Defense of the Confederation, in* G. Wood, *supra* note 1, at 174. An impli-cation for Rush was the people could exercise their sovereignty on election day but did not retain any power to instruct legislators not to exercise their sover-eignty if delegated power were abused. *Id.*

37. The more radical Whigs insisted on the immediacy of the sovereignty of the people precisely because they feared despotism even from their own elected representatives. *See* G. Wood, *supra* note 1, at 375–76. For the radical Whigs, only laws actually approved by the populace were truly legitimate, with the implica-tion that only the people could properly judge the merits of any law. "For the peo-ple to be enslaved, either to their rulers, or even their own laws, as not to be able to exercise their essential right of sovereignty for their own safety and welfare, is as inconsistent with civil liberty, as if they were enslaved to an army, or to any

foreign power." M. Hemmenway, *A Sermon, Preached before His Excellency John Hancock* (1784), *quoted in* G. Wood, *supra* note 1, at 375.

38. Defenders of Pennsylvania's 1776 constitution, the most democratic in the country, opposed various reforms to check legislative power on the ground that "the grand objection to our present Constitution is, that it retains too much power in the hands of the people, who do not know how to use it, as well as gentlemen of fortune." Calling the Conventions of 1776–1790, at 78–79, *quoted in* G. Wood, *supra* note 1, at 440. The proposed reforms included a proposal for a bicameral legislature with longer terms of office in the upper house and the elimination of a requirement that bills be referred to the people-at-large before they became law. G. Wood, *supra* note 1, at 439. *See, e.g.,* F. McDonald, *supra* note 2, at 165–66, 172–73, 183; Corwin, *supra* note 5, at 64.

39. Julius Goebel has observed that "the inexorable tide of democracy" had "blunted the edges of certain pronouncements of principle in the constitutions, *e.g.,* the separation of powers and the even more fundamental precept of the supremacy of the constitution." J. Goebel, *supra* note 8, at 142.

40. At the Philadelphia Convention, Madison stood behind the Virginia Plan, which included the proposed negative on state laws as a means both to secure the purposes of union and to check the perceived abuses of the states. *See* 1 M. Farrand, *supra* note 16, at 164 (June 8, 1787) (justifying "negative" by reference to state tendencies to "encroach on the federal authority" and to "oppress the weaker party within their respective jurisdictions"). Sherry observes that on June 8, 1787, Madison stated that he knew of no other mechanism to prevent such mischiefs other than resort to coercion, an indication that as of that date Madison remained skeptical of the propriety or efficacy of the institution of judicial review, or both. Suzanna Sherry, *The Founders' Unwritten Constitution,* 54 U. Chi. L. Rev. 1127, 1147 (1987), *citing* Madison's Notes for June 8, 1787. Madison also provided the classic argument for the advantages of an extended republic in The Federalist No. 10. *See* F. McDonald, *supra* note 2, at 165–66 & n. 42; Gordon S. Wood, *Democracy and the Constitution, in* How Democratic Is the Constitution? 1, 10–12 (Robert A. Goldwin & William A. Schambra, eds., 1980).

41. U.S. Const. Art. VI., cl. 2.

42. As Julius Goebel has observed, laws repugnant to the Constitution were "excluded from the imperative of obedience," and the clause "was directed equally at any law-making body and at all judges, the ultimate arbiters of enforcement and of enforceability." J. Goebel, *supra* note 8, at 239. *See also* Sherry, *supra* note 40, at 1147–1150.

43. G. Wood, *supra* note 1, at 304 ("most Americans were too fully aware of the modern conception of statutory law, too deeply committed to consent as a basis for law, and from their colonial experience too apprehensive of the possible arbitrariness and uncertainties of judicial discretion to permit themselves easily to allow Judges to set aside the law made by the representatives of the people").

44. Many thoughtful revolutionaries shared Jefferson's opposition, for example, to the exercise of broad discretion in equity jurisdiction because of the re-

sulting uncertainty it created in the law. G. Wood, *supra* note 1, at 304. Many thus contended that if judges followed the spirit rather than the letter of the law, and thus made legal interpretation dependent on the will of the judge, the result would be despotism. *Id.* at 301.

45. G. Wood, *supra* note 1, at 301–04, 455. Madison himself gave voice to the view in asserting that judicial review "makes the Judiciary Department paramount in fact to the Legislature, which was never intended and can never be proper." *Madison's Observations on Jefferson's Draft of a Constitution for Virginia (1788),* 6 Jefferson Papers 315 (Julian P. Boyd, ed., 1950), *quoted in* G. Wood, *supra* note 1, at 304.

46. Trenton N.J. Gazetteer, Apr. 18, 1781, *quoted in* Wood, *supra* note 1, at 302.

47. For the perspective that the framers had adopted a view of legislative sovereignty, but reconciled this view with one embracing the power of courts to give effect to constitutions as supreme law, see Goldstein, *supra* note 5, at 69–84.

48. Blackstone became the most important spokesman for a view inclined toward natural law, but committed to Parliamentary sovereignty. Grey, *supra* note 22, at 152. Wood concludes that there was "no logical or necessary reason why the notion of fundamental law, so common to Englishmen for over a century, should lead to the American invocation of it in the ordinary courts of law." G. Wood, *supra* note 1, at 292. The American doctrine of judicial review was at least in part "the product of their conception of a constitution as a higher law embodied in a written document." *Id.*

49. *See* G. Wood, *supra* note 1, at 453–63.

50. *Id.* 456.

51. *See* Grey, *supra* note 21, at 156–57.

52. The small number of cases are treated *infra* notes 58–131 and accompanying text.

53. As has been noted, "invalidation of legislation" was "rare and unpopular," but there is little doubt that they were influential cases and known by those at the Philadelphia Convention that drafted the Constitution. *See generally* Gerald Gunther & Kathleen M. Sullivan, Constitutional Law 14 & nn. 2, 3 (13th ed. 1991). For the view that judicial review was engaged in prior to the famous decision in *Marbury v. Madison,* which formally adopted this reading of the Constitution, and that the Court's adoption of judicial review could not have come as a surprise, see David P. Currie, The Constitution in the Supreme Court 69–74 (1985).

54. Sherry, *supra* note 40, at 1134–46; Grey, *supra* note 21, at 157–59, 165–68.

55. Sherry, *supra* note 40, at 1134–35, 1138; Grey, *supra* note 21, at 157–59.

56. For a treatment of the cases in these terms, see *infra* notes 60–63, 73–82, 90–92, 97–101, 102–106, 118–19. *Compare* Sherry, *supra* note 40, at 1135–46.

57. *Id.* at 1134.

58. Though unreported, the court's decision is found in 1 The Law Practice of Alexander Hamilton 392 (J. Goebel, ed., 1964) [hereinafter cited as Hamilton's Law Practice].

59. Goebel, *supra* note 8, at 133.

60. Hamilton, *Defendant's Brief No. 6*, in 1 Hamilton's Law Practice, *supra* note 58, at 373, *quoted in* Sherry, *supra* note 40, at 1136.

61. Hamilton, *Defendant's Brief No. 6*, in 1 Hamilton's Law Practice, *supra* note 58, at 367.

62. *Id.* at 367–68. *See* Sherry, *supra* note 40, at 1137. *But see infra* note 68 and accompanying text (court relied exclusively on state constitutional provision adopting the common law while ignoring Hamilton's argument based on universal society).

63. Sherry, *supra* note 40, at 1137. At one point Hamilton goes so far as to assert that a legislative act intended to violate the law of nations is void, I Hamilton's Law Practice, *supra* note 58, at 382; but there is room for doubt as to how literally this statement should be taken when read in context.

64. 1 Hamilton's Law Practice, *supra* note 58, at 380–91. But Sherry fails to acknowledge that Hamilton set forth this statutory construction defense as a separate argument from his contention that the law of nations controlled over the terms of the statute.

65. 1 Hamilton's Law Practice, *supra* note 58, at 395–97, 416–19. Calvin Massey has correctly observed that "[t]he court employed an artful dodge that seems typical of the period." Calvin R. Massey, Silent Rights: The Ninth Amendment and the Constitution's Unenumerated Rights 41 (1985).

66. *Id.* at 400. *See also* Sherry, *supra* note 40, at 1138.

67. 1 Hamilton's Law Practice, *supra* note 58, at 404. *But see infra* note 68 (treating the court's hedging on whether the law of war in question here was actually within the category of the immutable "necessary law of nations"). Herein that court was actually addressing the question whether the law of nations may be altered so as to deprive a foreigner "of his appeal to them." *Id.* at 403. The language could be construed as asking whether a nation may as matter of moral right abrogate the law of nations, rather than whether a nation has such a power within its own legal system.

68. *Id.* at 402. The court's treatment of the law of nations was further obscured, moreover, by its treatment of the issue whether the state of New York might properly have abrogated its commitment to the law of war at issue in the case under customary law, a question that turned on whether the law of war belonged to "the necessary law of nations" or fit within the "usages" that nations were at liberty to reject. *Id.* at 404–05. The court declined to resolve the issue of the status of the law of war at issue in the case but suggested that any power to abrogate the laws or usages of nations resided solely in Congress, *id.* at 405. Its treatment of the nature and status of the law of nations as fundamental law within the municipal law of a nation must be viewed, in any event, as dictum rather than holding.

69. *Id.* at 415. As Calvin Massey accurately pointed out, "[t]he court imitated Blackstone almost verbatim in declaring that, if the legislature 'think fit positively to declare a law, there is no power which can control them.' " C. Massey, *supra* note 65, at 233 n. 76. And as Helen Michael correctly observes, Judge Duane "rejected the premise that judges possess the power to invalidate *unambiguous* legislation conflicting with *express* constitutional terms; he asserted that judges possess only the limited power to interpret ambiguous legislation to avoid unreasonable results." Helen K. Michael, *The Role of Natural Law in Early American Constitutionalism: Did the Founders Contemplate Judicial Enforcement of "Unwritten" Individual Rights?*, 69 N.C L. Rev. 421, 455 (1991).

70. G. Wood, *supra* note 1, at 457. Sherry observes that "[t]he court's judgment essentially operated to deny effect to a statute repugnant to the unwritten but fundamental law of nations." Sherry, *supra* note 40, at 1137; *accord* J. Goebel, *supra* note 8, at 137.

71. Sherry, *supra* note 40, at 1137.

72. 5 U.S. (1 Cranch) 137 (1803).

73. The court stated: "The supremacy of the Legislature need not be called into question; if they think fit *positively* to enact a law, there is no power which can controul them." Alexander Hamilton, I Hamilton's Law Practice, *supra* note 58, at 415. As Gordon Wood observed, the opinion of the court "carefully avoided any direct confrontation between the court and the legislature, or between legislative law and any other law." G. Wood, *supra* note 1, at 458.

74. It is thus misleading to emphasize that "[t]he court characterized Hamilton's defense as contending that 'statutes against law and reason are void.' " Sherry, *supra* note 40, at 1138 (*quoting* I Hamilton's Law Practice, *supra* note 58, at 395.) Sherry suggests that the court's language lends support to viewing *Rutgers* as "firmly within the English opposition tradition." *Id.* In reality, the court omitted Hamilton's voidness argument, but purported to reconcile Hamilton's argument for a reasonable or equitable construction of the statute with the plaintiff's insistence that courts should not exercise discretion in construing the statute. I Hamilton's Law Practice, *supra* note 58, at 414–15. After rejecting the idea that courts might reject a law because it was unreasonable, the court concluded that the general words employed here rendered the statute unclear, giving the court "liberty to expound the statute by *equity,* and only *quoad hoc* to disregard it." *Id.* at 415.

75. The case is unreported, but is described in James Varnum, The Case, *Trevett v. Weeden*: On Information and Complaint, for refusing *Paper Bills* in payment for *Butcher's Meat,* in Market, at Par with Specie (1787).

76. *See* J. Varnum, *supra* note 75, at 38–39.

77. *See* Sherry, *supra* note 40, at 1139 (citing Plucknett, *Bonham's Case and Judicial Review*, 40 Harv. L. Rev. 30, 66 (1926) (relying on contemporary newspaper articles).

78. Sherry, *supra* note 40, at 1139. One of the judges even objected to the legislative inquiry by distinguishing between the defendant's plea, based on the

constitution, and the court's generally stated judgment; he concluded that "it appears that the plea hath been mistaken for the judgment." Varnum, *supra* note 75, at 39.

79. *See* J. Varnum, *supra* note 75 , at 33.

80. *Id.* at 11.

81. *See* Sherry, *supra* note 40, at 1139–41. We can only assume that Varnum's monograph provided an essentially accurate account of his argument to the court, given that it was prepared after the event. Goebel observes that Varnum's treatment "may well embody some afterthoughts." Goebel, *supra* note 8, at 138.

82. Sherry, *supra* note 40, at 1139. The quoted language does not clarify whether Sherry is claiming that Varnum's argument evidences the standard legal analysis of the day or reflects merely that such arguments were sufficiently current to be drawn upon by competent advocates. But in summarizing the confederation-era cases, Sherry asserts that they suggest "that for American judges in the late eighteenth century, the sources of fundamental law were as open-ended as they were in English opposition theory." *Id.* at 1145.

Although Sherry's treatment emphasizes Varnum's understanding, she claims that Varnum's analysis "illustrates the eighteenth century reliance on multiple sources of fundamental law." *Id.* at 1138. Notice that the analysis here distinguishes between the analysis of courts and advocates in characterizing the historical significance of a case.

83. Grey, *supra* note 21, at 157. For a similar view of Varnum's analysis, see Corwin, *supra* note 5, at 66–67.

84. *See* Varnum, *supra* note 76, at 14; Goebel, *supra* note 8, at 139–40.

85. *See* Goebel, *supra* note 8, at 139 (in merely altering the denomination of government "it might be supposed that these [charter] limitations had been accepted"). Goebel acknowledges, of course, that the legislature in Rhode Island had proceeded as though that charter no longer imposed any meaningful limitations on its powers, and the state's attorney general apparently defended the statute based upon the lack of a bill of rights in the state's legal charter. *Id.* at 138. But this tendency to assume legislative sovereignty in the post-independence setting follows the pattern of republican legislatures throughout the states, and the Rhode Island experience merely reinforces that such attitudes preceded rather than followed the creation of republican oriented constitutions in a number of states.

86. Varnum, *supra* note 75, at 14–15.

87. Goebel, *supra* note 8, at 139 ("Varnum conceived that jury trial was one of such rights [of Englishmen], confirmed by Magna Carta").

88. Varnum, *supra* note 75, at 15.

89. Although Varnum states that a 1663 statute was "declaratory of the rights of the people," *id.*, *see* Sherry, *supra* note 40, at 1140, he continues in that same sentence " . . . as derived through the Charter from their progenitors, time out of mind." Varnum, *supra* note 75, at 15. Although the argument refers to the ancient British constitution, its essential thrust is that a statute had clarified that the jury trial right was among the rights secured by the Charter.

90. Goebel observes that during the confederation period, "[t]he one area where [courts] seemed free to act boldly was the protection of the guarantee of jury trial," and he attributes this to the "popular sensitivity regarding any tampering with the 'inestimable' right of jury trial." Goebel, *supra* note 8, at 141. While courts did address other issues, it is clear that the right to a jury was the most common issue for appellate courts to confront despite countless legislative acts that thoughtful spokesmen viewed as contrary to natural justice and the proper role of legislatures.

91. Varnum, *supra* note 75, at 21.

92. *Id.*

93. *See* Sherry, *supra* note 40, at 1139 (suggesting that Varnum's argument presents the period's standard argument); *see also* Grey, *supra* note 21, at 157.

94. Varnum, *supra* note 75, at 24–25.

95. *Id.*

96. *Id.* at 21. Varnum emphasized, for example, that the laws enacted by the legislature, should "be not contrary and repugnant unto . . . the laws of this realm of England." *Id.* at 22. He concluded that compliance with the laws of England is required "by invariable custom and usage," and hence laws here should comport with those "which governed the realm of England at the time of the grant." *Id.* at 23.

97. This is true even though, as Corwin observes, in the aftermath of the controversy generated in *Weeden*, "interested attention was naturally directed . . . to the franker and more extensive claims of counsel." Corwin, *supra* note 5, at 73. Given the difficulty that would have faced anyone trying to justify the lack of a right to trial by jury, one is hard pressed to see in *Weeden* the basis for the idea of an unwritten constitution.

98. As we shall discover in chapter 4, moreover, it is quite clear what the framers believed would be the result of a deliberate decision to include a right to trial by jury in criminal cases and to leave the matter for legislative decision making as to civil cases, even though they argued for a constitutional right to civil juries in connection with the revolution. *See* chapter 4 *infra*, notes 111–20.

99. Kirby 444 (Conn. Super. Ct., 1785).

100. *Id.* at 447.

101. *Id.* at 452.

102. *Id.*

103. *See* Sherry, *supra* note 40, at 1142.

104. The case is unreported, but a description of relevant historical documents is provided in Scott, *Holmes v. Walton: The New Jersey Precedent,* 4 Am. Hist. Rev. 456 (1899).

105. N.J. Const. art. XXII (1776), *in* 5 The Federal and State Constitutions, Colonial Charters, and Other Organic Laws of the States, Territories and Colonies Now or Heretofore Forming the United States of America 2598 (Francis Newton Thorpe, ed., 1909) [hereinafter State Constitutions].

106. Sherry, *supra* note 40, at 1141. Sherry's summary is, however, somewhat misleading. From the Scott summary of court documents, we learn that counsel relied upon an alleged requirement of a twelve-man jury and also asserted that a six-man jury was "contrary to law" and the New Jersey constitution. *See* Scott, *supra* note 104, at 457–58. But the argument from "the constitution, practices and laws of the land"referred to "the proceedings and trial" without any specific reference to the lack of jury trial. *Id.* at 458.

107. Sherry, *supra* note 40, at 1141 (*citing* Scott, *supra* note 104, at 458–59).

108. Sherry, *supra* note 40, at 1141 (*citing* Scott, *supra* note 104, at 458–59).

109. *See* Scott, *supra* note 104, at 458 ("it may be proper to inquire with what color of right the counsel could urge his plea against the constitutional validity of the statute").

110. *Id.* at 459.

111. Unless the claim that denial of a twelve-man jury violated the "laws of the land" amounted to a general due process argument (a supposition that requires guesswork), it is not clear how it is distinguished from counsel's apparently separate claim that a six-man jury was "contrary to law." *See* Scott, *supra* note 104, at 458. And if Sherry correctly presumed that the final reason quoted by Scott refers to the denial of the right to trial by jury, counsel simply recombined the claim that the jury violated the constitution and "laws of the land." *Id.* We have no reason to presume that these various formulations amount to anything more than legal verbiage. *Id.* at 464.

112. Scott, *supra* note 104, at 464.

113. *Id.*

114. As noted above, we are very clear that those who adopted the federal Constitution did not believe that it had made any provision for a right to a jury trial in civil cases. *See* chapter 4 *infra*, notes 111–19 and accompanying text. In that setting at least, they would not have expected to be rescued by the courts in the absence of an express constitutional guarantee.

115. Mart. 42 (N.C. 1787).

116. 4 Call 5 (Va. 1782).

117. 1 Mart., *supra* note 115, at 45.

118. Sherry, *supra* note 40, at 1143. Indeed, at least one modern commentator concludes that the court "relied exclusively on the express terms of North Carolina's Constitution." Michael, *supra* note 69, at 449.

119. Call, *supra* note 116, at 7 (argument of counsel), 11–13 (Wythe, J.), 15–16 (other judges).

120. Sherry, *supra* note 40, at 1144–45.

121. *Id.* But Michael seems on the mark in stating that "one can only speculate about his views on [noninterpretivist judicial review]." Michael, *supra* note 69, at 453.

122. *Id.* at 1145. Sherry is somewhat tentative here, suggesting that Judge Pendleton's use of such language indicates that he "might have viewed the writ-

ten constitution as most relevant in cases involving the structure of government."
Id.

123. 4 Call, *supra* note 116, at 7 (argument of counsel).

124. *Id.* at 8.

125. *Id.*

126. *Id.* Wythe also seems to associate rather than to distinguish individual rights and government structure issues when he asserts that "if it was [a judge's] duty to protect a solitary individual against the rapacity of the sovereign, surely, it is equally mine, to protect one branch of the legislature, and consequently, the whole community, against the usurpations of the other." *Id.* at 8. For a treatment viewing this statement as reflecting Wythe's recognition of the case as involving only the function of mediating between the claims of rival branches of government, see Sherry, *supra* note 40, at 1144.

127. 4 Call, *supra* note 116, at 8.

128. Clearly, for example, Wythe's statement quoted in text would apply equally to the provisions securing individual rights contained within the Virginia declaration of rights.

129. 4 Call, *supra* note 116, at 17.

130. *Id.*

131. *Id.* at 17–18. While Pendleton's fellow judges expressed greater confidence than he that courts could exercise the power of judicial review, *id.* at 20, the state's attorney general, Edmund Randolph, argued that courts were not authorized to declare laws void because in conflict with the constitution. *Id.* at 7.

132. F. McDonald, *supra* note 2, at 156; 1 Hamilton's Law Practice, *supra* note 58, at 312–15. One of the leading opponents of this exercise of judicial power was Melancton Smith, who was later a leading Antifederalist opponent of the proposed federal Constitution. 1 Hamilton's Law Practice, *supra* note 58, at 313.

133. F. McDonald, *supra* note 2, at 156. Sherry claims that this controversy was directed at the court's reliance on a power of judicial review and concludes that "the spirit of the English opposition vision of fundamental law" was congenial to the public as well as to the courts. Sherry, *supra* note 40, at 1138. But the vehement public reaction to perceived judicial excess was hardly an endorsement of unwritten fundamental law. Indeed, it seems logical to suppose that those fearing the undermining of legislative power would be even more averse to judicial review on behalf of unwritten higher law principles than on behalf of the plainly expressed will of the people set down in a written constitution.

134. *Id.* Grey observes that the legislature nonetheless repealed the statute that had been stricken by the court. Grey, *supra* note 21, at 158. While the history supports Grey's further conclusion that the judges had "refused to bow to legislative pressure," *id.* at 157, it is difficult to see how this record indicates that the court "more or less prevailed." *Id.*

135. Letter from Richard Spaight to James Iredell, in 2 Life and Correspondence of James Iredell 168, 169 (G. McRee, ed., 1949).

136. *Id.*

137. *See, e.g.,* Corwin, *The Debt of American Constitutional Law to Natural Law Concepts,* in 1 Corwin on the Constitution, *supra* note 5, at 195, 199–201.

138. Corwin, *The "Higher Law" Background of American Constitutional Law,* in 1 Corwin on the Constitution, *supra* note 5, at 79, 107–17.

139. Robin v. Hardaway, Jeff. 109 (Va. 1772), *quoted in* Corwin, *supra* note 5, at 199.

140. Corwin, *supra* note 5, at 201.

141. *See id.*

142. *See supra* notes 121–126 and accompanying texts. Gouverneur Morris also relied on this sort of rationale in describing the holding of *Holmes v. Walton* in 1785. *See supra* note 113 and accompanying text.

143. Hamilton's argument in *Rutgers v. Waddington* arguably provides an example of this sort of reliance on natural right and justice. Without conceding the constitutional argument, Hamilton contended that the applicability of the law of nations "results from the relations of Universal Society." A. Hamilton, *supra* note 58, at 367. Taken at face value, this argument should imply that the law of nations would bind New York's courts even if the state's constitution specifically purported to reject its applicability within the state.

144. *Robin v. Hardaway,* Jeff., *supra* note 139, at 114.

145. According to this view, the constitution binds even if it departs from the higher law. Thomas Grey, for example, appears to conclude that the founding generation probably embraced such a view. He concludes that the written constitution took priority over natural principles of justice where it clearly spoke to an issue, and he thus allows that the Constitution accepted the institution of slavery. Grey, *supra* note 21, at 164. Sherry's description of the confederation period suggests that she believes that the founding generation would have given priority to unwritten principles of liberty, implying that she would give priority to unwritten principles of justice over even the written constitution. Sherry, *supra* note 40, at 1160, 1167–68, 1177.

146. James Iredell to Richard Spaight, Aug. 26, 1787, in 2 G. McRee, *supra* note 135, at 172.

147. *Id.* at 173.

148. *Id.* at 174.

149. *Id.* at 172.

150. Sherry, *supra* note 40, at 1143.

151. The balance of Iredell's letter presents the heart of his argument for judicial review. Moreover, in a contemporaneous pamphlet, *see* 2 G. McRee, *supra* note 135, at 145–49 (Aug. 1786), Iredell presented an argument for judicial review based upon the written constitution without alluding to any other potential limitation on legislative power. *Id.* at 172. Even Grey acknowledges that this statement "favorably contrasted judicial review founded on a positive constitution with more ethereal kinds." Grey, *supra* note 21, at 159.

152. 2 G. McRee, *supra* note 135, at 173.

153. *Id.* at 172. The narrowness with which Iredell probably viewed any natural justice exception to legislative power is illustrated as well by his treatment of the scope of judicial review under a written constitution. Iredell contends that "[i]n all doubtful cases, . . . the Act ought to be supported," and that "it should be unconstitutional beyond dispute before it is pronounced such." *Id.* at 175. Even if this "clear error" doctrine has not, in the long run, carried the day, Iredell's formulation reflects that judicial review was viewed, even by many of its most ardent supporters, as a grave and exceptional power which should be employed sparingly. It seems doubtful that Iredell in 1787 would have embraced anything approaching the sort of open-ended commitment to judicial review on behalf of developing moral and political ideals that characterizes so much of modern constitutional theory. For one thing, Iredell capitalizes "Constitution" throughout the letter, strongly suggesting that he equates "Constitution" for purposes of his discussion with North Carolina's written constitution. *Id.* at 174.

154. *Id.* at 456–57.

155. *Id.* at 83.

156. *Id.* at 169–70.

157. 3 Dall. 386, 398–99 (1798) (arguing for both a narrow construction of the power of judicial review *and* rejection of any limitation of legislative power beyond the limits stated in the written constitution). As Grey observes, *supra* note 21, at 171 n. 15, Iredell also made a similar argument with respect to a case arising out of North Carolina in June of 1798, in which he contended that the written constitution would have stated a general natural law limitation had one been intended. *Minge v. Ginnour*, 17 Fed. Cas. 440, 443–44 (C.C.D.N.C., 1798). Grey suggests, however, based on Iredell's 1787 letter to Spaight, that "Iredell himself was not yet an Iredellian in 1787." Grey, *supra* note 21, at 160. The analysis above suggests that he may well have held a consistent view throughout the period in question, but if there is doubt about his views in 1787, by 1788 he rather clearly held the positivist view.

158. *E.g.*, 4 Debates in the Convention of the Commonwealth of North Carolina on the Adoption of the Federal Constitution 149 (July 28, 1788) [hereinafter Elliot's Debates].

159. Michael observes that, as a member of the federal bench, Iredell "consistently adhered to a textualist conception of judicial review" and directly rejected reliance on unwritten rights. Michael, *supra* note 69, at 451–52.

160. Interestingly, although Hamilton supplied the argument from unwritten law in *Rutgers*, he is better known for his defense of judicial review that emphasized that there "was no clearer principle than that every act of a delegated authority contrary to the tenor of the commission under which it is delegated is void." J. Goebel, *supra* note 8, at 313. Goebel is referring to Hamilton's defense of judicial review in The Federalist No. 78.

161. Stourzh, *supra* note 5, at 169. It cannot be surprising, therefore, that even a recent advocate of recognizing unenumerated rights through the Ninth Amendment acknowledges that "[t]he state precedents from the 1780s establish that judi-

cial review was employed haltingly, sparingly, and with knowledge that its use would inspire popular opposition from dedicated radical egalitarians." C. Massey, *supra* note 65, at 43.

162. *Id.*

163. *Id.* at 169–70. Parliament held such a power notwithstanding that its exercise might well be viewed as abusive in a particular context. In some formulations at least, acts violating such basic principles were considered within Parliament's power even though such laws were viewed, in a sense, as "null, and void, being mere corruptions, and not [true] laws." *The Independent Citizen*, *quoted in* G. Wood, *supra* note 1, at 457.

164. Over the years, Parliament has continued to be viewed as obligated to preserve the rights and liberties of the English people, and the people are considered to be the ultimate judges of whether that duty is being fulfilled. The English people have thus continued to see the British constitution as embodying fixed principles of a fundamental nature despite the doctrine of legislative supremacy. J.W. Gough, Fundamental Law in English History 174–91 (1955); Stourzh, *supra* note 5, at 336.

165. Stourzh, *supra* note 5, at 336.

166. At the end of his classic study on the higher law background of the American Constitution, Corwin offers this compelling analysis:

Why, then, did not legislative sovereignty finally establish itself in our constitutional system?. . . In the first place, in the American *written Constitution*, higher law at last attained a form which made possible the attribution to it of an entirely new sort of validity, the validity of a *statute emanating from the sovereign people*. Once the binding force of higher law was transferred to this new basis, the notion of sovereignty of the ordinary legislative organ disappeared automatically, since that cannot be a *sovereign* law-making body which is subordinate to another law-making body. (Corwin, *supra* note 5, at 138–39.)

4

The Decision at the Philadelphia Convention: The Federal System as Bill of Rights

In the modern era, we have almost completely lost track of the relationship that the framers perceived between the structure of our federal system and protection of popular rights.[1] At least two obvious components of this confusion persist. First, as we have come to think of rights almost exclusively in terms of the claims of individuals against the government, we have lost the ability to hear the framers' voices referring to rights held by the people in their collective capacity, including the rights of the people within each of the sovereign states to be free from undue federal intrusion on their power of self-governance.[2] Second, our familiarity with the modern judiciary's reliance upon specific textual rights provisions as trumps against otherwise valid claims of legislative authority has blinded us to the fact that claims based on lack of governmental authority are also individual rights claims.[3] Most Americans, and even many legal thinkers, find it difficult to fathom that the framers of the unamended Constitution saw this limited grant of federal authority as an adequate alternative to a comprehensive statement of rights in a declaration or bill of rights.[4]

These modern tendencies of thought have been powerfully reinforced because the framers' expectations of significantly limited federal authority have been swept aside in the twentieth century. This expansion of federal power may have been inevitable, in which case the framers were wrong in assuming that the limited grant of authority would be a sufficient means for securing a wide range of rights in our system of fundamental law. However, even if it is true that expansion of federal power was inevitable, this does not warrant the modern tendency to denigrate the framers' position as disingenuous or implausible; the defenders of the Constitution engaged in their own form of argument for popular rights and limited federal authority.[5]

Our difficulty in seeing the ways in which the framers anticipated such great things from our federal system has obscured our vision of the Ninth Amendment.[6] In 1965 in *Griswold v. Connecticut*,[7] Justices Black and Stewart explained in separate dissenting opinions that the Ninth Amendment's reference to the other rights "retained by the people" alluded to the collective and individual rights that the people retained by virtue of the Constitution's grant of limited, enumerated powers to the national government.[8] Even though the overwhelming evidence supports this interpretation of the amendment, it has been widely rejected, and the single largest barrier to this interpretation's acceptance has been that the modern American mind has difficulty accepting the idea that the federal system was considered a sufficient guarantor of popular rights by those who drafted the Constitution.[9]

In my published works, I have defended the view that the purpose of the Ninth Amendment is to preserve the federal structure against a unique threat posed by the enumeration of significant limits on federal power.[10] In both works, a major task was to explicate how a structural or federalist reading of the Ninth Amendment is consistent with the undeniable fact that it is also a rights provision. The burden of those works was to show that the amendment was to foreclose a feared inference from the inclusion of a Bill of Rights: the fear that the rights-protective scheme of limited, enumerated powers was overthrown by the inclusion of a comprehensive system of rights and that the result would be a government of general legislative powers subject only to the specific restrictions stated in the Constitution and its amendments. Shocking as it seems to some modern minds, the idea was common to the debate over the proposed Constitution: it is the precise argument against a bill of rights offered by James Iredell in North Carolina.[11] We are so out of touch with the thinking of the framers, however, that the arguments that lend support to this reading of the Ninth Amendment are ignored and missed by those who are anxious to promote a more ambitious reading.[12]

The argument that the Ninth Amendment cannot be about limited powers begins by assuming that individual rights cannot be preserved structurally, by the granting and withholding of powers, even though the founding generation assumed the contrary.[13] But things do not always end up as they begin. At one point, to use a single example, Randy Barnett told us that the "Tenth Amendment does not speak of rights, of course, but of reserved 'powers,' "[14] with the apparent implication that its purpose is to protect states' powers, not secure the rights of the people. More recently, however, he has suggested that the Ninth Amendment secures unenumerated rights by providing a rule for construing federal powers, and the Tenth Amendment lends further support to the project.[15] Indeed, a host of commentators have come to see the federal system as part of the system for securing rights; but in each case, they have seen the federal system as part of the means chosen for affirmatively securing the rights of the people, rather than as an alternative, indirect way to secure the liberty of the people.[16] The purpose of this chapter is to show that these attempts to read modern fundamental rights law back into the structure of the Constitution partake of the same fallacious assumptions that prompted commentators to reject the idea that the federal structure could be the source of the other rights retained by the Ninth Amendment.

THE TENTH AMENDMENT AS A GUARANTEE OF FUNDAMENTAL RIGHTS

Traditionally the Tenth Amendment has been viewed as a structural guarantee designed to clarify the implications flowing from the Constitution's grant of limited powers to the national government.[17] It makes explicit what was already implicit in Article I of the Constitution: the federal government was to be a government of limited, rather than general, powers, and the states would continue to exercise power over the vast range of matters over which the national government was not granted authority. The amendment thus appears to provide a classic example of a declaratory provision—a provision included in a legal document to confirm an existing understanding of its meaning or implications.[18] James Madison confirmed this limited purpose when he presented a draft of what became the Tenth Amendment to the first Congress.[19]

It has been suggested, however, that the Tenth Amendment was not simply to reaffirm the federal structure, but also to guarantee fundamental rights limitations on the federal government.[20] It is observed that the amendment adopted by the states was not the same amendment Madison described as purely declaratory of the original federal design.[21] According to one commentator, "[t]he addition of the words, 'or to the people,' to the end of the Tenth Amendment as it was finally adopted . . . made that amendment not only a guarantor of federalism but also of the retained rights of the people."[22] We are to know that this additional language spelled out new limitations on the powers of Congress because we are to assume that this language was added to conform the meaning of the amendment to the Ninth Amendment, and we are told that because the people retained rights through the

Ninth Amendment we know that there were powers which neither the federal government nor the states possessed.[23]

The Text of the Tenth Amendment

The text of the Tenth Amendment seems to confirm Madison's assurance to Congress that the amendment restates what would already be a valid inference from the unamended Constitution.[24] The idea that Congress is limited to the powers granted and all other powers are reserved to the states is a reasonable inference from the language of Article I, Section 8 of the Constitution.[25] To begin with, Section 8 states that "[t]he Congress shall have Power" and then proceeds to provide a fairly substantial list of the various powers granted to Congress.[26] Considering that this enumeration of powers followed the practice established in the Articles of Confederation, which stated the exclusive powers of the national government, this is an appropriate place in which to apply the common law maxim of *expressio unius est exclusion alterius*—the inclusion of such a list of powers logically excludes others.

Moreover, the last clause of this section of the Constitution, the one we know as the Necessary and Proper Clause, further clarifies that this is indeed the correct inference, as it purports to acknowledge the existence of ancillary powers and to state the extent to which such powers may legitimately be exercised.[27] If the listing of powers was intended merely to exemplify or illustrate what was intended to be a general set of national powers, there would be no reason to state the power to execute the various named powers. The Necessary and Proper Clause rather obviously includes the pregnant negative, suggesting that if an act of Congress does not bear the stated relationship to one of the enumerated powers, Congress will have acted beyond the scope of its constitutional authority.

It might have been conceived, of course, that the fundamental rights secured by the Ninth and Tenth Amendments were not delegated to the nation because they could not be, even if a granted power might logically seem to encompass authority to invade such a right. At the very least, though, "powers not delegated" remains an unusual way to reference natural and inalienable rights which, as noted above, are conceived as rights that in their nature could not have been delegated to any government.[28] That the language of the Tenth Amendment did not have reference to affirmative limits on the powers granted the nation is confirmed by statements made by Madison himself.[29]

The Mischief to Which the Tenth Amendment was Addressed

The textual antecedent to the Tenth Amendment is, of course, Article II of the Articles of Confederation, the original American constitution. It provided that each state "retains every Power, Jurisdiction, and right, which is not by this confederation expressly delegated to the United States."[30] The Constitution's critics made the omission of this confederation language in the proposed Constitution a centerpiece of their argument against ratification.[31]

Given their fear that an all-powerful, consolidated form of government was the proper inference to draw from the omission of a general reservation of powers clause, Antifederalists concurred that such a provision would be "a summary of a bill of rights, which gentlemen are anxious to obtain."[32] Although the provision was drafted as a general reservation of power in favor of the states, it did not matter whether it was stated in favor of the states or the sovereign people. Patrick Henry, for example, demanded "that a general provision should be inserted in the new system, securing to the states and the people every right which was not conceded to the general government."[33] There is no reason to believe that Henry was referring to limits on powers granted the national government rather than a general reservation of the powers not granted to the new government.[34] It is little wonder that every state convention that offered proposed amendments to the Constitution included an amendment based on Article II of the Articles of Confederation.[35]

The "Remedy" Embodied in the Tenth Amendment

As we have noted, the critics of the Constitution expressed fears for the rights of the people and the states if the Constitution were adopted without a provision stating a general reservation of powers not granted to the federal government. This concern for the rights of both the people and the states is reflected in an amendment proposed by the New York Ratifying Convention: "Every power, Jurisdiction, and right, which is not by the said Constitution clearly delegated to the Congress of the United States, or the departments of the Government thereof, remains to the People of the several States, or to their respective State Governments to whom they may have granted the same. . . ."[36] These general reservation clauses were worded in several different ways. Most of the states that proposed constitutional amendments, including Virginia, worded the amendment in terms of the reserved rights and powers of the states.[37] These provisions, however, were as often touted as important guarantees of popular rights as those framed in terms of "the people," just as the New York provision could equally be described as a "state rights" proposal. In each case, the purpose was to state the basic principle embodied in Article II of the Articles of Confederation.

There was, of course, real significance to the reference to "the people" that some states employed. Proponents of the Constitution had relied upon the doctrine of popular sovereignty to justify the Philadelphia Convention's decision to draft a new Constitution, and they used the doctrine to explain how they had created governments of divided sovereignty.[38] The Constitution's defenders contended that the people held ample authority to reconsider their commitment to the Articles of Confederation and to withdraw power from the various state governments.[39] Madison was, on the one hand, an important proponent of the popular sovereignty rationale for the Constitution,[40] but he also served on the committee that drafted the reserved powers provision in Virginia in terms of powers reserved to the states.[41]

What little evidence we have from the first Congress confirms that the Tenth Amendment's language change reflected the preference for underscoring that it is the people who grant and reserve powers to both the federal and state governments. In the House of Representatives, the idea of stating the amendment in terms of the reserved powers of the people was objected to on the ground that "it tended to create a distinction between the people and their legislators."[42] The question of wording, however, arose again in the Senate, undoubtedly because the final version of the Tenth Amendment conforms more completely to the theory of the Constitution defended by its proponents.[43] There is widespread agreement that the language change in the Tenth Amendment was not significant.[44]

The fundamental-rights construction, by contrast, requires us to imagine, despite the lack of evidence to support the conclusion, that the first Congress inserted the language about powers reserved to the people to transform the provision to one that reinforced the doctrine of unenumerated rights.[45] When the two amendments were actually discussed together during the debate over the ratification of the Bill of Rights in Virginia, the governing assumption was that both provisions served as a "reservation against constructive power."[46] Randolph expressed concern that the Ninth Amendment had shifted language away from a prohibition of an inference of extended national powers from the enumeration of specific limits on granted powers.[47] But a member of the Virginia assembly, Hardin Burnley, contended that whether the Amendment was framed in terms of powers or rights, it would serve to prevent undue extensions of federal power only "if [Congress'] powers are not too extensive already."[48]

FUNDAMENTAL RIGHTS AND THE "PROPER" SCOPE OF THE NECESSARY AND PROPER CLAUSE

The traditional understanding of the Necessary and Proper Clause is that it performs the mundane task of affirming the idea that Congress may exercise reasonable discretion in enacting legislation to implement the powers granted by Article I, Section 8.[49] As suggested by its derogatory nickname, the "Sweeping Clause" generated great fears among those who were concerned that the Constitution portended a tyrannical federal government.[50] In its favor, defenders of the Constitution denied that the Necessary and Proper Clause carried the implication of unlimited power, contending that, if the principle set forth by the clause was not accepted, there would be no point in empowering the national government.[51]

The Text of the Necessary and Proper Clause

The Constitution's defenders, however, lacked the help of modern legal commentators, and thus missed the implication that the so-called Sweeping Clause was actually the most powerful limiting clause in the original Constitution.[52] As construed and applied by some modern commentators, the Sweeping Clause might have been better nicknamed the "Back Draft" Clause, considering that it was to serve as a virtually open-ended (and, thus, potentially destructive) jurisdictional limitation on the powers delegated to the national government by the Constitution—a limitation favoring principles of separation of powers, states' rights, and unenumerated individual rights.[53] If the framers had used the Necessary and Proper Clause as a weapon, their defense of the Supremacy Clause, the omission of a bill of rights, and the Constitution as a whole against charges that they would consolidate power behind an unlimited national government would have been greatly simplified. This simplicity would have been purchased, however, at the price of potentially undermining everything they had labored to accomplish during the long summer of 1787.

Lawson and Granger contend that the word "proper" in the clause was "understood as a significant limitation on legislative power" that was jurisdictional in nature.[54] The authors make clear their belief that the clause serves as a barrier to laws that would invade any of the individual rights held by the people, whether or not such rights are found specifically in any constitutional text.[55] Their assumption that the people's basic rights might not be stated in particular limiting provisions begins by making a "jurisdictional" leap that is not supported by statements of the framers or the experience under the state constitutions.[56] Under the state constitutions, the governments held general legislative powers, and it is commonly agreed that the people did not implicitly hold unstated rights against them.[57]

Nevertheless, in the context of a government of enumerated powers, Lawson and Granger contend that the word "proper" serves as a textual repository for the idea that laws executing federal powers are limited by norms found implicitly in the Constitution.[58] The Necessary and Proper Clause is thus contrasted with state and federal provisions describing the powers of government that are not limited to specific areas of legislative authority. They observe, for example, that the Territories Clause of the Constitution grants Congress power to make "all needful" rules and regulations respecting American territories; it does not limit Congress' authority to enacting laws "necessary and proper" for implementing some other power.[59] While they are clear that the clause is a source of otherwise unstated limits on federal legislative power, Lawson and Granger are far less clear as to the nature and source of these limits.[60]

The Purpose of the Necessary and Proper Clause

Lawson and Granger argue that the word "proper" was used in a "jurisdictional" sense, both because such a use of the term was common "in contexts involving the allocation of governmental powers"[61] and because it would avoid conflict with "the venerable legal maxim of document construction that presumes that every word of a statute or constitution is used for a particular purpose."[62] The other common meaning of "proper" referred to fitness or suitability, and, according to these authors, such a usage would render the word "proper" as redundant of "necessary," leaving the term "proper" without a meaningful function in the clause.

But the argument begs all the important questions. If the word "proper" was to fulfill a declaratory purpose, and its apparent redundancy was intended, we should not be shocked. Moreover, in his often-cited opinion, *McCulloch v. Maryland*,[63] Chief Justice Marshall applied maxims that are at odds with those stressing an independent role for legal texts and found that the term "proper" would not fit with the word "necessary" if "necessary" could only refer to a word with a strict and rigorous meaning. Based on the premise that "we may derive some aid from that with which [the word 'necessary'] is associated," Marshall finds it implausible that the framers would have used the term "proper" where its only possible effect "is to qualify that strict and rigorous meaning" and "to present to the mind the idea of some choice of means of legislation not straitened and compressed within the narrow limits for which gentlemen contend."[64] Marshall, then, finds it important to refrain from attributing contradictory purposes to the framers;

but this goal runs in tension with the common law maxim favoring a distinct purpose for different words.

The power-granting provision that most closely tracks the Necessary and Proper Clause is the provision of the Georgia Constitution of 1789, which states that "[t]he general assembly shall have power to make all laws and ordinances which they shall deem necessary and proper for the good of the State, which shall not be repugnant to this constitution."[65] Lawson and Granger read the constitution-limiting language as essential to avoid undermining "the otherwise general authority of the state legislature."[66] But it seems unlikely that the legislature was given the broad authority to judge its own constitutional authority. A more restrictive interpretation of "proper" enables an interpreter to leave to the legislature power to make an initial determination of the "fit" between proposed laws and the good of the state, while leaving to the state's highest court authority to determine whether a law violates a basic constitutional limit to legislative power. The more restrictive interpretation of "proper"enables an interpreter to recognize wide legislative discretion without engaging in the double-talk of recognizing legislative power to ignore the constitution absent a heroic rescue.

It seems reasonable to conclude that the word "proper" fits with all the common-law maxims and still displays an independent purpose. The term "proper" could have been used because it fits with the term "necessary," without radically altering its meaning, while also serving to remind us that Congress' power is only effective within the jurisdictional parameters of the Constitution.[67] On this reading, the Necessary and Proper Clause fits in well because it recognizes limits stated or implied elsewhere in the Constitution without turning a clause authorizing ancillary powers into a powerful new source of prohibitions on congressional power.

The Sweeping Clause, as construed by Lawson and Granger, amounts to exactly the sort of limiting provision that Chief Justice Marshall found to be implausible as a construction of a constitutional provision that purported to be one of the grants of power to Congress.[68] It is at least plausible, after all, to think that the framers of the Constitution intended a relatively narrow construction of ancillary powers to the end of ensuring that the national government remained a government responsible for the relatively few areas of concern specified in the Constitution; the result could have been the drafting of a power-granting provision designed to clarify the priority in favor of somewhat limited congressional discretion in pursuing national ends. As to limitations on the powers granted, the Constitution already included Article I, Section 9, which specified limits on congressional authority.[69] A provision intended to function as a supplement of these specified limits would logically seem to belong in this section of the Constitution.[70]

THE SWEEPING CLAUSE AND THE FRAMERS' CONCEPT OF LIMITED FEDERAL POWERS

While Lawson and Granger drew on the ratification-era debate on the Constitution, they failed to examine the scheme against the backdrop of the Articles of Confederation. Yet the Constitution's proponents drew heavily on the Articles in defending the Constitution.[71] They emphasized not only that the Articles of Confederation were limited in granting powers only the entire nation would exercise, but also that it lacked a comprehensive bill of rights.[72] In addition, the proposed Constitution granted limited powers to the national government, following the lead of its predecessor.[73]

As Madison put it, the standard defense of their enterprise was that "the Constitution is a bill of powers, the great residuum being the rights of the people."[74] This standard refrain harks back to the simple idea of granted and retained powers as embodied in the Articles of Confederation. When the Constitution's critics argued that it granted too much power to the national government, its defenders responded that "[t]he powers vested in the federal government are only Such as respect the common interests of the Union, and are particularly defined, so that each State retains [its] Sovereignty in what respects its own internal government."[75] The Constitution's defenders argued that the limited grant of national power protected both the states and the people, and the people's rights would receive additional security from the existence of the declarations of rights in their state constitutions. This is why Professor Amar has observed that the people of the United States saw it as their task to "conquer government power by dividing it between two rival governments, state and federal, a structural scheme textually reaffirmed by the Tenth Amendment."[76]

The Limited Powers Scheme and the Arguments against the Necessity of a Bill of Rights

Lawson and Granger enter the debate over the omission of a bill of rights in the middle, ignoring the dialogue that originated in an analogy to the Articles of Confederation. For example, they cite various statements denying that the Constitution included a "national power over speech and press."[77] Having reviewed these and other confident assertions about the limited scope of federal powers, they concluded that "the federalists must have believed that the Sweeping Clause does jurisdictional work."[78]

Yet those who defended the Constitution set forth the document's grant of powers as though they were a key to justifying the document. For example, James Iredell defended the Constitution, claiming that it included "such a definition of authority as would leave no doubt" that "any person by inspecting [the Constitution] may see if the power claimed be enumerated."[79] Those who defended the proposed Constitution spoke as though a person could determine by a careful reading whether a particular power had been granted.[80] If their arguments for a restrained understanding of national powers were really based on a jurisdictional reading of the Necessary and Proper Clause, we would expect those advancing such arguments to clarify the point. But they say nothing that would clarify their point or prompt readers to give these arguments a new or closer look.

The same point can be made by looking at the arguments advanced by the Constitution's critics. In his well-known, *Letters from a Federal Farmer*, an opponent of the Constitution argued: "[t]he people's or the printers' claim to a free press, is founded on the fundamental laws, that is, compacts, and state constitutions, made by the people. The people, who can annihilate or alter those constitutions, can annihilate or limit this right. This may be done by giving general powers, as well as by using particular words."[81] The Federal Farmer made his point, but it did not go unanswered. One of the Constitution's leading defenders, James Wilson, freely acknowledged, as today's interpreters of the Necessary and Proper Clause would not, that if Congress had been granted the power "to regulate literary publications," this general regulatory power would have given Congress power to abridge freedom of the press.[82] But Wilson contended that no power to regulate the press had been granted to Congress by the Constitution.[83]

The sides agreed that the basic question concerned the powers of Congress. The Federal Farmer argued that one could rely on a limited delegation of powers if there were grounds for confidence that "the particular enumeration of the powers given adequately draws the line between them and the rights reserved."[84] But such was not the case when it came to the proposed Constitution.[85] The sides of the debate were unlikely to agree that the proposed Constitution adequately drew the line between the powers granted and the rights reserved.[86]

James Madison and the Necessary and Proper Clause

Lawson and Granger suggest that the jurisdictional interpretation of the clause avoids seeing the framers as "fools and knaves who concocted a desperate defense of a flawed document."[87] Yet the view that the framers spoke too harshly of those who advocated a bill of rights was admitted even by one of the Constitution's key defenders, James Madison.[88] Madison made the following argument:

I admit that these arguments [from enumerated powers] are not entirely without foundation; but they are not conclusive to the extent which has been supposed. It is true that the powers of the general government are circumscribed, they are directed to particular objects; but even if government keeps within those limits, it has certain extraordinary powers with respect to the means, which may admit of abuse to a certain extent ... because in the constitution of the United States there is a clause granting to Congress the power to make all laws which shall be necessary and proper for carrying into execution all the powers vested in the government of the United States. ... Now, may not laws be considered necessary and proper by Congress, for it is for them who are to judge of the necessity and propriety to accomplish those special purposes which they may have in contemplation. ... . The general government has a right to pass all laws which shall be necessary to collect the revenue; the means for enforcing the collection are within the discretion of the legislature: may not general warrants be considered necessary for this purpose, as well as for some purposes which it was supposed at the framing their state constitutions had in view. If there was reason for restraining the state governments from exercising this power, there is reason for restraining the federal governent.[89]

Madison argued that just as the general grant of power to state legislatures may "admit of abuse ... to an indefinite extent," so might the more limited grants of power to Congress "admit of abuse to a certain extent," within the boundaries suggested by the limited objects as to which it might regulate.[90] Madison concludes that the prohibition on general warrants, as provided in what became the Fourth Amendment, is justified for precisely the same reasons that such a provision was considered necessary "for restraining the State Governments from exercising this power."[91] Madison's analysis strikes a fair balance between the somewhat inflated claims about the rights-protective capacity of enumerated powers and the overblown claims that the Constitution portended an unlimited national government.[92]

The Threat to Rights Presented by a Bill of Rights

After contending that the Constitution granted the federal government no control over the press, James Wilson argued that a free-press provision might even be construed "to imply that some degree of power was given, since we undertook to define its extent."[93] A premise of his argument is that a bill of rights serves to "limit and qualify the powers of government, by excepting out of the grant of power those cases in which the government ought not to act, or to act only in a particular mode."[94] According to Wilson the inclusion of a bill of rights presents the risk of reversing the governing premise of enumerated powers—that all not granted was retained.[95] Thus a slogan became that, under the proposed Constitution "every thing not granted is reserved," while an attempt to include a bill of rights would raise the inference "that every thing omitted is given to the general government."[96]

Edmund Randolph, who supported the Constitution, posed the following question to James Madison: "Does not the exception as to a religious test [for any office under the authority of the United States] imply that Congress by the general words had power over religion?"[97] His implication was clear: he wondered how the Federalists could contend that there is no need for a general provision securing freedom of religion when the text of the Constitution creates an exception or limitation on a power of Congress on the subject of religion. Madison responded that the provision under consideration meant "nothing more than that without that exception, a power would have been given to impose an oath involving a religious test as a qualification for office. The constitution of necessary offices being given to Congress, the proper qualifications seem to be evidently involved."[98] Madison's implicit suggestion to Randolph, then, was that the limitations included in the Constitution, in contrast to many that might be included in the proposed bill of rights, were necessary "exceptions" to authority contained in the granted powers, not "exceptions" to nonexistent powers that might give rise to an inference of their actual existence to the detriment of the enumerated powers scheme.[99]

Madison's analysis implicitly acknowledges that such abuses as religious tests were not necessarily prohibited by the grant of limited powers.[100] Accordingly, even though a comprehensive bill of rights would be superfluous, and even dangerous, the specific limits included in the proposed Constitution were neither. Randolph took Madison's insight and ran with it. At the Virginia Ratifying Convention, he provided analysis of the Constitution's limiting provisions and attempted to show that each one "is an exception, not from general powers, but from the particular powers therein vested."[101] There was no reason, on this view, to see the limits stated in the proposed Constitution as an attempt to provide a comprehensive bill of rights and thus no ground for inferring new or enlarged powers.

Randolph's logic was impeccable, and, contrary to some modern suggestions, constituted more than a desperate back and fill operation. Even so, there are real problems with Randolph's argument and reasons why it did not end the debate over a bill of rights. First, Randolph and others did not ever quite acknowledge in so many words that a number of fundamental rights not secured by the written Constitution could just as plausibly be thought to be threatened by the specific powers granted, which at least suggests that the drafters had not gone far enough in securing rights.[102] At least some amendments in favor of rights should have been able to be adopted without even raising the danger postulated by Federalist arguments against a bill of rights. Whether other fundamental rights, such as freedom of the press or freedom of conscience, could also have been threatened by some potential reaches of enumerated power, would only be answered over a period of time. To a certain extent, then, these questions could only be answered as the scope of federal power, including implied power, was fleshed out; and under such circumstances, it was hardly unreasonable that many would be demanding security in the face of reasonable doubt.

The only way to bring James Madison and Patrick Henry together was to agree to amend the Constitution to include additional individual rights guarantees, as Henry insisted, and to add an unprecedented provision that would prohibit any inference extending Congress' powers from the inclusion of specific exceptions without begging the question as to whether any particular guarantee was an essential exception to a granted power or an arguably unnecessary limit on an unintended power.[103]

The Sweeping Clause, the Bill of Rights, and the Balance between Government "Energy" and the Protection of Individual Rights

Lawson and Granger assert not only that their jurisdictional interpretation of the Necessary and Proper Clause provides the most reasonable explanation of the framers' insistence that the enumerated powers scheme secures fundamental rights, but that it "is consistent with almost everything we know about the Constitution's design."[104] But the framers of the Constitution would not have thrown a wild card into the system of delegated and reserved powers. If we take the time to study carefully their thinking about how to strike the balance between government effectiveness and the protection of individual rights, we will discover that they did not rely upon a single provision to accomplish their goals.

While the parties engaged in a highly formal debate about the necessity for a bill of rights, there is no question that the debate only partly reflected the real differences between them. The defenders of the Constitution made it their priority to create a government of great efficiency. They justified that priority by emphasizing that a stronger government could better protect rights.[105] They also observed that "liberty may be endangered by abuses of liberty, as well as by the abuses of power," and "the former rather than the latter is apparently most to be apprehended by the United States."[106] They concluded that the people must necessarily cede some of their natural rights "to vest [government] with requisite powers."[107]

The Constitution's critics believed that their opponents held too much regard for the necessity of empowering government and too little for the need to preserve the people's rights.[108] One of their central themes was the idea that individuals enter the social contract to obtain greater security for their rights, not to relinquish them to government.[109] But given their own commitment to balancing the need to limit government with the need to empower it, the framers would have opposed a proposal to include a general limiting provision on behalf of popular rights, precisely because it would have presented a serious risk of skewing the balance.[110] This is why Madison wrote to Jefferson that "I am inclined to think that absolute restrictions in cases that are doubtful, or where emergencies may overrule them, ought to be avoided."[111]

Civil Juries and Standing Armies: The Rights Omitted

The Constitution's advocates deliberately omitted some rights that others viewed as crucial. The classic example is the right to have a jury in civil cases. It had been considered one of the crucial rights under the English constitution.[112] It was so fundamental that Lawson and Granger suggest that the right to trial by jury in civil cases was secured by the Necessary and Proper Clause.[113]

Yet defenders of the Constitution wrote and spoke in defense of a deliberate decision to omit the right to juries in civil cases. The reason for this is clear. The Constitution specifically provided for jury trials in federal criminal cases, and this was taken as a necessary exception to the power of Congress to establish the procedures governing criminal trials.[114] More generally, given that trial by jury appears to fall within the powers granted to Congress, the apparent consensus that rights could only be secured in fundamental law by inclusion in the written Constitution suggests that the right to a civil jury trial would not have legal protection.[115]

But defenders of the Constitution argued against providing such constitutional protection. One problem was the lack of uniformity among the states with respect to the scope of the jury trial right.[116] A related difficulty was that cases involving foreign parties raised unique difficulties for imposing a jury trial right.[117] To defenders of the Constitution, it also appeared that by retaining the flexibility of governing the matter through ordinary law, Congress could adapt the right to a changing society. Alexander Hamilton made this point:

The best judges of the matter will be the least anxious for a constitutional establishment of the trial by jury in civil cases, and will be the most ready to admit that the changes which are continually happening in the affairs of society, may render a different mode of determining questions of property, preferable in many cases, in which that mode of trial now prevails. . . . I suspect it to be impossible in the nature of the thing, to fix the salutary point at which the operation of the institution ought to stop; and this is with me a strong argument for leaving the matter to the discretion of the legislature.[118]

An assumption of those defending this decision was that a right to trial by jury in civil cases is not really a fundamental guarantee of liberty, as was the case with jury trials in criminal cases.[119] The Constitution's defenders, at any rate, assured their opponents that Congress would make provision for a right to trial by jury in civil cases.[120] A governing assumption may well have been that specific constitutional guarantees are not as important as "the general genius of a government" and that constitutional limitations "have far less virtue and efficacy than are commonly ascribed to them."[121]

John Philip Reid has written that there were "few principles better established in eighteenth century law than that a standing army was unconstitutional."[122] Positions against standing armies were also found in pre-1787 state constitutions.[123] Such limitations were also among the amendments proposed by state ratifying conventions,[124] and they were offered by such important figures as Thomas Jefferson and Richard Henry Lee.[125] Little wonder that Leonard Levy lists the prohibition on standing armies as among the "positive rights . . . deriving from the social compact that creates government" that he claims the Ninth Amendment was intended to secure.[126]

Lawson and Granger suggest that the jurisdictional limitation they find in the Sweeping Clause prohibited the enactment of laws that violated any of the rights that would later be included in the Bill of Rights, as well as "those rights the violation of which the general public in 1789 would have thought 'improper.' "[127] In these terms, it is difficult to imagine a more fitting candidate for inclusion among the unenumerated rights secured by a broad jurisdictional reading of the Necessary and Proper Clause. For example, there is no provision in the Constitution that purports to relinquish this right. Even Congress' powers to declare war and to raise an army could readily be construed, given the internal limits established by a generally worded jurisdiction-defining clause, as not including authority to engage in the improper act of creating a standing army in peacetime.

There is a problem, however. Congress was deliberately granted the discretion to keep a standing army,[128] and this delegation of authority was universally acknowledged even though it was cast as a general grant of power rather than as an express relinquishment of a right.[129] Moreover, the attempt to amend the Constitution was rejected by Madison, the initial draftsman of a bill of rights, and ultimately rejected by the Congress that recommended amendments.[130]

Equally important, when Madison wrote to Jefferson of his concerns about inflexible prohibitions, he used the issue of standing armies in peacetime as a primary example.[131] If Britain or Spain established armies near America's borders, such constitutional prohibitions would not be heeded.[132] Roger Sherman argued that such a ban could "embarrass the public concerns and endanger the liberties of the people" so that "it might become improper strictly to adhere to" such a ban.[133] Hamilton put the argument as a chilling question: "With what colour of propriety could force necessary for defense, be limited by those who cannot limit the force of offense?"[134] As Isaac Kramnick has perceptively observed, Hamilton's preference for a standing army reflected both a liberal skepticism as to the viability of expecting a citizen militia to adequately provide security of frontiers and a conviction that the future of the nation lay in becoming a powerful commercial state that was capable of protecting its interests around the world.[135]

The Content of the Bill of Rights: The Rights Not Added

Madison drafted the Bill of Rights with an approach that can only be characterized as cautious. He stated that his purpose was to "proceed with caution" so as to make the "revisal" of the Constitution "a moderate one."[136] Madison reassured colleagues that he intended to support inclusion of constitutional safeguards "against which I believe no serious objection has been made by any class of constituents" and as to which "they have been long accustomed to have interposed between them and the magistrate who exercised the sovereign power."[137] Madison's goal was to provide for all essential rights, but to omit all others, and this determination became a source of debate in Congress.

A classic example is the proposed clause that would have exempted from military service anyone who conscientiously objected to bearing arms in a military setting.[138] The proposal was opposed by some, however, on the grounds that conscientious objection is not a natural right, given the claim of civil society on individuals to defend the community against external threat, and some opposed curtailing legislative discretion.[139] Such opposition did not so much reflect hostility to the interest involved as it demonstrated the amount of trust there was in the legislative branch to balance the competing values.

A similar set of feelings was reflected in the discussion of a proposed antimonopoly amendment. Some state declarations of rights had included such a limitation,[140] and Thomas Jefferson included the antimonoply limitation among six provisions to which the people are entitled under any constitution.[141] The problem was that Madison believed that the power to create monopolies was one that governments should exercise reluctantly, but it was a power they nevertheless required.[142] Madison omitted a prohi-

bition on the granting of monopolies, and when such a limitation was proposed in the first Congress, it was rejected.[143]

STATE POWER TO CREATE AND PROTECT
FUNDAMENTAL RIGHTS FROM FEDERAL INTRUSION

A final theory linking the federal system to fundamental rights is the
most novel—and perhaps the least plausible—of the group. In its most ex-
treme form, this state grounded theory has worked as a kind of "Reverse
Preemption Clause."[144] On this view, fundamental rights would trump inconsistent acts of Congress, despite the Supremacy Clause, because the inclusion of a right in a state constitution would assure its status as a right
retained by the people and limit the scope of federal power.[145] This claim
that the Ninth Amendment secures state created rights as affirmative limitations on federal power had not been advanced by a single commentator between 1789 and the 1980s.

As originally set forth in the work of Russell Caplan, upon which Professor Massey relied, the state law thesis was an attempt to reinforce the close
historical link between the Ninth and Tenth Amendments. The thesis posited that the Ninth Amendment took the role of securing the rights, existing
under state law, that had been guaranteed by Article II of the Articles of
Confederation.[146] Caplan's article suggested that the rights referred to and
secured by Article II of the Articles of Confederation were the individual-
right guarantees found within state law, whether constitutional or statutory.[147] For Caplan, Article II was a rights guarantee in exactly the same
sense that the Tenth Amendment is a rights guarantee; it secured for the
states sovereign power, including the authority to recognize rights in state
law, to the extent that federal powers did not preclude the exercise of state
authority.[148]

Professor Massey culled from Caplan's analysis the bare conclusion that
the Ninth Amendment was at least in part "an attempt to be certain that
rights protected by state law were not supplanted by federal law simply because they were not enumerated."[149] Contrary to Caplan's analysis, however, Massey found that the Ninth Amendment's state law rights trump
federal powers in the event of conflict.[150] He rested this conclusion on two
assumptions: (1) the textual position that if the unenumerated state law
rights limit only state power and not federal power, these unenumerated
rights would be disparaged compared to the enumerated rights;[151] and (2)
the historical claim that since the Antifederalists were seeking to limit federal power, they would not have agreed to a provision that did not protect
fundamental state law rights against federal power.[152]

In truth, Massey's state law rights thesis and Caplan's analysis begin at fundamentally opposed starting points for understanding the project embodied in the Ninth Amendment. Caplan sees the Amendment as an outgrowth of Article II and, therefore, as a complementary provision to the Tenth Amendment's general reservation of all power not granted to the national government. Massey sees the Amendment as an expansion of the limiting provisions of the first eight amendments and, thus, as complementary to the idea of stating affirmative limitations on powers granted to government. While they appear at first blush to be similar views, virtually every bit of evidence that would support Caplan's reading would undermine Massey's, and vice-versa.[153]

A key is to understand that questions about state law rights and the Bill of Rights concerned the fear of displacement of state law and the risk of a consolidated national government. Caplan is correct in asserting that the Constitution's opponents were insistent that there be the equivalent of Article II of the Articles of Confederation.[154] Caplan is wrong, however, that the provision called for by this debate is the Ninth Amendment; rather, it is the Tenth Amendment. In both the ratification-period debate, as well as in the proposals offered by the state ratifying conventions, the demand for a general reservation provision was cast in terms of reserved powers or reserved rights, as well as in terms of "rights, powers, and jurisdiction" (the language of Article II). In every case, the reservation of sovereign power would secure rights guaranteed by state law to the extent that the powers granted the national government did not conflict with them.

The Ninth Amendment protected exactly the same rights, but from an entirely different potential threat. Federalist critics feared that a bill of rights could threaten the rights secured structurally by creating the inference that the federal government was limited only by the specific rights contained in the bill of rights.[155] A related argument was that the inclusion of fundamental rights as to which no power had been granted could itself raise an inference that unintended powers had been granted.[156] The Ninth Amendment secured the rights reserved by the Constitution's enumerated powers scheme against the danger of an inference of extended national powers from the enumeration of specific clauses limiting the exercise of federal powers, clarifying that such limiting clauses could well be cautionary provisions that did not qualify any power actually granted.[157]

If the goal of the Ninth Amendment was to ensure that state law rights secured by reserved state sovereignty remained unthreatened, the rights referred to in the Ninth Amendment would in no sense be disparaged. They would only be disparaged if, contrary to the amendment's command, interpreters inferred enlarged federal powers from the enumeration of specific limitations in the Constitution and Bill of Rights.[158]

NOTES

1. "Popular rights" is used purposefully to include rights that were held by the people collectively as well as rights that are usually called "individual rights."

2. Indeed, some tension exists between the idea of collective rights, in particular the idea of popular rule, and the idea of human rights—rights which make claims against the authority of the people. But part of the point of our federal system (and partly our Bill of Rights) was to secure collective rights (including the right of local popular governments). Walter Berns, *The Constitution as Bill of Rights, in* How Does the Constitution Secure Rights? at 50, 58 (Robert A. Goldwin & William A. Schambra, eds., 1985) (observing that for framers of American constitutions, both state and federal, "[t]he right to share equally in this decision [on the form, organization and powers of the government instituted to secure the rights of all] is the most important human right because government is the means by which all other rights are secured").

3. *Compare* United Pub. Workers v. Mitchell, 330 U.S. 75, 96 (1947) (referring to rights reserved by Ninth and Tenth Amendments), *with* Randy Barnett, *Reconceiving the Ninth Amendment,* 74 Cornell L. Rev. 1, 6 (1988) ("[t]he Tenth Amendment does not speak of rights, of course, but of reserved 'powers.'"), *and* Calvin R. Massey, Silent Rights: The Ninth Amendment and the Constitution's Unenumerated Rights 11 (1995) (arguing that "the Ninth Amendment is pretty clearly concerned with '*rights* retained by the people' while the Tenth is equally explicit that its focus is upon governmental '*powers* . . . reserved to the States respectively, or to the people' "). According to one scholar, if an act is within a federal grant of authority, Congress may legislate "even at the cost of individual rights." Sanford Levinson, *Constitutional Rhetoric and the Ninth Amendment,* 64 Chi.-Kent L. Rev. 131, 142 (1988). The assumption is that an individual's claim of immunity from a federal statute on the ground that it exceeded granted powers is not properly described as presenting a rights claim. The framers held a different view. *See* James Madison, *Debates in the House of Representatives* (June 8, 1789), *in* Creating the Bill of Rights: The Documentary Record from the First Federal Congress 69, 82 (Helen E. Veit et al., eds., 1992) [hereinafter Creating the Bill of Rights] (describing the Constitution as creating a "bill of powers" with the "great residuum" being the rights reserved to the people).

4. *But see* Madison, *supra* note 3, at 82 (describing enumerated powers scheme as playing a critical role in Madison's conception of rights). "[I]t follows that all [the powers] that are not granted by the constitution are retained," *id.,* for "the constitution is a bill of powers, the great residuum being the rights of the people." *Id.*

5. *See* Leonard Levy, Original Intent and the Framers' Constitution 156 (1988) (arguing that there is difficulty thinking the framers "actually believed

their own arguments to justify the omission of a bill of rights"); Levinson, *supra* note 3, at 140 (suggesting that Alexander Hamilton's reliance on limited powers scheme to defend omission of a bill of rights "does not fit altogether well with his defense of implied power only four years later in relation to the chartering the Bank of the United States"); Gary Lawson & Patricia B. Granger, *The "Proper" Scope of Federal Power: A Jurisdictional Reading of the Sweeping Clause*, 43 Duke L.J. 267, 325 (1993) (calling omission of a bill of rights "a major blunder" and referring to a standard view that that framers were "fools and knaves who concocted a desperate defense of a flawed document"). *But see* Berns, *supra* note 2, at 52 (concluding that "history has vindicated the Federalists, who insisted that, so far as the federal government was the object of concern, a bill of rights was unnecessary"); Arthur E. Wilmarth, *The Original Purpose of the Bill of Rights: James Madison and the Founders' Search for a Workable Balance between Federal and State Power*, 26 Am. Crim. L. Rev. 1261, 1275 (stating the view that Federalists "genuinely believed that the rights of state citizens would not be threatened by the Constitution"). A more moderate assessment of the Federalist argument is found in this chapter.

6. The Ninth Amendment reads: "The enumeration in the Constitution, of certain rights, shall not be construed to deny or disparage others retained by the people." U.S. Const. amend. IX.

7. U.S. 479 (1965).

8. *See id.* at 519–20 (Black, J., dissenting) (stating that the Ninth Amendment was to protect against the false idea that federal government held powers in addition to those enumerated in its text); *id.* at 530–31 (Stewart, J., dissenting).

9. The objection begins with a reference to the text, which refers to seemingly unenumerated "rights" and makes no reference to federal powers. Thomas B. McAffee, *A Critical Guide to the Ninth Amendment*, 69 Temple L. Rev. 61, 65 (1996). Moreover it has been asserted that "[a]ny provision that has survived [the amending] process must be presumed by interpreters of the Constitution to have some legitimate constitutional function, whether actual or only potential." Randy E. Barnett, *Introduction: James Madison's Ninth Amendment*, in 1 The Rights Retained by the People: The History and Meaning of the Ninth Amendment 2 (R. Barnett ed., 1989). To Barnett it is clear that the traditional reading of the Ninth Amendment, that would limit the additional rights to those defined by the limited grant of federal powers, effectively "denies it any role in the Constitutional structure." *Id.* Barnett's argument begins with the assumption that the framers of a constitution would see no need for "declaratory" provisions that would serve to reinforce an existing understanding and prevent misconstructions.

10. McAffee, *A Critical Guide*, *supra* note 9, at 61; Thomas B. McAffee, *The Original Meaning of the Ninth Amendment*, 90 Colum. L. Rev. 1215 (1990). This narrower reading of the Ninth Amendment has not received the widespread support of the more expansive reading, but thoughtful constitutional commentators have raised significant doubts about the expansive reading as a construction of what the provision meant to those who framed it and ratified it. *See, e.g.,*

McAffee, *A Critical* Guide, *supra* note 9, at 61, 64 n. 16 (collecting sources); Akhil Reed Amar, The Bill of Rights: Creation and Reconstruction 123–26 (1998).

    11. Iredell argued that a bill of rights could have been both proper and necessary if the Constitutional Convention had created a federal government that was like the governments that existed in the states. In such a case, a bill of rights "would have then operated as an exception to the legislative authority in such particulars"; in the contrary case, in which the framers had "expressly defined" legislative "powers of a particular nature, . . . [a bill of rights] is not only unnecessary, but . . . absurd and dangerous." James Iredell, *Debates in the Convention of the Commonwealth of North Carolina on the Adoption of the Federal Constitution* (July 28, 1788), *in* 4 The Debates in the Several State Conventions on the Adoption of the Federal Constitution 144, 149 (J. Elliot, ed., 2d ed. 1866) [hereinafter Elliot's Debates].

    12. *See* Archibald Maclaine, 4 Elliot's Debates, *supra* note 11, at 139, 141 (insisting that we "retain all those rights which we have not given away to the general government"); Samuel Spencer, 4 Elliot's Debates, *supra* note 11, at 163 (contending that if the Constitution contained a guarantee that "every power, jurisdiction, and right, which are not given up by it, remain in the states," there would be no need for a bill of rights).

    13. Typical is Professor Laycock's claim that a clause referencing "rights retained by the people" *cannot* be one "allocating powers between the state and federal governments." Douglas Laycock, *Taking Constitutions Seriously: A Theory of Judicial Review*, 59 Tex. L. Rev. 343, 352 (1981). Laycock not only assumes that structural provisions cannot be about rights, but also forgets that the Tenth Amendment by its terms reserves powers both to the people and to the states. The people, however, did not reserve merely the collective power to govern through the jurisdiction of the state governments; they also reserved to themselves, as rights, powers that they might have ceded up to the national government. *See* James Wilson, Address to the Pennsylvania Ratifying Convention (Nov. 28, 1787), *in* 2 The Documentary History of the Ratification of the Constitution 387, 388 [hereinafter Ratification of the Constitution] ("A bill of rights annexed to a constitution is an enumeration of the powers reserved."). By contrast to Laycock, Wilson argued that Article I's enumerated powers worked more effectively than a traditional bill of rights because an imperfect "enumeration of the powers of government reserved all implied power to the people," while an imperfect statement of rights might implicitly concede dangerous powers to government. *Id.* Wilson's entire argument proceeded on the assumption that strictly limited grants of power are as plausible a way to retain rights ("the powers reserved") as affirmative limitations on powers in favor of specified rights.

    14. Barnett, *supra* note 9, at 6.

    15. Randy E. Barnett, *Necessary and Proper*, 44 U.C.L.A. L. Rev. 745, 776–77, 786 n. 149 (1997) (defending unenumerated rights by reliance on limiting constructions that are lent support by both the Ninth and Tenth Amendments).

16. *See generally* Barnett, *supra* note 15, at 745; Steven J. Heyman, *Natural Rights, Positivism and the Ninth Amendment: A Response to McAffee*, 16 S. Ill. U. L.J. 327, 327 (1992); David N. Mayer, *The Natural Rights Basis of the Ninth Amendment: A Reply to Professor McAffee*, 16 S. Ill. U. L.J. 313, 313 (1992); Suzanna Sherry, *Natural Law in the States*, 61 U. Cin. L. Rev. 171, 180 (1992).

17. *See* U.S. Const. amend. X ("The powers not delegated to the United States by the Constitution, nor prohibited by it to the States, are reserved to the States respectively, or to the people.").

18. As a member of the Court wrote, "There is nothing in the history of [the Tenth Amendment's] adoption to suggest that it was more than declaratory of the relationship between the national and state governments as it had been established by the Constitution." *United States v. Darby*, 313 U.S. 100, 123–24 (1941).

19. *See* Madison, *supra* note 3, at 85 (acknowledging his understanding that reserved powers amendment "may be considered as superfluous," but arguing that "there can be no harm in making such a declaration, if gentlemen will allow that the fact is as stated").

20. *See* Mayer, *supra* note 16, at 316–17 n. 13 (arguing that the Tenth Amendment serves a dual role as guarantor of federalism as well as guarantor of retained rights of the people); Norman G. Redlich, *"Are There Certain Rights . . . Retained by the People?"*, 27 N.Y.U. L. Rev. 787, 806–07 (1962) (asserting that the text of the Tenth Amendment implied that people possess powers that neither federal government nor state governments possess).

21. Madison Resolution (June 12, 1789), in Creating the Bill of Rights, *supra* note 3, at 11, 14 ("The powers not delegated by this constitution, nor prohibited by it to the states, are reserved to the states respectively."). On September 7, 1789, the Senate added "or to the people" to the language describing the powers "not delegated." *See id.* at 41 n. 23.

22. Mayer, *supra* note 16, at 317 n. 13. Mayer's formulation assumes that there is an important distinction between guaranteeing federalism and guaranteeing "the retained rights of the people." *Id.* One need not, however, posit a new and dramatic purpose of implying additional qualifications of the powers granted by the Constitution to recognize that the Tenth Amendment belongs squarely in the Bill of Rights as a guarantee of the rights reserved to the people when they granted only limited powers to the national government.

23. *See* Redlich, *supra* note 20, at 807. Initially Mayer endorsed this analysis by Professor Redlich. Mayer, *supra* note 16, at 317 n. 13. More recently, however, Mayer has suggested only that the additional language in the Tenth Amendment had transformed it "from a reservation of powers to the states to a more general rule for construing federal powers." David N. Mayer, *Justice Clarence Thomas and the Supreme Court's Rediscovery of the Tenth Amendment*, 25 Cap. U. L. Rev. 339, 351 (1996). He does not explain, however, how it is that the Tenth Amendment can serve as a rule of strict construction of federal powers and, at the same time, serve affirmatively to limit the scope of federal powers.

24. U.S. Const. amend. X ("The powers not delegated to the United States by the Constitution, nor prohibited by it to the States, are reserved to the States respectively, or to the people.").

25. *See* U.S. Const. art. I, § 8 (enumerating powers of Congress).

26. *Id.*

27. *Id.* at art. I, § 8, cl. 16.

28. Individual rights guarantees like those included in the federal Bill of Rights were sometimes described as "powers" withheld from government. *See* Wilson, *supra* note 13, at 388 (describing a bill of rights as "an enumeration of the powers reserved"). Even so, it seems unlikely that the framers would have used the phrase "powers not delegated" to refer simultaneously to the residuum of the powers granted, in referring to the states' reserved powers, and to unspecified fundamental rights limitations in referring to powers reserved by the people. This, however, is the thesis that the fundamental rights reading asks us to adopt.

29. Madison referred to the system of enumerated powers as being rights-protective, but in the plain sense that "it follows that all [the powers] that are not granted by the constitution are retained," and thus "the constitution is a bill of powers, the great residuum being the rights of the people." Madison, *supra* note 3, at 82. For Madison at least, the "powers not granted" referred to the residuum that would be defined by reference to the enumerated powers; they did not refer to additional limitations on the exercise of granted powers. *See id.* (discussing meaning of "powers not granted").

30. *See generally* Articles of Confederation (1777).

31. *See* McAffee, *Original Meaning, supra* note 10, at 1244–45 (discussing Antifederalist arguments based on the omission of Article II of the Articles of Confederation).

32. Samuel Adams, *Debates in the Commonwealth of Massachusetts on the Adoption of the Federal Constitution* (Feb. 1, 1788), *in* 2 Elliot's Debates, *supra* note 11, at 130, 131.

33. Patrick Henry, *Debates in the Convention of the Commonwealth of Virginia on the Adoption of the Federal Constitution, in* 3 Elliot's Debates, *supra* note 11, at 150.

34. *See Id.* at 446 (contending that without provision similar to the one found in the Confederation "that every right was retained by the states, respectively, which was not given up to the government of the United States," it would follow, "by a natural and unavoidable implication," that the people give up all their rights to the general government).

35. *See* McAffee, *Original Meaning, supra* note 10, at 1242 ("[A] provision like the Tenth Amendment is the only one that appears in the proposals of every ratifying convention that offered any.").

36. Bernard Schwartz, The Bill of Rights: A Documentary History 911–12 (1971); *see The Ratifications of the Twelve States Reported in the General Convention* (Rhode Island) (June 16, 1790), *in* 1 Elliot's Debates, *supra* note 11, at 334 (substantially same amendment as New York's).

37. *See The Ratifications of the Twelve States Reported in the General Convention* (Massachusetts) (Feb. 7, 1788), *in* 1 Elliot's Debates, *supra* note 11, at 322 ("All powers not expressly delegated . . . are reserved to the several states. . . .").

38. James Wilson, for example, argued that true sovereign power, "from which there is no appeal, and which is therefore called absolute, supreme and uncontrollable," resides "with the people." Wilson, *supra* note 13, at 340, 348.

39. Forrest McDonald, Novus Ordo, Seclorum: The Intellectual Origins of the Constitution 277–81 (1985) (summarizing the popular sovereignty response to arguments that the Constitution sought to divide sovereignty).

40. *See* James Madison, The Federalist No. 46, at 315 (Jacob E. Cooke, ed., 1961) (stating that governments of nations and states were "different agents and trustees of the people, instituted with different powers, and designated for different purposes").

41. *See* McAffee, *Original Meaning*, *supra* note 10, at 1236 (describing Madison's service on the Virginia drafting committee). When he served in the first Congress, Madison drafted a proposed Tenth Amendment that also reserved powers to the states. *See* Madison Resolution (June 12, 1789), *supra* note 21, at 11, 14.

42. Debates in the House of Representatives (Aug. 22, 1789), in Creating the Bill of Rights, *supra* note 3, at 192, 193 (Rep. Daniel Carroll).

43. We know that Richard Henry Lee, for one, objected to the change of language. Letter from Richard Henry Lee to Patrick Henry (Sept. 14, 1789), *in* Creating the Bill of Rights, *supra* note 3, at 295, 295–96 (claiming that insertion of "the people" suggested that reservation was on behalf of "[the] People of the United States, not of the Individual States," and this reflected an intent "to deny it to the people of the Indiv. States"). But this was a standard objection to the Constitutional plan and reflected the Antifederalist preference for a state centered system.

44. *See* Charles Lofgren, *The Origins of the Tenth Amendment: History Sovereignty, and the Problem of Constitutional Intention,* in Government from Reflection and Choice: Constitutional Essays on War, Foreign Relations and Federalism 108–09 (1986) (suggesting that "or to the people" was added to Tenth Amendment because similar language proposed for the preamble was not adopted; indicating that its purpose may have been to clarify that the Constitution was not premised on the notion of legislative sovereignty). *See id.* at 113 (concluding that the Tenth Amendment was "[d]eclaratory of the overall constitutional scheme" and "had no independent force as originally understood").

45. One might have expected the logic to run in the opposite direction. Given the evidence that the reservation of sovereign power in the Tenth Amendment was viewed as a means of securing popular rights, it would make sense to consider whether the other rights retained by the people in the Ninth Amendment are not the same reservation from granted powers referred to in the Tenth Amendment, rather than implied limits on government.

46. Letter from Hardin Burnley to James Madison (Nov. 28, 1789), *in* 2 B. Schwartz, *supra* note 36, at 1188 (quoting Edmund Randolph). Similarly, a Vir-

ginia judge, Richard Parker, wrote to Richard Henry Lee that he considered a bill of rights unnecessary because "the States claim & have all power but what they have given away." Letter from Richard Parker to Richard Henry Lee (July 6, 1789), *in* Creating the Bill of Rights, *supra* note 3, at 260 . Even so, he stated that he had "no objection to such a bill of Rights as has been proposed by Mr. Madison because we declare that we do not abridge our Rights by the reservation but that we retain all we have not specifically given." *Id.*

47. *See* Letter from Hardin Burnley to James Madison, *supra* note 46, at 1188.

48. *Id.* (stating that if powers of Congress are not too extensive "the rights of the people & the States" will be secured by the Ninth Amendment as finally adopted). Madison agreed. Letter from James Madison to George Washington (Dec. 5, 1789), *in* 2 B. Schwartz, *supra* note 46, at 1189, 1190 ("If a line can be drawn between the powers granted and the rights retained, it would be the same thing, whether the latter be secured . . . by declaring that they shall, . . . or that the former shall not be extended."). For review of the Burnley and Madison letters, see McAffee, *Original Meaning, supra* note 10, at 1287–93.

49. *See* U.S. Const. art. I, § 8, cl. 16 ("The Congress shall have Power . . . [t]o make all Laws which shall be necessary and proper for carrying into Execution the foregoing Powers, and all other Powers vested by this Constitution in the Government of the United States, or in any department or Officer thereof.").

50. *See* George Mason, *Objections to the Government Formed by the Convention* (1787), *in* 2 The Complete Anti-Federalist, 11, 13 (Herbert J. Storing, ed., 1981) (noting that under the Necessary and Proper Clause, "the State Legislatures have no Security for the Powers now presumed to remain to them; or the People for their rights"); Aristocrotis, The Government of Nature Delineated (1788), *reprinted in* 3 The Complete Anti-Federalist, *supra*, at 196, 208 n. 2 (clause as evidence of scheme to create aristocratic rule); *Essay of Brutus XI*, N.Y.J., Jan. 31, 1788, *reprinted in* 2 The Complete Anti-Federalist, *supra*, at 417, 421 (clause will lend itself to "an equitable construction" of the Constitution in which the most important powers will be "unlimited by any thing but the discretion of the legislature"). For some, the Sweeping Clause threatened liberty by granting an extremely wide discretion in implementing already broad powers; others went further, reading the clause as making Congress the sole judge of the scope of its own powers based on its language.

51. James Madison, The Federalist No. 44, *supra* note 40, at 305 (stating that clause was included to remove "a pretext which may be seized on critical occasions for drawing into question the essential powers of the Union"); Alexander Hamilton, The Federalist No. 33, *supra* note 40, at 205–06 (clause was introduced "for greater caution, and to guard against all caviling refinements in those who might hereafter feel a disposition to curtail and evade the legitimate authorities of the Union"); Letter from C. William Cranch to John Quincy Adams (Nov. 26, 1787), *in* 14 Ratification of the Constitution, *supra* note 13, at 224, 226 ("If they

had not the power to 'make all laws which shall be necessary & proper for carrying into execution the foregoing powers' . . . the powers would be of no service").

52. *See* Lawson & Granger, *supra* note 5, at 271 (clause requires "executory laws to be peculiarly within Congress's domain or jurisdiction—that is, by requiring that such laws not usurp or expand the constitutional powers of any federal institution or infringe on the retained rights of the states or of individuals"); *id.* at 270–71 (Sweeping Clause "is not, nor did the Framers think it to be, a grant of general legislative powers").

53. *See id.* at 297, 299 (stating the view that jurisdictional construction of the Sweeping Clause requires that executory laws be consistent with principles of separation of powers, federalism and individual rights).

54. Lawson & Granger, *supra* note 5, at 314.

55. *Id.* at 271–272 ("[L]aws [must] be peculiarly within Congress's domain [and] not usurp . . . retained rights . . . of individuals.").

56. *See id.* at 274 (contending that the "word 'proper' serves a critical, although previously largely unacknowledged, constitutional purpose by requiring executory laws to be peculiarly within Congress's domain or jurisdiction"). They conclude that the clause is a "vital part of the constitutional design." *Id.* Yet there is nothing more pervasive in dicussion of the Necessary and Proper Clause than the idea that it serves a function that is purely declaratory of the Constitution without the clause.

57. A few weeks after the Constitutional Convention, James Wilson explained that under the state constitutions the people had "invested their representatives with every right and authority which they did not in explicit terms reserve," James Wilson, *Speech in the State House Yard,* Pa. Herald, Oct. 9, 1787, *reprinted in* 2 Ratification of the Constitution, *supra* note 13, at 167, 167–68. *See* George Nicholas, *Debates in the Convention of the Commonwealth of Virginia on the Adoption of the Federal Constitution* (June 14, 1788), *in* 3 Elliot's Debates, *supra* note 11, at 449, 450 (contrasting the case of Virginia, where "all powers were given to the government without any exception," with "the general government, to which certain special powers were delegated for certain purposes"); Edmund Randolph, *Debates in the Convention of the Commonwealth of Virginia on the Adoption of the Federal Constitution* (June 5, 1788), *in* 3 Elliot's Debates, *supra* note 11, at 463, 467 (distinguishing state legislatures that have "no limitation to their powers" from legislatures "with certain delineated powers" and contending that while a bill of rights is "necessary in the former, it would not be in the latter" because "the best security that can be in the latter is the express enumeration of its powers"). The pervasive fears of the Antifederalists that their rights were forfeited by the proposed Constitution indicates that traditional and natural rights did not in general hold the status of well-established jurisdictional limitations in a legal sense—a fact that cuts sharply against the view that the word "proper," to the extent that it textually grounds well-established jurisdictional limits on the exercise of power, would have been understood to include these traditional and natural rights limitations on government.

58. Lawson & Granger, *supra* note 5, at 273 ("[T]he Sweeping Clause's requirement that laws be 'proper' means that Congress never had delegated power to violate those rights in the first instance.").

59. *Id.* at 310–11 (contrasting Congress' power to make "all needful Rules and Regulations" with its more restricted power to make laws that are both "necessary and proper").

60. *See id.* at 330 ("The task of identifying those unenumerated rights, if any, that the Sweeping Clause and the Ninth Amendment jointly protect is beyond the scope of our inquiry.")

61. *Id.* at 291.

62. *Id.* at 290.

63. U.S (4 Wheat.) 316 (1819).

64. *Id.* at 418–19.

65. Ga. Const. of 1789, art. I, § 16.

66. Lawson & Granger, *supra* note 5, at 314.

67. Constitutional limits would include all those found in Article I, Section 9, as well as limitations implicit in the system of separation of powers and federalism.

68. *See* Lawson & Granger, *supra* note 5, at 285–99 (arguing for a reading of the word "proper" that goes "well beyond [the] requirement of a telic relationship between means and ends" suggested by word "necessary").

69. U.S. Const. art. I, § 9 (prohibiting Congress from suspending writ of habeas corpus, passing bills of attainder or *ex post facto* laws, or imposing taxes or duties on state exports).

70. Lawson and Granger acknowledge the existence of the Constitution's limiting provisions, but fail to address why the Necessary and Proper Clause would not have been included there if it were a limiting provision. Proponents of the Constitution justified the provisions of Article I, Section 9, as essential exceptions to the powers granted by the Constitution—an argument that contradicts the idea that fundamental rights were already implicit in the requirement that executory laws be proper as well as necessary. *See generally* Spencer Roane, Roane's "Hampden" Essays, Richmond Enquirer, June 11–12, 1819, *reprinted in* John Marshall's Defense of *McCulloch v. Maryland* 106, 125–38 (Gerald Gunther, ed., 1969).

71. *E.g., The Report of Connecticutt's Delegates to the Constitutional Convention*, New Haven Gazette, Oct. 25, 1787, *reprinted in* 13 Ratification of the Constitution, *supra* note 13, at 470, 471 (defending the Constitution because federal powers "extend only to matters respecting the common interests of the Union, and are specially defined, so that the particular states retain their Sovereignty in all other matters").

72. *E.g.,* An American Citizen IV: On the Federal Government, Pa. Gazette, Oct. 21, 1787, *reprinted in* 13 Ratification of the Constitution, *supra* note 13, at 434 (observing that the "old [Federal] Constitution contained many of the same

things, which from error or disingenuousness are urged against the new one," and that "[n]either of them have a bill of rights").

73. Charles Jarvis, *Debates in the Convention of the Commonwealth of Massachusetts on the Adoption of the Federal Constitution* (Feb. 4, 1788), *in* 2 Elliot's Debates, *supra* note 11, at 153 ("The first article proposed . . . is an explicit reservation of every right and privilege which is nearest and most agreeable to the people."); Maclaine, 4 Elliot's Debates, *supra* note 11, at 141 (describing Necessary and Proper Clause as "an express clause which . . . clearly demonstrates that [Congress is] confined to those powers which are given them").

74. 1 Annals of Cong. 455 (1789) (Joseph Gales, ed., 1834).

75. Letter from Roger Sherman to Unknown (Dec. 8, 1787), *in* 14 Ratification of the Constitution, *supra* note 13, at 387.

76. A. Amar, *supra* note 10, at 123. Amar correctly finds it "wholly unsurprising that, alone among the successful amendments, the Tenth was the only one proposed by every one of the state ratifying conventions that proposed amendments." *Id.*

77. Lawson & Granger, *supra* note 5, at 319.

78. *Id.* at 323.

79. James Iredell, Debates in the Convention of the Commonwealth of North Carolina on the Adoption of the Federal Constitution (July 29, 1788), *in* 4 Elliot's Debates, *supra* note 11, at 170, 171–72.

80. *See, e.g.,* James Wilson, Proceedings and Debates of the Pennsylvania Convention, *reprinted in* 2 Ratification of the Constitution, *supra* note 13, at 455 (challenging opponents to show "what part of this system puts it in the power of congress to attack [the rights of conscience]").

81. *Letter from a Federal Farmer* XVI, *in* 2 The Complete Anti-Federalist, *supra* note 50, at 329.

82. James Wilson, Speech in the State House Yard, *reprinted in* 2 Ratification of the Constitution, *supra* note 13, at 168.

83. *Id.* at 167–68.

84. *Letter from a Federal Farmer* XVI, *in* 2 The Complete Anti-Federalist, *supra* note 50, at 324.

85. He wrote "[t]he distinction, in itself just, that all powers not given are reserved, is in effect destroyed by this very constitution, as I shall particularly demonstrate—and even independent of this, the people, by adopting the constitution, give many general undefined powers to congress, in the constitutional exercise of which, the rights in question may be effected." (*Id.* at 325.)

86. *See id.* at 324 ("People, and very wisely too, like to be express and explicit about their essential rights, and not to be forced to claim them on the precarious and unascertained tenure of inferences and general principles. . . .").

87. Lawson & Granger, *supra* note 5, at 325.

88. *See* Letter from James Madison to Thomas Jefferson (Oct. 17, 1788), *in* 11 The Papers of James Madison 299, 300 (William T. Hutcheson et al., eds.,

1962) (acknowledging that Madison did not view a bill of rights as superfluous to the extent that other federalists had).

89. Madison, *supra* note 3, at 82–83.

90. *Id.*

91. *Id.*

92. Lawson and Granger focus on Madison's description of potential abuses as involving laws that "in themselves are neither necessary nor proper," and they conclude that the Sweeping Clause only reinforced such powers by its potential for misconstruction. Lawson & Granger, *supra* note 5, at 323 n. 229 (using the misconstruction argument to question Madison's general warrant example). But Madison is clearly referring to what he considered to be a potential abuse of a power actually granted by the Constitution.

93. James Wilson, Speech in the State House Yard, *reprinted in* 2 Ratification of the Constitution, *supra* note 13, at 167–68.

94. *See* Madison, *supra* note 3, at 81.

95. James Wilson, 2 Ratification of the Constitution, *supra* note 13, at 382, 387–88, 389 (arguing against a bill of rights).

96. James Madison, *Debates in the Convention of the Commonwealth of Virginia on the Adoption of the Federal Constitution* (June 24, 1788), *in* 3 Elliot's Debates, *supra* note 11, at 616.

97. Edmund Randolph to James Madison (Feb. 29, 1788), *quoted in* Robert J. Morgan, James Madison on the Constitution and the Bill of Rights 141 (1988).

98. James Madison to Edmund Randolph (April 10, 1788), *in* 9 Ratification of the Constitution, *supra* note 13, at 730, 731.

99. In his letter, Madison specifically referred to the provision under discussion as an "exception to a power granted by the Constitution." *Id.*

100. This of itself belies the claims of some modern commentators. Given that a religious test would have affected a fundamental natural right, freedom of conscience, many would contend that Madison should patiently have explained to Randolph that no power to affect religion had been granted to Congress, contending that the ban on religious tests was purely cautionary. But there is not a hint of such a view in Madison's response.

101. 3 Elliot's Debates, *supra* note 32, at 464. *See id.* at 464–65.

102. The most obvious example is that the procedural protections relating to the legal system seem to have required security as much as the right to trial by jury in criminal cases, as was guaranteed by Article III.

103. *See, e.g.,* Letter from James Madison to Thomas Jefferson, *supra* note 88, at 300 (stating that Madison would be in favor of a bill of rights if "it be so framed as not to imply powers not meant to be in the enumeration"). Little wonder that Professor Amar says that the central purpose of the Ninth Amendment, as originally conceived, was to warn readers "not to infer from the mere enumeration of a right in the Bill of Rights that implicit federal power in fact exists in a given domain." A. Amar, *supra* note 10, at 124.

104. Lawson & Granger, *supra* note 5, at 315.

105. *See* James Wilson, 3 Elliot's Debates, *supra* note 11, at 35, 37 (arguing that there is "no quarrel between government and liberty" because government "is the shield and protector" of liberty and war is "between government and licentiousness, faction, turbulence, and other violations of the rules of society, to preserve liberty"); Edmund Randolph, Virginia Ratifying Convention (June 16, 1788), *in* 2 B. Schwartz, *supra* note 36, at 775, 777 (stating the proposed government "secures the liberty of the citizen" and checks "that excessive licentiousness which has resulted from the relaxation of our laws"); John Marshall, Debates in the Convention of the Commonwealth of Virginia on the Adoption of the Federal Constitution, *in* 3 Elliot's Debates, *supra* note 11, at 222, 226 (noting that "friends of the Constitution are as tenacious of liberty as its enemies," and that government is empowered "to secure and protect it").

106. James Madison, The Federalist No. 63, *supra* note 40, at 422, 428–29.

107. John Jay, The Federalist No. 2, *supra* note 40, at 8.

108. *See Letter from a Federal Farmer* XVI, *supra* note 50, at 323, 329 ("[M]any of us are quite disposed to barter [our freedom] away for what we call energy, coercion, and some other terms we use as vaguely as that of liberty.").

109. *See, e.g., A Columbian Patriot: Observations on the Constitution* (Feb. 1787), *reprinted in* 16 Ratification of the Constitution, *supra* note 13, at 272, 278 (quoting Blackstone that "the principal aim of society is to protect individuals in the absolute rights which were vested in them by the immediate laws of nature").

110. Thus at the Philadelphia Convention, the Committee of Detail stated in an introduction to a draft of the Constitution that one of its purposes was "[t]o insert essential principles only, lest the operations of government should be clogged by rendering those provisions permanent and unalterable, which ought to be [accommodated] to times and events." 2 The Records of the Federal Convention of 1787, at 137 (Max Farrand, ed., 1911).

111. Letter from James Madison to Thomas Jefferson, *supra* note 88, at 300. *See also* Philip A. Hamburger, *The Constitution's Accommodation of Social Change*, 88 Mich. L. Rev. 239, 277 (1989).

112. *E.g.,* John Phillip Reid, Constitutional History of the American Revolution: The Authority of Rights 47–48 (1986) (observing that Blackstone thought trial by jury to be "as fundamental as anything else in British constitutional law").

113. Lawson & Granger, *supra* note 5, at 320–21.

114. *See Letter from a Federal Farmer* XVI, in 2 The Complete Anti-Federalist, *supra* note 50, at 323, 326–27.

115. *See id.* (observing that the Constitution would be "the supreme act of the people" and hence it would be "improper to refer to the state constitutions" to establish claim to a civil jury; noting more generally that these rights must be "secured and established by the constitution or federal laws"). Notice that this thoughtful critic of the Constitution presumed that there could not be an implied constitutional right, even with respect to government of limited, and enumerated, powers.

116. *E.g.,* Alexander Hamilton, The Federalist No. 83, *supra* note 40, at 565–71.

117. *See id.* at 568 (relating problems with jury trial in cases concerning foreign nations).

118. *Id.* at 573.

119. *See, e.g.,* James Wilson, *Speech at a Public Meeting in Philadelphia* (Oct. 6, 1787), *in* 13 Ratification of the Constitution, *supra* note 13, at 341 (arguing that "the oppression of government is effectually barred, by declaring that in all criminal cases the trial by jury shall be preserved").

120. *See id.* at 340–341 (stating the claim that "trial by jury is abolished in civil cases" is "disingenuous" and the right is secured because Congress "is a faithful representation of the people").

121. Alexander Hamilton, The Federalist No. 83, *supra* note 40, at 574. Hamilton observed that, although civil juries were controlled by legislative discretion in Great Britain as well as in Connecticut, the right to trial by jury had been less abused in those places than in New York in the years since the American Revolution, even though the New York constitution provided for it. *See id.* 573–74.

122. John Phillip Reid, The Concept of Liberty in the Age of the American Revolution 49 (1988).

123. Virginia Declaration of Rights, *reprinted in* The Federal and State Constitutions, Colonial Charters, and Other Organic Laws of the States, Territories, and Colonies Now or Heretofore Forming the United States of America [hereinafter State Constitutions], at 3814 (providing "that standing armies, in time of peace, should be avoided, as dangerous to liberty"). *See also* Pa. Const. of 1776, art. XII, *reprinted in* 3 State Constitutions, *supra*, at 3083; N.C. Const. of 1776, art. XVII, *reprinted in* 5 State Constitutons, *supra*, at 2788.

124. *See* Amendments Proposed by the States, in Creating the Bill of Rights, *supra* note 3, at 16, 17 (New Hampshire); *id.* at 17, 19 (Virginia); *id.* at 21, 22, 25 (New York).

125. Letter from Thomas Jefferson to James Madison (Dec. 20, 1787), *in* 14 Ratification of the Constitution, *supra* note 13, at 482 (listing it as among the rights that should be included in a bill of rights); Richard Henry Lee, Proposed Amendments (Oct. 16, 1787), *in* 8 Ratification of the Constitution, *supra* note 13, at 65 (proposing a super-majority requirement and describing it as among the individual rights that he would insert into the Constitution).

126. Leonard Levy, *supra* note 5, at 278–79.

127. Lawson & Granger, *supra* note 5, at 330.

128. *See* U.S. Const. art. I, sec. 8, cl. 12. For a helpful summary of the convention's thinking about military matters, confirming that they made a definite decision to permit Congress to keep an army when they saw fit, *see* Joyce Lee Malcolm, To Keep and Bear Arms 151–55 (1994).

129. In defending this decision, Madison framed the issue this way: "[W]as it necessary to give an indefinite power of raising troops, as well as providing fleets; and of maintaining both in peace, as well as in war?" James Madison, The Federalist No. 41, *supra* note 40, at 270.

130. *See* Creating the Bill of Rights, *supra* note 3, at 30 n. 16, 36 n. 13 (noting that both congressional houses rejected proposed amendments restricting Congress' power to create standing armies). Nor was any such proposal included among Madison's proposed amendments. Madison Resolution (June 12, 1789), *in* Creating the Bill of Rights, *supra* note 3, at 11, 14.

131. Letter from James Madison to Thomas Jefferson (Oct. 17, 1788), *supra* note 88, at 299, 300.

132. *Id.*

133. Roger Sherman, *The Letters of a Countryman, reprinted in* Essays on the Constitution 222 (Paul Ford, ed., 1892).

134. Alexander Hamilton, The Federalist No. 41, *supra* note 40, at 270.

135. Issac Kramnick, *The Discourse of Politics in 1787: The Constitution and Its Critics on Individualism, Community, and the States, reprinted in* To Form a More Perfect Union: The Critical Ideas of the Constitution, at 166, 173–74, 210–11 (Herman Belz, et al., eds., 1992). Kramnick observed that Hamilton's argument "was a further blow to the ideal civic virtue, which had always seen professional armies as evil incarnate, undermining the citizen's self-sacrificial participation in the defense of the public realm that had been the premise of the militia." *Id.* at 173–74. In an environment of such fundamental differences in perspective and philosophy which created disagreements about the necessity for including what many viewed as a fundamental protection, it seems especially unlikely that there would be agreement about a general limiting provision.

136. Madison, *supra* note 3, at 79.

137. *Id.*

138. *See* The Ratification of the New Federal Constitution (Augustine Burke, ed., 1788), *reprinted in* Contexts of the Bill of Rights 135 (Stephen L. Schechter & Richard B. Bernstein, eds., 1990) (containing Virginia's nineteenth proposed amendment in a declaration of rights, which provided that "any person religiously scrupulous of bearing arms ought to be exempted upon payment of an equivalent to employ another to bear arms in his stead"). It was included in the House Resolution proposing amendments. House Resolution and Articles of Amendment (Aug. 25, 1789), in Creating the Bill of Rights, *supra* note 3, at 37, 38; and the Senate voted to amend the proposed article to eliminate the conscientious-objection guarantee. *See id.* at 38–39 n. 13.

139. *See, e.g.,* James Jackson, *Debates in the House of Representatives* (Aug. 17, 1789), *in* Creating the Bill of Rights, *supra* note 3, at 182, 183 (arguing that the provision "was unjust" to others "unless the constitution secured an equivalent"); Roger Sherman, *Debates in the House of Representatives* (Aug. 17, 1789), *in* Creating the Bill of Rights, *supra* note 3, at 182, 183 (stating that he did "see an absolute necessity for a clause of this kind," given that "[w]e do not live under an arbitrary government" and considering that, without such clause, many members of religious sects opposed to war "will turn out" and "defend the cause of their country"). Representative Benson concluded that they should leave the matter alone because it "ought to be left to the discretion of the government," given the

likelihood that the legislature will be likely to "indulge" such persons. Egbert Benson, *Debates in the House of Representatives* (Aug. 17, 1789), *in* Creating the Bill of Rights, *supra* note 3, at 184.

140. *See* Md. Const. of 1776, art. XXXIX, *reprinted in* 3 State Constitutions, *supra* note 123, at 1690 (stating that "monopolies are odious, contrary to the spirit of a free government, and the principles of commerce; and ought not to be suffered"); Mass. Const. of 1789, pt. 1, art. VI, *reprinted in* 3 State Constitutions, *supra* note 123, at 1890 (stating that "[n]o man, nor corporation, or association of men, have any other title to obtain advantages, or particular and exclusive privileges, distinct from those of the community, than what arises from the consideration of services rendered to the public"); N.C. Const. of 1776, art. XXIII, *reprinted in* 5 State Constitutions, *supra* note 123, at 2788 (stating "[t]hat perpetuities and monopolies are contrary to the genius of a free State").

141. Letter from Thomas Jefferson to James Madison (Dec. 20, 1787), *in* 14 Ratification of the Constitution, *supra* note 13, at 482.

142. Letter from James Madison to Thomas Jefferson, *supra* note 88, at 300.

143. Additional Articles of Amendment, *in* Creating a Bill of Rights, *supra* note 3, at 41. Jefferson wrote to Madison expressing disappointment that a limiting provision as to monopolies was not included. Letter from Thomas Jefferson to James Madison (Aug. 28, 1789), *in* 2 B. Schwartz, *supra* note 36, at 1143.

144. C. Massey, *supra* note 3, at 123–73.

145. Calvin R. Massey, *The Anti-Federalist Ninth Amendment and its Implications for State Constitutional Law,* Wis. L. Rev. 1229, 1233 (1990) (stating that "state citizens have the power, through their state constitutions, to preserve areas of individual life from invasion by the federal Congress in the exercise of its delegated powers").

146. *See* Russell Caplan, *The History and Meaning of the Ninth Amendment,* 69 Va. L. Rev. 223, 262 (1983) ("[T]he ninth and tenth amendments both derived from Article II of the Articles of Confederation.").

147. *See id.* ("The Articles of Confederation recognized that the country's fundamental law consisted of the states' fundamental laws.").

148. *See id.* at 262–63 (arguing that the Ninth and Tenth Amendments were each derived from Article II of the Articles of Confederation and "were paired in the final version of the Bill of Rights probably because of their analogous residual purposes").

149. C. Massey, *supra* note 3, at 121–22.

150. *Id.* at 124. Massey admits that "[t]his is radical stuff, for it seemingly amounts to a form of reverse preemption." *Id.* at 125. In fact as he acknowledges, if it is to be justified at all, it is only by considering "the alterations over time to the allocations of power between state and federal governments," *id.*(justifying the judicial imposition of new affirmative limits of governmental power from an initial unwillingness to read the original grants of power in a restrained fashion).

151. *See id.* at 124 (stating that the Ninth Amendment forbids interpreters to "deny or disparage" other rights retained by the people).

152. Massey, *supra* note 145, at 1244. Massey concludes that "[g]iven the evident and overriding concern of the Anti-Federalists on this point, it is highly unlikely that the Anti-Federalists would have acceded to an amendment so ill-suited to their purpose." *Id.*

153. Difficulty in perceiving that different readings are irreconcilable and actually head in opposite directions is a pervasive problem in Ninth Amendment studies. *Cf.* A. Amar, *supra* note 10, at 348 n. 3 (citing both an article on the Ninth Amendment by Professor McAffee, that links the amendment—correctly, according to the author—to the federal system of enumerated powers, as well as a law journal note that begins with the premise that the Ninth Amendment is a source of unenumerated rights that "trump" even constitutional amendments adopted by the sovereign people; nevertheless, finding the law journal note as focusing appropriately on the phrase "retained by the people" and the theme of popular sovereignty, matters of which McAffee's article is said "to glide too quickly past").

154. Caplan, *supra* note 146, at 245 (stating that "antifederalists pointed out that Article II of the Articles of Confederation had embraced individual as well as state rights, and argued that a bill of rights was necessary to guarantee individuals the same protection under the proposed Constitution").

155. *See, e.g,* James Iredell, 4 Elliot's Debates, *supra* note 11, at 149 (North Carolina Ratifying Convention) ("A bill of rights, as I conceive, would not only be incongruous, but dangerous.").

156. *E.g.,* Alexander Hamilton, The Federalist No. 84, *supra* note 40, at 579 (a bill of rights "would contain various exceptions to powers which are not granted; and, on this very account, would afford a colourable pretext to claim more than were granted").

157. *See* 2 B. Schwartz, *supra* note 36, at 844 (discussing Virginia's seventeenth proposal). It read: "That those clauses which declare that Congress shall not exercise certain powers, be not interpreted, in any manner whatsoever, to extend the powers of Congress; but that they be construed either as making exceptions to the specified powers where this shall be the case, or otherwise, as inserted merely for greater caution." *Id.*

158. No one claims that rights are not secured by Article I's enumerated powers, nor that the rights antifederalists sought to protect in the Tenth Amendment are disparaged simply because they flow from the truism that all not granted is reserved to the states or the people. These are all, however, unenumerated rights of a sort. Professor Amar is correct, moreover, in asserting that "the federalism roots of the Ninth Amendment, and its links to the unique enumerated power strategy of Article I, help explain why no previous state constitution featured language precisely like the Ninth's—a fact conveniently ignored by most mainstream accounts." A. Amar, *supra* note 10, at 124.

5

The Ratification-Era Debate over the Omission of a Bill of Rights: The Constitution as Fundamental Positive Law

Despite claims to the contrary, the ratification debate over the proposed Constitution included the founding period discussions that are most directly relevant to assessing whether the idea of natural or customary rights as inherently enforceable constitutional norms was predominant at the time of the framing and adoption of the Constitution.[1] The debate concerned whether the proposed Constitution adequately secured the rights of the people or, to the contrary, had actually granted them away. Even though much of the discussion focused on the unique nature of a *federal* constitution, as contrasted with constitutions for a government of general jurisdiction as existed in the states, as well as on the merits of the specific features of this particular federal Constitution, it is also true that the discussion necessarily concerned basic questions of constitutional theory, including the central question whether the adoption of a republican constitution, general or federal, raises a presumption in favor of fundamental rights.

The opponents of the Constitution, the Antifederalists, made the omission of a bill of rights a central issue of the debate over ratification of the Constitution.[2] They contended that the omission of a bill of rights made manifest the intent to create an all-powerful central government and established that the national government had been granted plenary power to invade the people's natural rights.[3] On the other hand, the Federalists, who defended the Constitution, insisted that the proposed Constitution created a government of limited powers that adequately secured the people's fundamental rights. Despite their disagreements, however, in general the opposing camps shared remarkably similar premises that it was important that the Constitution secure the fundamental natural rights and that the natural rights did not operate as inherent, enforceable limitations on government power.[4] Based on their ratification-era arguments, neither group would have contended that written protections contribute only the additional security of explicitness in defining the natural rights or the certainty that a particular right would be included.

The debate had an air of artificiality about it precisely because, as a purely legal debate, it often ignored the real wellsprings of motivation of the parties, as for example the Constitution supporters' apparent concerns about the potential divisions that might become associated with drafting and adopting a bill of rights or their suspicion that many critics saw the issue as a stalking horse for more fundamental grounds of opposition. The context of a ratification struggle no doubt influenced the debate as well. Thus some defenders of the Constitution were deep skeptics of the value of a bill of rights, but these views were not given the same emphasis as the legal arguments because they understood that bills of rights in general were extremely popular in America.

THE WRITTEN CONSTITUTION AS THE SUPREME LAW OF THE POPULAR SOVEREIGN

For American constitutional law to develop, as Gerald Stourzh has observed, it was essential for fundamental law to make a transition to enforceable constitutional law inasmuch as the functioning eighteenth-century British constitution had come to recognize "certain imperatives or prohibitions as fundamental elements of the laws of the land *without* thereby creating a special category of legal norms."[5] Although England's doctrine of Parliamentary sovereignty should not be confused with the idea that such fundamental law principles have no significance in their political and constitutional order,[6] it is the special category of "constitutional" norms that bind even the legislature that most clearly distinguishes American from British constitutionalism. England's experience demonstrates, moreover, that it is possible to speak of fundamental law that, at least from the perspective of the modern legal positivist, does not appear to be truly "law" at all inasmuch as it is viewed as having no force or effect in the ordinary legal system. Given that it is harmonized with legislative sovereignty, such fundamental law might well be seen as having only a moral or political effect—in effect, it operates as a starting point for principled political discourse and may even be altered quite informally by an evolving political and legislative consensus.

Historically an important contribution of American constitutional law was its effective establishment of a higher law "in the technical sense that it cannot be abrogated or changed by normal legislative procedure."[7] This creation of a special category of legal norms that the British constitution lacked was accomplished by giving the higher law roots in a document that proceeded from the people—the fountain of all political power.[8] In thus reducing the higher law (whether "fundamental law" or philosophical "natural law," if distinguished at all) to positive constitutional law—what German authors call "Positiviering des Naturrechts" ("transforming natural law into positive law")[9] —America put into political practice what had been only a dissenting theory and revolutionary doctrine as to British constitutionalism. In light of Stourzh's analysis, it appears that although the state constitutions and declarations of rights represented a critical step in the direction of creating meaningful positive constitutional law limitations on government, they embodied an ambiguous middle ground between unwritten higher law which lacked a meaningful status in the practical workings of the legal order and the federal Constitution's unequivocal establishment of an enforceable, positive higher law. As we have seen, the state constitutions (1) were adopted, at least initially, by the legislatures, with the arguable implication that the legislatures stood in the place of the people and could alter the constitution at will, (2) made no express provision for judicial enforcement of their fundamental law norms, and (3) stated their declarations of rights generally in the language of obligation rather than of command. Taking their cues from these features and from a radical democratic view, the state legislatures often acted upon the assumption of their own illimitable power, and most often this confident assertion of power had gone unchallenged. These constitutions clearly enjoyed the status of fundamental law, but this was a fundamental law that might be reconciled with the doctrine of legislative supremacy.[10]

As we saw in chapter 3, while some courts and commentators relied upon the tradition of unwritten limitations or took the view that the written constitutions were enforceable super-statutes adopted by the people, many thoughtful Americans presumed the Blackstonian doctrine of legislative sovereignty, or at least an idea of a legislative supremacy that differed little in practice, and opposed (or in other cases held deep reservations about) the idea of judicial review.[11] For such thinkers, fundamental law continued to enjoy a status close to, if not identical with, the status it enjoyed in English law. Moreover, in the world of practice, the state constitutions did not succeed in establishing effective limits on the legislative branch.

The Invented Constitution?

Professor Suzanna Sherry has supplied a compelling and insightful account of the founders' clarification of the Constitution's status "as a *sui generis* form of positive law" during the course of the Philadelphia Convention.[12] Sherry suggests that the convention notes reveal the refining of two ideas critical to establishing the Constitution as an effective form of higher, positive law: the idea of self-referential enforceability and the notion of extra-legislative origin.[13] According to Sherry, the federal Constitution gained the quality of self-referential enforceability by the transition from a proposed congressional negative on state laws[14] to the Supremacy Clause that affirmatively declared the Constitution as the supreme law of the land.[15] Similarly, the idea of the extra-legislative origin of the Constitution came to the center as the arguments for popular ratification of the Constitution (which varied the pattern established by the Articles of Confederation) evolved from practical justifications to the contention that popular ratification reflected the recognized principle that the people held plenary power to change their form of government at will.[16] When these insights were integrated together, the convention brought to a new level of clarity the understanding of the Constitution as a distinctive form of higher law positively enacted by the people and binding on all levels of government.[17]

These developments at the convention, says Sherry, marked a transition from government by consensus to government by command and from government as the embodiment of community morality to a more limited view of government that separates the functions of law and morality.[18] They embodied, in short, "the transition from a classical republican outlook to a modern liberal one."[19] In this sense, the federal Constitution is described by Sherry as "the invented Constitution," inasmuch as it fully develops the notion of a constitution created by an act of will rather than one that is simply a description of established and time tested customary rights, practices, and expectations. Even so, Sherry contends that these developments fell short of establishing an exclusively positivist system inasmuch as the founders conceived of this new structure as complementing rather than displacing the older tradition of enforceable natural rights—a tradition which, as we have seen, she identifies with a malleable constitution or frame of government and a body of unalterable norms located in a declaration of rights.[20] Accordingly, Sherry concludes that "[t]he innovation of the summer of 1787 was to explain why a written constitution was a part of fundamental law, not to redefine the whole of fundamental law."[21]

Sherry's analysis of developments at the convention—and especially the convention's innovation in employing self-referential enforceability—calls useful attention to the continuing process by which the transition to a full conception of constitutions as binding enactments of the sovereign people was completed. At the same time, Sherry's analysis at once overstates the extent of altered understanding of basic constitutional principles revealed in the convention notes while misapprehending the extent to which the "innovations" in question grew mainly out of confronting issues of federalism that had to be faced. Even so, as we will discover, it is perhaps an interesting twist of history that federalism concerns may have added impetus to forms of thought essential to constitutionalism's transition to supreme and enforceable law.[22]

Supremacy, Popular Sovereignty, and the Structure of Federalism—Innovations or Adaptations?

Sherry is clearly correct in perceiving that during the summer of 1787 the founders crystallized the theory of the written constitution's central role in generating binding and enforceable fundamental law, though to say that the theory explained why a written constitution was "a part of fundamental law" overstates this point. What she most clearly fails to confront, however, is that this sharpening of understanding of the role of the written constitution suggests (and reflects) a theory of fundamental law (and what makes it enforceable) that is difficult to reconcile with a theory of unwritten constitutionalism.

Sherry's analysis of the federal convention and the debate over ratification seeks to determine whether the special status of individual rights norms, as reflected in the state declarations of rights and the tradition of unwritten limitations, was adversely affected by the achievement of what she describes as "the invented Constitution."[23] As shown in chapter 2, Sherry had advanced two closely related claims. She claimed, first, that the adopters of the state constitutions presumed the existence of inherent rights against government which would be part of the body of constitutional law, whether or not embodied in the written constitution. Second, she asserted that these rights were conceived of as more fundamental than issues of structure and the allocation of powers, and that, therefore, to the extent they were embodied in writing, they were placed in declarations of rights and conceived of as being beyond the ordinary processes of constitutional amendment.

An extended analysis of these original claims, however, calls into question Sherry's claim that the state constitutions presumed the legal enforceability of inherent and unchangeable individual rights limitations (whether or not embodied in any text) and the related division between provisions allocating governmental powers (as embodied in the frames of government) and provisions securing individual rights (as embodied in the declarations of rights). In the first place, the declarations included nonfundamental as well as communal rights and provisions dealing with governmental structure and were not treated as a distinctive body of uniquely immutable norms.[24] And while constitutional founders in general sought to draft documents comprised of provisions that would be permanent and unchanging, the evidence does not support the view that they saw any body of constitutional norms as existing without being subject to the decisions of the sovereign populace.[25]

Beyond the general claim that the framers believed that the Constitution included implied constitutional rights, Sherry more specifically insists that they viewed nontextual natural rights as enforceable because these rights were inherent and unalterable limitations on government power. In this section, we will examine the text and structure of the 1787 Constitution to determine in general whether the proposed dichotomy between mutable and immutable constitutional norms is confirmed or refuted.

An initially striking feature of the proposed federal Constitution is its failure to follow the typical confederation-era pattern of separating the frame of government from a declaration or bill of rights. Rather, rights provisions were included in the same document as allocation of powers provisions, and a bill of rights was omitted. While the omission of a bill of rights of itself generated intense controversy that will also bear on the issues we are addressing, the point here is simply that the omission of a separate bill of rights of itself suggests that the framers of the 1787 Constitution did not conceive of the Constitution as including two different orders of norms: those changeable portions relating to governmental structure and allocation of powers and those fixed portions embodying first principles such as the natural rights of individuals.[26]

This feature, moreover, can hardly be explained away on grounds that the *federal* Constitution naturally focused on the allocation of powers to and within the national government, leaving the security of natural rights to the states.[27] After all, Sherry and others insist that the Constitution *implicitly* included fundamental rights.[28] More fundamentally, it is clear that, although the proposed Constitution did not include a comprehensive bill of rights, it did include specific limitations on government in favor of individual rights.[29] It is thus striking that, if the Constitution were comprised of two different orders of norms (whether each was always embodied in a text or not), the document itself provides not a clue that this is the case.

The omission of any reference to such a doctrine, moreover, presents potential for confusion that should not be lightly attributed. For example, Sherry contends that at least one of the rights provisions included in the proposed Constitution, the prohibition on ex post facto laws, was viewed by the framers as a violation of natural law that would have been preserved whether or not embodied in the text of the Constitution.[30] According to

Sherry's analytical scheme, such rights retain their status as constitutional norms, whether or not embodied in any text, and are not subject to repeal by amending the written Constitution. But it seems especially implausible that the framers would have provided for the explicit protection of such inherent rights without clarifying the unique status they were thought to hold in our system of fundamental law.[31] The document itself quite straightforwardly appears to permit the elimination of such a right by the use of Article V, and if the written Constitution were intended not only to complement but also to give way to the broader fundamental law tradition, one would have expected that principle to be set forth.[32]

Moreover, Sherry also suggests that the Bill of Attainder Clause was not viewed as securing a natural right, but as enacting only a positive right.[33] But if the framers really did draw such a distinction between the two clauses, which is unlikely considering that they largely serve the same ends,[34] it seems a doubtful proposition that they would have done nothing to clarify the radically different status of these clauses in our system of fundamental law. If the prohibition on *ex post facto* laws would survive even repeal by constitutional amendment, but not so the ban on bills of attainder, the placing of these provisions in such close proximity would create only confusion about the nature of their status as fixed or malleable features of our fundamental law.

Sherry's claim that a "constitution" in America during the founding period consisted of both constitutional text and the unwritten tradition seems contradicted by the references to the "Constitution" within the text of the federal Constitution itself. In the Preamble, the Judiciary Article, the Amendment Article, and in the Article VI Supremacy Clause, references to the Constitution use the term to refer to the written constitution which the people "ordain[ed] and establish[ed]."[35] The constitutional text, moreover, conforms to the developing practice as of 1787 of using the term "constitution" to refer to the written constitution. At the very least, these uses of the term create a dilemma for Sherry: if these references are properly read inclusively enough to incorporate the implied natural rights limitations, the text of Article V would appear to subject them to the amending power, while under the narrower reading there is doubt raised as to how the broader fundamental law would be cognizable in federal court or as to how it manages to limit the reach of the Supremacy Clause of Article VI.[36]

Popular Sovereignty and the Scope of the People's Constitutive Power

If the text and structure of the Constitution raise serious doubts about the existence of two orders of constitutional norms, the extrinsic materials dealing with the doctrine of popular sovereignty strongly confirms those doubts. As noted previously, during the period leading up to the Philadelphia Convention critics of state constitutional practice had frequently underscored the people's role in constituting government, both to support efforts at reformation of existing constitutions and to oppose unlimited democracy. But as the Constitution's proponents defended the convention's decision to create a new form of government with provisions for popular ratification and an extended republic based on popular representation, they placed renewed emphasis on the plenary power of the people to change their forms of government at will.[37]

At the Pennsylvania Ratifying Convention, Wilson began a speech in defense of the Constitution by focusing on the Preamble's declaration that the Constitution was established by "We, the People of the United States."[38] Wilson continued: "What is the necessary consequence? Those who ordain and establish have the power, if they think proper, to repeal and annul."[39] According to Wilson, this power to reject as well as to ordain was implicit in the people's sovereignty understood in the classic sense: "In all governments, whatever is their form, however they may be constituted, there must be a power established from which there is no appeal and which is therefore called absolute, supreme, and uncontrollable."[40] Whereas in Great Britain this power resided in Parliament, Wilson contended that in the United States it resided in the people.[41]

As Gordon Wood has observed, Wilson's argument went beyond the traditional idea "that all governmental power was *derived* from the people" to the conclusion "that all government was only a temporary and limited agency of the people—out, so to speak, on a short-term, always recallable, loan."[42] The new division of power in the proposed Constitution, which appeared to attempt the impossible in seeking to create two sovereign powers in the nation and the states, could thus be justified on the ground that the people "may take from the subordinate governments powers with which they have hitherto trusted them, and place those powers in the general government."[43]

Wilson, moreover, also made explicit the implication that the people's sovereignty reached as far as Parliament's had within the British system, which included the plenary power to determine the content of their Constitution:

The truth is, that, in our governments, the supreme, absolute, and uncontrollable power *remains* in the people. As our constitutions are superior to our legislatures; so the people are superior to our constitutions. Indeed the superiority, in this last instance, is much greater; for the people possess, over our constitutions, control in *act*, as well as in right.

The consequence is, that the people may change the constitutions whenever and however they please. This is a right, of which no positive institution can ever deprive them.[44]

The Federalists were thus enabled to appeal to the people's power not only to ordain and establish the Constitution, but also to change it should it prove disadvantageous. As Iredell argued in North Carolina, "[t]hose in power are [the people's] servants and agents; and the people, without their consent, may new-model their government whenever they think proper."[45]

In thus relying upon, and arguably expanding, the doctrine of popular sovereignty, the Federalists powerfully reinforced the trend of perceiving the Constitution as fundamental law enacted by the people. At the same time, these arguments cut sharply against any idea of unalterable constitutional norms, whether written or unwritten.[46] The basically positivist idea of sovereignty, which in Great Britain had been attributed to Parliament, had now been attributed by the Constitution's leading defenders to the people of the United States. Their plenary power over their own constitutions, including we may presume any principles viewed as implicit in those constitutions, was here fully acknowledged. To this extent at least, constitutionalism in the United States had completed the transition to positivism.[47]

At the same time, it is possible that the founders were sufficiently committed to popular sovereignty to give preeminence to the written constitution, but nevertheless gave at least a presumption in favor of the continuing validity of customary or natural law norms where they had not been rejected or displaced by the written constitution.[48] Moreover, such natural law norms could have been thought of as binding fundamental law within a body of federal common law and as thus having a continuing status within our constitutional order, but without being conceived of as part of the "constitution" itself (given an evolving usage of that term). It thus remains important to determine whether the framers might have considered natural rights to be either implicit in the Constitution, or to have an independent significance, subject only to the sovereign people's power to manifest a contrary view by specific provision in the written Constitution.

THE DEBATE OVER THE NECESSITY OF A BILL OF RIGHTS

The Antifederalists were emphatic that a bill of rights was absolutely necessary and argued, on the basis of general constitutional theory and specific textual claims, that the proposed Constitution effectively relinquished all the basic rights of the people. Each specific argument to advance these claims proceeded from the decidedly positivist premises that the people might foolishly exercise their sovereignty so as to grant away their natural rights and that whether they had done so in fact depended on a fair reading of the written Constitution without resort to any presumption in favor of the constitutional status of such rights.[49] In each case the Federalists responded to the specific charges advanced against the proposed Constitution without disputing the essentially positivist premises underlying these charges. While the idea of inherent rights was invoked on a few rare occasions, in the main the debate over the omission of a bill of rights was classic lawyers' argument from beginning to end, replete with advocacy of the appropriate inferences to be drawn from the text and structure of the written Constitution. Each of these arguments will be treated in turn.

The Argument from General Constitutional Theory and Constitutional Design

Antifederalist spokesmen repeatedly argued "that all nations have adopted this construction—that all rights not expressly and unequivocally reserved to the people are impliedly and incidentally relinquished to rulers, as necessarily inseperable from the delegated powers."[50] In thus contending for the strict necessity of a bill of rights as a matter of general constitutional theory, Antifederalists offered a clear resolution of the confusion implicit in arguments as to the inherent nature of rights that was often combined with arguments as to the need to reduce basic rights to writing—a confusion that Gordon Wood suggests had characterized the postrevolutionary period.[51] These Antifederalist arguments contradict what Thomas Grey and Suzanna Sherry have claimed was the overwhelmingly predominant view during the confederation era—that the natural rights were viewed as presumptively enforceable whether or not embodied in any text.

Some Antifederalists placed the argument for the need of a bill of rights on the nature of the proposed Constitution itself rather than on a principle of general constitutional theory. As an example, the author of *Letters from a Federal Farmer* questioned the existence of a broad principle that the people necessarily delegate what they have not in express terms reserved.[52] Indeed, he suggested that as to a government established "to manage a few great national concerns," it had been thought "easier to enumerate particularly the powers to be delegated to the federal head, than to enumerate particularly the individual rights to be reserved."[53] It was possible in theory, then, to secure rights by reserving them as a residuum from a grant of limited powers, at least provided the reservation of all rights and powers not granted was expressly provided for.[54]

But in making room for the special case of a government of carefully limited and well-defined powers, such Antifederalists were a long ways from arguing for a strong presumption in favor of individual rights limitations. As to a government to which the people had granted broad, indefinite, or general legislative powers, these thinkers agreed that it was essential that the people reserve their fundamental rights as specific limitations on government power.[55] Indeed, these thinkers concurred in the dictum that what was not reserved in the written constitution was presumed to have been granted when it was applied to the state governments to which the people had given general legislative powers—a view directly contrary to the presumption in favor of individual rights which modern commentators claim American constitutions, including the state constitutions that preceded the United States Constitution, were thought to embody.[56] They also agreed that an enumerated power included all authority that would logically fall under such a granted power, including the authority to invade what might have been perceived as basic rights, in the absence of a specific limiting provision in the written constitution. Thus Congress' power to regulate the federal judiciary, together with its authority to enact criminal laws pursuant to its legitimate authority, would logically include the power to deny traditional procedural guarantees to criminal defendants unless such rights were stated as limitations in the Constitution.[57]

The Antifederalists powerfully reinforced their argument by what they took to be the obvious implications of the Supremacy Clause. For example, George Mason, the draftsman of the Virginia Declaration of Rights,[58] stated that "the Laws of the general Government being paramount to the Laws and Constitutions of the several states, the Declarations of Rights in the separate states are no Security."[59] Considering that the Supremacy Clause by its terms limits its grant of supreme law status to *constitutional* federal laws (laws adopted "pursuant to" the Constitution), Mason could not have feared its implications had he accepted a broad doctrine of inherent constitutional limits in favor of natural rights. Yet Mason's argument became a standard objection to the Constitution[60] and was joined by Samuel Chase, a person who is now famous for advocating inherent constitutional rights.[61]

Considering their objections to the proposed Constitution, one would have expected its critics to read implied limitations on federal power into the federal Constitution. In fact, Mason and others viewed the Supremacy Clause as a real threat to their state constitutional rights, as well as to customary and natural rights they believed people should have against government. On the other hand, one might have expected the Federalists to dispute the implications of the Supremacy Clause if they were advocates of inherent constitutional rights. But this is not the case. Alexander Hamilton argued in *The Federalist* that federal power would clearly be supreme and that this followed from the very idea of national power.[62] The debate revolved around whether the national government had been limited to the powers that a nation should have. Hamilton answered the Antifederalist concern with the observation that "it will not follow from this doctrine that acts of the larger society which are *not pursuant* to its constitutional powers but which are invasions of the residuary authorities of the smaller societies will become the supreme law of the land."[63] The Antifederalist opponents of the Constitution had correctly stated the implications of the Supremacy Clause, but had overestimated the reach of federal powers.[64]

Arguments based on the doctrine of implied powers, and the Necessary and Proper Clause, have already been confronted in an earlier treatment of the arguments leading to adoption of the Constitution.[65] It is no accident, however, that the Federalists did not rely on the doctrine of inherent limits to answer objections based on the Necessary and Proper Clause. To have invoked inherent limitations on government to resolve the dangers posed by implied powers would have undercut the Federalist argument for the uniqueness of the federal system and contradicted the refrain that the demand for a bill of rights manifested a failure to apprehend the distinction between governments of general and of limited powers.[66]

It appears, however, that at least one Federalist fell into this very trap. Alexander Contee Hanson, a Maryland legislator and judge who wrote under the pseudonym of Aristides, initially defended the proposed Constitution by reference to the standard Federalist distinction between governments of general and of specific powers.[67] If the Constitution had granted general powers, argued Aristides, the lack of a bill of rights would have implied that there were no limits on the authority granted; but under the proposed Constitution, power was limited because the Constitution "ascertains and defines the powers delegated."[68] Subsequently, however, Aristides offered an argument that appears to contradict his initial reliance on the standard Federalist argument from enumerated powers.

Aristides first confessed that it was "impossible to divine" the scope of Congress' particular powers, let alone what laws might be necessary and proper "at all times." Then he advanced a solution to the problem: "this we may say—that, in exercising those powers, Congress cannot legally violate the natural rights of an individual."[69] In thus apparently shifting from reliance on the unique features of the federal Constitution to the rhetoric of inalienable natural rights, Aristides' "interesting (if dubious) argument"[70] seems to place him in the position of contradicting the main thrust of Federalist argument as well as his own prior writing.[71]

Partly for this reason, there is room for doubt about the precise force of the argument proffered by Aristides. There is an alternative reading that would reconcile his arguments, but in a way that modern thinkers would likely find problematic. If he began with the assumption, held by many in his era, that the inalienable natural rights, whether included in a bill of rights or not, serve as limiting principles without necessarily giving rise to enforceable legal rules, his claim could amount only to the argument that Congress would act beyond its legitimate and, in that sense, lawful, authority if it invaded natural rights even though the Constitution adopted by the people did not itself forbid it. As Blackstone and others reasoned, an act could be unlawful in this "natural law" sense, without giving rise to enforceable remedies and without violating the Constitution.

In one sense, Congress could act with impunity in cases in which implied powers granted discretion because of the lack of a limit in the Constitution itself (reflecting as Aristides stated of a constitution without a bill of rights, that there was "no [strictly legal and constitutional] limitation on its authority"[72]). Yet at the same time, given that abusive acts would violate a natural right and be "unlawful" in that sense (if bills of rights stated principles mainly to influence political dialogue rather to effectuate legal enforcement), it would remain true, as Aristides asserts, that "this again is all you could say, were there an express constitutional avowal of those rights."[73] On this reading, Aristides is committed to inherent rights with a status equal to fundamental law rights, but he need not have viewed either as creating strict legal limits on government that could be enforced in court. If this sort of reconciliation of his arguments is not possible, the implication would be that Aristides advances arguments that contradict each other, and that he dissents from the views of virtually all of his colleagues defending the Constitution. Not surprisingly, then, others did not follow his lead.

Modern Responses to the Antifederalist Argument

It is a strange feature of the debate over inherent, unwritten consitutional rights that the overwhelming number of proponents of the view that such rights were taken for granted by the founders have never seriously confronted these Antifederalist arguments from general constitutional theory and the text of the proposed Constitution. These rather clear and straightforward arguments have been ignored, misdescribed, or (more rarely) acknowledged but denigrated without serious analysis. Thus Professor Sherry traces the idea of inherent, unenumerated rights through the debate over ratification of the Constitution by focusing exclusively on statements by defenders of the Constitution without so much as acknowledging that the Antifederalist arguments for the absolute necessity of a bill of rights directly contradict her claim that inherent rights were universally considered to be an implicit feature of American constitutions as of 1787.[74] Indeed, whereas Sherry contends that the constitutional status of fundamental rights did not require their stipulation in the text of the preexisting state constitutions,[75] the Antifederalists were adamant that the issue of necessity for a bill of rights would be established if the state constitutions were the guiding precedent. And, as we will discover, their opponents agreed.[76]

A typical formulation was the one offered in *Letters of Agrippa*, which concluded that "a constitution does not in itself imply any more than a declaration of the relation which the different parts of the government have to each other, but does not imply security of the rights of individuals."[77] This view was powerfully reinforced, moreover, by the unique standing of the people of the United States as the adopters of a new social contract, first as the people of each state adopted their respective state constitutions and, ultimately, as they accepted the proposed federal Constitution. The most thoughtful Antifederalist writer, the Federal Farmer, thus referred to the Constitution as the people's "last and supreme act," from which it would follow that "wherever this constitution, or any part of it, shall be incompatible with the ancient customs, rights, the laws or the constitutions heretofore established in the United States, it will entirely abolish them and do them away."[78]

Other scholars have called attention to the commitment of Antifederalist thinkers to natural rights[79] and suggested that the arguments under consideration may not have been a majority view[80] or intimated that these arguments perhaps reflected fear of pretextual (and hence illegal) usurpation of power.[81] But in each and every case, the suggestion appears as a bare assertion that the views expressed by Antifederalists lend support to the unwritten constitution/inherent rights idea. There is no attempt to show how this suggestion can be reconciled with the pervasive Antifederalist statements, found in carefully constructed writings as well as in speeches before the state ratifying conventions, that rest on the view that fundamental and natural rights must be secured by the written constitution.

To date, only a single commentator, so far as research has shown, has attempted more than a bare, unsupported assertion for reconciling the Antifederalist arguments against the proposed Constitution with the idea of inherent constitutional rights constituting the standard position of the day. Professor David N. Mayer documented the Antifederalist commitment to the concept of natural rights and then offered two explanations for the Antifederalists' uniform inisistence that fundamental rights must be secured in the text of the Constitution.[82] First, he suggested that, given their Whig tendencies toward deep distrust of government, Antifederalists may have "feared that without express stipulation for rights, written constitutions would be used as pretext for invading natural rights."[83] Second, he suggests that arguments about the strict necessity of bills of rights under the state constitutions may have reflected the partisan nature of the ratification debate rather than a carefully considered philosophical and constitutional theory.[84]

The historical evidence, however, lends little support to either point, so that the theses rest finally on unsupported assumptions about what it means to believe in preexisting and inalienable natural rights. One basic problem with the "pretext" or "illegal conspiracy" argument is that the advocates in question were fully capable of arguing for the advantages of defining and securing rights as a hedge against pretext, abuse, or changing political conceptions over time and thus need not have included stronger, legally grounded arguments about the *constitutional* effect of failing to amend the Constitution. For example, someone as sophisticated as George Mason, the principal draftsman of the Virginia Declaration of Rights, was undoubtedly concerned about the need to define limits on government to avoid pretextual and perhaps unwarranted abuse of power, and some of his criticisms, especially of the Necessary and Proper Clause, regarded in part precisely such risks.[85] But Mason went much further, contending that the omission of a provision similar to Article II of the Articles of Confederation ceded "many valuable and important rights," and he further argued that the Supremacy Clause meant that federal law enacted under the Constitution would override the guarantees included in the state declarations of rights.[86] Implicit in Mason's argument is the assumption that the constitutional status of natural rights came by virtue of their inclusion in the state constitutions; since those constitutions were inferior to the federal constitution, it followed that the natural rights would be forfeited to the extent that federal powers were construed broadly enough to reach them.[87]

Moreover, the legal arguments on behalf of bills of rights had tap roots reaching deeper than the debate over ratification, a fact that cuts against viewing them as purely pragmatic ratification inventions. As we noted in chapter 2, in an important work on the early state constitutions, Professor Donald Lutz observed that the people responsible for those constitutions "assumed that government had all power except for specific prohibitions contained in a bill of rights."[88] The logic of the position was clear and rested on both the notion of the people, as sovereign, granting and retaining portions of their limitless power, as well as the tendency to speak of "rights" in terms of the "power" to act in specified ways.[89] It was this standard way of speaking that was reflected as early as September 27, 1787, when the Constitution was briefly considered by Congress for transmittal to the states.

Nathaniel Gorham of Massachusetts explained that there was no need to insert a bill of rights because "a bill of rights in state governments was intended to retain certain power [in the people] as the legislatures had unlimited powers."[90] His characterization of the state constitutions was not contradicted, but instead Richard Henry Lee responded that a bill of rights remained necessary because the proposed Constitution did not preclude "constructive power" in the manner of the Articles of Confederation.[91]

It is probably true that the argument for the strict necessity of a bill of rights advanced a more compelling case for rejection of the Constitution than one based merely on the need to provide additional security for accepted rights. This could conceivably have provided some incentive to advance that argument rather than the more moderate, but less forceful one. But there is also a compelling downside. It would not have been possible to underscore the need for the safeguard that constitutional text supplies without at the same time supplying fodder for opponents of future claims of right in the event the Constitution was adopted without amendment. We should also pause and consider whether the evidence warrants imputing a compromise of basic constitutional principle by the Constitution's opponents, especially considering such a compromise's devastating long-term effects.

After all, while the ratification debate aroused great passion, the advocacy in question did not consist of stump speeches or what today we would call "sound bytes." Antifederalist advocates supplied full-blown restatements of the basic elements of social contract political theory, explaining the justification for entering civil society as well as the need to cede to government some natural rights while retaining those considered fundamental or inalienable. Such authors were equally clear that, though there are rights that cannot, as a matter of moral theory, be ceded to government even by the sovereign people, the failure to give effect to those rights in the written Constitution would amount to "resigning" those rights to government as a matter of law.[92] Far from suggesting that such spokespersons unwittingly or expediently compromised natural rights social contract theory that was opposed to the Constitution, these carefully drafted essays confirm instead that commitment to natural rights theory does not preclude commitment to an intelligently considered positivist understanding of fundamental law that comports with a meaningful concept of popular sovereignty.

The Federalist Response Based on the Unique Nature of the Federal Constitution

If there had existed a universal understanding, or even an overwhelming consensus, that America's republican constitutions gave inherent status to inalienable or fundamental rights, the Antifederalist argument would also have been an extremely risky one. The full-blown legal argument that the people were at risk of ceding up their most cherished rights could readily have been dealt a death blow by the invocation of fundamental constitutional understanding.[93] Instead, James Wilson, speaking for Federalist defenders of the Constitution, labored to distinguish the proposed federal Constitution from the constitutions that provided the models for Antifederalist constitutional theorizing: the British constitution and the constitutions of the states.[94]

Relying on the doctrine of popular sovereignty, Wilson and others contended that under the Constitution the people retained control over all their rights and, by contrast to the constitutions of the states, had immediately reserved all they had not granted to the general government.[95] The Federalists thus concurred with the Antifederalist assumption that the state constitutions granted limitless legislative power unless the people reserved power in a bill of rights.[96] Under the proposed Constitution, however, the government would be one of limited and delegated powers, and the people would retain their natural rights because the federal government had not been given powers that would enable it to invade them. In short, the opposing parties in the debate over ratification of the Constitution shared the premise that unless the people reserve rights to themselves by carefully defining the powers they grant to government, their rights will be subject to government invasion unless specifically reserved in a bill of rights.[97]

The Federalists thus turned the debate over a bill of rights into a debate over whether the proposed Constitution was in important ways analogous to the Articles of Confederation—a document that lacked a bill of rights, to no one's great displeasure. As briefly noted above, many Antifederalists placed great weight on the omission from the Constitution of a provision like Article II of the Articles of Confederation, expressly reserving to the states all rights, powers, and jurisdiction not granted to the national government.[98] The failure to include a similar provision was used both as evidence of the framers' design to create a consolidated government in which the rights of the states and people were given to the national government and as evidence of bad faith in the Federalist argument defending the omission of a bill of rights.[99] The Federalists responded in two ways. Many argued that the reservation of rights and powers not granted was implicit in the general theory of the Constitution and Article I's enumerated powers scheme, insisting that the Antifederalist arguments rested on confusion about general theory.[100] Others responded that the enumeration of powers and the Necessary and Proper Clause provided express textual foundation for the Federalist refrain that all not granted was reserved.[101] Even if it were essential that rights be expressly reserved, the federal Constitution effectively supplied an express general reservation of rights and powers.

While the Federalists thus disputed the notion that the federal Constitution was properly read as resting on a presumption in favor of government power, a number of Federalists expressed agreement with the idea that if the people did not take care to ensure that they retained the rights which they possessed by virtue of their sovereign power, they might well grant them away.[102] But there was no reason for concern, Federalists reasoned, because the enumerated powers scheme effectively limited power and thereby defined rights. In the words of Roger Sherman, "[t]he powers vested in the federal government are only Such as respect the common interests of the Union, and are particularly defined, So that each State retains its Sovereignty in what respects its own internal government."[103] More specifically as to individual rights, James Iredell argued against a bill of rights before the North Carolina Ratifying Convention with the claim that the powers enumerated in the Constitution provided "such a definition of authority as would leave no doubt" so that "any person inspecting [the Constitution] may see if the power claimed be enumerated."[104] The analogy to the Articles of Confederation was never far off, as reflected in James Wilson's query: "Is there any increase of risk, or rather are not the enumerated powers as well defined here, as in the present Articles of Confederation?"[105]

Arguing that the Federalist Defense Rested on the Idea of Implied Limits on Congress' Powers

Some have contended that all these arguments from enumerated powers rested in fact on the assumption that the powers would be construed against a background idea of implied limitations on government or even that laws that conflicted with customary or natural rights would be invalidated as "improper" laws under the Necessary and Proper Clause.[106] But these contentions are misreadings based on statements taken out of the context of the flow of the ratification debate. If the Federalist argument were really based on implied limitations, the statements defending the adequacy with which the enumerated powers were drafted (some of which are quoted above) would lack coherence. The drafting of the grants of power would be largely irrelevant because the limiting principle, inevitably read into the power grant on this reading, or perhaps the word "proper" would be doing the real work.[107]

Under this strained implied limitations reading of enumerated powers, the same lack of coherence would characterize the Federalist demands to be shown the provisions in the Constitution that granted power to Congress to invade certain fundamental rights. For example, before the Pennsylvania Ratifying Convention, James Wilson demanded in response to an argument that the Constitution failed to secure the rights of conscience: "I ask the gentleman, what part of this system puts it in the power of Congress to attack these rights?"[108] If the Constitution's grants of power were all to be construed as subject to inherent limitations, such a question is sheer nonsense; no grant of power could authorize invasion of a right (the right of conscience) deemed by almost everyone to be among the inalienable natural rights.[109] But Wilson took the question, and the possibility of a grant of power that could lend itself to abuse, very seriously. In an October speech, he had acknowledged that if the Constitution had delegated to Congress power "to regulate literary publications," it would have been essential to include a freedom of the press provision as an exception to, or limitation on, this general regulatory power.[110] Indeed, in further contrast to his own exposition of the Constitution's enumerated powers scheme, Wilson freely acknowledged that some specific provision would need to be made to secure freedom of the press in the District of Columbia inasmuch as the legislative power of Congress with respect to the District would be general in nature.[111] These statements directly contradict the modern contention that the Federalists contemplated that the enumerated powers would be construed through a filter of inherent rights.

Some commentators have argued that the Federalists relied on enumerated powers, understood in a straightforward way, to protect individual rights in general, but nevertheless perceived the powers as also subject to the limitations logically imposed by the idea of a few inalienable natural rights—whether enumerated or not.[112] On this view, customary rights such as the right to trial by jury would be forfeited if not secured by the written Constitution, but not the most fundamental freedoms such as speech or religion.[113] But the examples pointed to above, concerning freedom of conscience and freedom of the press, both of which were considered to be inalienable rights under social contract natural rights theory, belie even this somewhat narrowed version of the implied constitutional rights theory.

NATURAL AND INALIENABLE RIGHTS AND THE NINTH AMENDMENT

The claim that the Ninth Amendment secures at least the rights considered "inalienable" by social contract theory pervades the debate over the amendment's meaning.[114] Indeed, for a large number of commentators, the framers' recognition of natural law is the key assumption that undergirds the "straightforward" reading of the text.[115] Evidence from the ratification debate, however, undercuts the idea that enforceable natural rights constituted the background assumption illuminating the Federalist objection to the inclusion of a bill of rights in the Constitution. To be sure, the concept of the people's sovereignty was rooted in both contractual and natural law thinking. In Pennsylvania, Wilson contrasted systems of government which required a bill of rights, either as a "grant" from the king or by virtue of a "compact" with a sovereign legislature, with the American system of natural rights.[116] And the debate over a bill of rights largely revolved around the question of how best to secure the people's natural, inalienable rights.

But as we have noted, the debates were based on the assumption that alternative legal systems might more or less adequately secure basic rights and the concern that some constitutional arrangements would have the effect of granting away even rights that should not be granted to government. Patrick Henry, for example, insisted in Virginia, that: "If you intend to reserve your unalienable rights, you must have the most express stipulation; for, if implication be allowed, you are ousted of those rights."[117] Even though Federalists rejected Henry's conclusion about the Constitution, they did not disagree with his premise that even inalienable rights may be granted away. James Wilson conceded that in a Constitution that granted to government a general legislative power, the people's most fundamental rights would be presumed to be granted unless specifically reserved.[118]

Professor David A. J. Richards has relied on the founders' theory of inalienable rights and sought to enlist James Iredell in support. He quotes at length from Iredell's speech at the North Carolina Ratifying Convention to reinforce this view.[119] Richards claims that Iredell prophetically anticipated the philosophy of Judge Robert Bork "that would anachronistically limit the protection of rights to those enumerated rights protected in 1787 or 1791."[120] Iredell's speech is highly relevant because it was delivered in the midst of a debate of how best to secure inalienable rights.[121] But Richards missed the thrust of Iredell's critique of a bill of rights. Within the very material Richards quoted, Iredell explained that his fear of a negative inference as to omitted rights rested on the prediction that a later generation would logically deduce from a bill of rights that "the people did not think every power retained which was not given,"[122] a clear allusion to enumerated powers and reserved rights. According to Iredell, natural rights are secured if there is "such a definition of authority as would leave no doubt"[123] so that "any person by inspecting [the Constitution] may see *if the power claimed be enumerated*."[124] In the course of defending the Constitution, Iredell emphasized that a bill of rights would be both "necessary" and "proper" if "we had formed a general legislature" after the pattern of the state constitutions.[125] The only reason there was no real need for a bill of rights under the

Constitution drafted in Philadelphia is that the powers granted to the federal government were enumerated and all the rest were reserved.

Advocates of the inherent rights reading of the Ninth Amendment assume that the Antifederalists, as proponents of inalienable rights, conceived of the bill of rights simply as supplying additional security to rights that already held status as fundamental law. David Richards, for example, quotes at length from the well-known *Letters from a Federal Farmer*, a powerful critique of the Constitution by a thoughtful exponent of natural rights.[126] But the Federal Farmer was as committed to a positivist reading of the Constitution as he was to natural rights.[127] Among other things, the Federal Farmer believed that the Constitution had not adequately limited and defined federal powers.[128]

But the Federal Farmer offered a potential solution to his problems that in many ways anticipated the Ninth and Tenth Amendments:

When we particularly enumerate the powers given, we ought either carefully to enumerate the rights reserved, or be totally silent about them; we must either particularly enumerate both, or else suppose the particular enumeration of the powers given adequately draws the line between them and the rights reserved, particuarly to enumerate the former and not the latter, I think most advisable; however, as men appear generally to have their doubts about these silent reservations, we might advantageously enumerate the powers given, and then in general words, according to the mode adopted in the 2d art. of the confederation, declare all powers, rights and privileges, are reserved, which are not explicitly and expressly given up.... But admitting, on the general principle, that all rights are reserved of course, which are not expressly surrendered, the people could with sufficient certainty assert their rights on all occasions, and establish them with ease, still there are infinite advantages in particularly enumerating many of the most essential rights reserved in all cases; and as to the less important ones, we may declare in general terms, that all not expressly surrendered are reserved.[129]

Though steeped in the tradition of natural rights, the Federal Farmer engaged in careful analysis of how best to secure those rights in a system of positive constitutional law. His answer was to enumerate "the most essential rights" and to express explicitly the general principle of reserved rights and powers to supplement the protection offered in the Constitution's partial enumeration of rights.[130] It is significant that the Federal Farmer does not refer to any independent legal or constitutional status for natural or inalienable rights.[131]

Indeed, in the midst of the ratification-era debate over the advantages and disadvantages of express and implied reservations and enumerated powers and rights, there was virtually no discussion of the force of natural rights standing alone. Such discussion was passed over because the crux of the debate was how best to secure these rights in positive law. It would be strange indeed if the central underlying premise of those who participated in the process of adopting the federal Constitution were a doctrine that was a background assumption that participants did not feel compelled to address. This is especially true when one considers that the Federalist proponents of the Constitution consistently expressed doubts as to the efficacy of bills of rights, considering that they represented mere "parchment barriers" to government action that could affect those rights.[132]

THE FEDERALIST CLAIM THAT A BILL OF RIGHTS WOULD PRESENT A DANGER TO RIGHTS

The Federalists went beyond denying the necessity of having a bill of rights. They contended that a bill of rights would be dangerous, inasmuch as it would present the risk of reversing the principle of the federal Constitution that all not granted was reserved.[133] The result would be a government of general powers to which a bill of rights excepted particular rights.[134] James Wilson, for one, concluded that a free press provision could backfire because it could be construed "to imply that some degree of power was given, since we undertook to define its extent."[135] Thus Samuel Parsons contended that "establishing any other bill of rights [than the one already established by the Constitution's scheme of limited powers] would be dangerous, as it would at least imply that nothing more was left with the people than the rights defined and secured in such bill of rights."[136] Summing up his argument before the Pennsylvania Ratifying Convention, James Wilson stated: "In short, sir, I have said that a bill of rights would have been improperly annexed to the federal plan, and for this plain reason, that it would imply that whatever is not expressed was given, which is not the principle of the proposed Constitution."[137]

If the Federalist arguments against a bill of rights had rested on the doctrine of inherent rights, Wilson's argument about the "danger" of a bill of rights should have applied equally well to the state constitutions and would not have been limited, as his argument was, to the impact of a bill of rights on "the federal plan."[138] Wilson's statement reflects that the Federalist argument against a bill of rights rested on the enumerated powers scheme, not a notion of inherent or implied rights, and indicates that the "danger" he feared was the result of reversing the assumption of limited powers that he thought would result from the insertion of a bill of rights. The Federalist position became that, just as under the proposed Constitution "every thing not granted is reserved," an attempt to enumerate the people's rights, as sug-

gested by the enterprise of adopting a bill of rights, would raise the inference "that every thing omitted is given to the general government."[139] Even
if we find the Federalist argument doubtful for some reason, there is no room
to doubt that this was their standard line.[140]

Modern Misreadings of the Federalist Argument

Advocates of inherent rights have wrenched Federalist arguments from
the larger debate, understanding them to express fears of losing unenumerated rights. Thus modern commentators persistently rely upon James Wilson's classic formulation of the argument that since all rights secured by the
Constitution could "not be particularly enumerated," the inevitably partial
enumeration would raise an inference that the rest were "presumed to be
given" and the people's rights "would be rendered incomplete."[141] Without
any explication at all, Wilson's argument is taken to mean that inherent limits that would be implied under the Constitution would be forfeited if not included in a bill of rights.[142]

But when the debate that produced this argument is carefully reviewed,
the Federalist "danger" argument provides powerful confirmation that the
leading contestants in the ratification debate did not presume inherent constitutional rights against government. If Wilson's argument is highly debatable, as explicated above,[143] it is almost inexplicable when it is understood
as suggested by advocates of an inherent rights reading of the Constitution.
For one thing, it is difficult to determine the source of the initial rights interpretation of the Constitution. It is true that Wilson was deeply committed to
the concept of natural rights, as were most participants in the ratification debate, but he was clearly on record that no inference in favor of inherent
rights existed under the constitutions of the states.[144]

The state constitutions were undoubtedly the most important source for
general thinking about constitutionalism available to the framers and ratifiers, and neither Wilson nor any Federalist ever advanced an argument as to
why unwritten customary or inalienable natural rights would remain "imperfect" (i.e., not legal or constitutional) rights under the state constitutions,
but would hold a different status under the federal Constitution. Had such a
view been their position we would expect to see an argument in its defense.
Wilson, moreover, had nowhere articulated a view of the federal system as a
source for a different view as to inherent constitutional limitations than the
one holding under the state constitutions, except to contend that the people
had retained as "rights" all the "powers" not granted by Article I.

Equally baffling, interpreters never explain how it would be that Wilson
or others could believe that the existence of a written consitution would

pose no threat to rights, given that they are inherent (and perhaps "inalienable"), but an enumeration of rights would pose such a threat. Wilson's argument does not provide a clue to answering such a question, even though it makes no sense without an explication of the distinction being relied upon to separate different constitutions. But the argument makes perfect sense, without any additional explanation, if one understands it as expressing the view that a comprehensive bill of rights woud be taken as a substitute for the protection intended to be given by the enumerated powers scheme of the Constitution.

Understanding the Federalist "Argument of Danger"

The Antifederalists responded to the Federalist "danger" argument as one concerning the viability of the enumerated powers scheme in a setting in which rights limitations are being articulated as well. Thus the Federal Farmer also picked up Wilson's concern that the inclusion of a right where there is no corresponding power to be limited might raise an inference of unenumerated powers. He argued along these lines in considering the prohibition in Article I, Section 9 on granting titles of nobility: "Why then by a negative clause, restrain congress from doing what it would have no power to do? This clause, then, must have no meaning, or imply, that were it omitted, congress would have the power in question, either upon the principle that some general words in the constitution may be so construed as to give it, or on the principle that congress possesses the powers not expressly reserved."[145] As with Wilson's similar argument about a free press clause, the concern is that the statement of a limiting provision might be taken as raising an inference that there must exist some power that the adopters believed required such a limitation.

At a more general level, the Antifederalists argued that the Federalist "danger" argument gave away the whole game. Taking Article I, Section 9, setting forth limits on Congress in favor of individual and states rights, as well as other limitations that were sprinkled in the Constitution as proposed, the Antifederalists contended that the proposed Constitution already included the very partial enumeration of rights that Wilson's argument presumed to carry such ominous implications. Patrick Henry took the matter up, arguing that the Constitution's list of limitations "reverses the position of the friends of this Constitution, that every thing is retained which is not given up; for, instead of this, every thing is given up which is not expressly reserved."[146] And Arthur Lee drew the same inference, contending that "exceptions in the Body of [the Constitution], . . . in which no power is expressly given, implies that every thing is given."[147] The inclusion of various rights limitations, in other words, created Wilson's partial bill of rights, and the proper inference was that the Constitution was intended to grant great or even general powers. A bill of rights would supply the only rights Americans could be sure of. Such reasoning, in parody of Federalist argument, supported the Antifederalist theme that a bill of rights "could do no harm, but might do much good."[148]

The Federalists needed to justify the limitations included in the body of the proposed Constitution and distinguish such limitations from the feared partial bill of rights. They attemped to do this, and the manner by which they did tells us a great deal about their original argument. The Federalists argued that they had included specific exceptions to granted powers where they were needed to safeguard fundamental rights; to go further, and to attempt to provide a comprehensive bill of rights, would be to raise an inference of powers held by the national government that were never intended to be granted.[149]

THE DRAFTING AND RATIFICATION PROCESS: FULFILLMENT OR REVISION?

Virginia answered concerns that the proposed Constitution did not reserve powers to the states and to the people and that there could be a danger presented by the attempt to specify rights limitations.[150] In particular, Virginia's seventeenth proposal spoke directly to the Federalist argument that enumerating rights would threaten the principle of limited powers. It provided "[t]hat those clauses which declare that Congress shall not exercise certain powers, be not interpreted, in any manner whatsoever, to extend the powers of Congress; but that they be construed either as making exceptions to the specified powers where this shall be the case, or otherwise, as inserted merely for greater caution."[151] Until recently, it was generally agreed that Madison drafted the Ninth Amendment from these state proposed amendments.[152]

A close look at the Virginia proposal and Madison's initial draft confirms that this conclusion is sound.[153] Madison joins the states in forbidding an inference of enhanced federal power, or of diminished rights, from the enumeration of specific exceptions to granted powers. In both cases, the proposed clauses forbid one construction and express another; in each case, they provide a concise rebuttal to the suggestion that including rights implies enhanced powers or diminished rights. At least one modern commentator, however, has argued that Madison's draft of the Ninth Amendment is indistinguishable from the various proposals for a provision like the Tenth Amendment: proposed amendments "that made explicit the enumerated powers rule of construction."[154] These proposals, it is claimed, were "not excited by guarantees of personal rights in the Constitution," and since they all predated inclusion of the bill of rights, they were "responsive to the draft Constitution itself; they did not depend upon the prospect of such a listing-out of rights."[155]

But this analysis is wrong. The New York and Virginia proposals that preceded the adoption of a bill of rights anticipated that amendments to the Constitution would be adopted. The prohibition on a move to "extend the powers of Congress"[156] from a statement of limits on those powers tracks with James Wilson's reference to individual rights provisions as "powers reserved"[157] and Hamilton's reference to such individual rights guarantees as "exceptions" to granted powers.[158] The Virginia proposal, moreover, states that limiting clauses may "be construed either as making exceptions to the specified powers where this shall be the case, or otherwise, as inserted for greater caution."[159] Notice how this language steers through the troubled waters of the bill of rights debate, leaving the "necessity" issue unresolved while offering reassurance to Federalists that the Constitution would not be read, even if it included a bill of rights, as creating a federal government of general powers. To the extent that national powers are read broadly enough to threaten basic rights, the enumeration of rights would act as "exceptions" to the specified powers. To the extent that the powers are construed so as to leave an area of human liberty unaffected, such apparently limiting provisions would perform the more limited role of being inserted "for greater caution."[160]

It is true that Madison added to the amendment proposed by Virginia by referring not only to a feared enhancement of federal power, but by prohibiting an inference "to diminish the just importance of other rights retained by the people."[161] One view is that Madison may have offered here an original contribution to the bill of rights drama.[162] On this view, Madison adds something when he refers to the risk of diminished rights, but not necessarily when he refers to the possibility of enhanced federal power. It is noteworthy that Madison refers to the potential impact on rights and powers of "exceptions here or elsewhere in the Constitution, made in favor of particular rights" before specifying the inferences that may not be drawn from such provisions.[163]

Madison explained his drafted language in this way:

It has been objected also against a bill of rights, that, by enumerating particular exceptions to the grant of power, it would disparage those rights which were not placed in that enumeration; and it might follow by implication, that those rights which were not singled out, were intended to be assigned into the hands of the General Government, and were consequently insecure. This is one of the most plausible arguments I have ever heard urged against admission of a bill of rights into this system; but, I conceive, that it may be guarded against. I have attempted it, as gentlemen may see by turning to the last clause of the fourth resolution [the proposed Ninth Amendment].[164]

Given the context, it is suprising that some commentators have read this statement as unambiguously referring to rights as exceptions to powers—and that such rights might be lost.[165] But when they are read in the context of the bill of rights debate, Madison's remarks lend support to the view that his goal was to reinforce the purpose of the amendment as first embodied in the state proposals.

The question is whether Madison's reference to rights being "assigned into the hands of the General Government" refers to the power to invade affirmative rights or to the evisceration of the enumerated powers scheme. Madison begins by indicating that he is summarizing an objection that had been proffered by opponents of a bill of rights. As we have seen, these opponents had contended that a bill of rights would destructively tear away the system of enumerated powers. Madison himself had earlier posed this question to the Virginia Ratifying Convention: "[i]f an enumeration be made of our rights, will it not be implied that every thing omitted is given to the general government?"[166] The proposed amendment, moreover, clearly speaks to the feared enlargement of powers that had been the heart of the Federalist objection to a bill of rights. If one reads Madison as referring only to the loss of rights, understood as implied limits to the granted powers, it would mean that Madison defended his proposed Ninth Amendment without even making reference to the fear of extended powers that we know he and others feared from a bill of rights.

The Ratification Debate in Virginia

In November of 1789, the proposed bill of rights came up for ratification in Virginia. This presented Madison with an opportunity to explain and defend changes that Congress had made to the amendment that Madison had drafted. On November 28, 1789, Hardin Burnley reported to Madison that the amendment had prompted debate before the Virginia assembly. Objections had come from Edmund Randolph:

[Randolph's] principal objection was pointed against the word retained in the eleventh proposed amendment, and his argument if I understood it was applied in this manner, that as the rights declared in the first ten amendments were not all that a free people would required [sic] the exercise of; and that as there was no criterion by which it could be determined whether any other particular right was retained or not, it would be more safe, & more consistent with the spirit of the 1st. & 17th. amendments proposed by Virginia, that this reservation against constructive power, should operate rather as a provision against extending the powers of Congress by their own authority, than as a protection to rights reducable [sic] to no definitive certainty.[167]

    Randolph's argument, as summarized by Burnley and repeated by Madison, makes key assumptions that go unchallenged. First, Randolph linked together the idea that the provision might not be sufficiently protective of rights with the idea that it was to be a "reservation against constructive power."[168] Second, Randolph assumed that it might actually be a safer constitutional provision if it were stated as "a provision against extending the powers of Congress . . . than as a protection to rights reducable [sic] to no definitive certainty."[169]

    Randolph's argument, as well as the Federalist position, is clarified when we study Burnley's and Madison's responses. Burnley made this statement to Madison: "But others among whom I am one see not the force of the distinction, for by preventing an extension of power in the body from which danger is apprehended safety will be insured if its powers are not too extensive already, & so by protecting the rights of the people & of the States, an improper extension of power will be prevented & safety made equally certain."[170] He appears to reject Randolph's notion that there was even a meaningful distinction between the Virginia and congressional proposals. In fact, he explicitly defines the other rights "retained by the people" in terms of the grants of power : "if [Congress'] powers are not too extensive already," the "rights of the people & of the States" will be secured against the "improper extension of power" that Randolph professed to fear.[171] To Burnley the goal was the same, that of preventing "an extension of power," but he could not see why the language of retained rights in the proposed Ninth Amendment did not accomplish this end.

    Madison went even further in rejecting Randolph's proposed distinction between the Virginia proposed amendment and the one offered by Congress. He wrote:

The difficulty stated agst. the amendments is really unlucky, and the more to be as it springs from [Randolph,] a friend to the Constitution. It is a still greater cause of regret if the distinction be, as it appears to me, altogether fanciful. If a line can be drawn between the powers granted and the rights retained, it would seem to be the same thing, whether the latter be secured ["whether" stricken out] by declaring that they shall ["be not be abridged violated" stricken out], or that the former shall not be extended. If no line can be drawn, a declaration in either form would amount to nothing.[172]

As with Burnley, Madison recognizes that the purpose of the amendment is to preserve the rights reserved to the people by the system of enumerated powers. Notice, though, that Madison does not see the distinction between guaranteeing rights and declaring that national powers shall not be extended. Under either form that the amendment might take, it would "amount to nothing" if the line between rights and powers were not adequately drawn in the drafting of the Constitution.[173]

NOTES

1. *See, e.g.,* Suzanna Sherry, *The Founders' Unwritten Constitution*, 54 U. Chi. L. Rev. 1127, 1161 n. 143 (1987).

2. *E.g.,* Leonard Levy, Original Intent and the Framers' Constitution 148 (1988); Jack Richon Pole, *Introduction, in* The American Constitution: For and Against 3, 18 (J. R. Pole, ed., 1987). For an overview of the ratification debate with respect to the omission of a bill of rights, see Thomas B. McAffee, *The Original Meaning of the Ninth Amendment*, 90 Colum. L. Rev. 1215, 1227–37 (1990).

3. *See generally* Thomas B. McAffee, *supra* note 2, at 1228–29, 1243–44.

4. This point will be documented throughout the balance of this chapter. For views differing from those presented here, see Calvin R. Massey, Silent Rights: The Ninth Amendment and the Constitution's Unenumerated Rights (1995); Thomas C. Grey, *The Original Understanding and the Unwritten Constitution, in* Toward a More Perfect Union: Six Essays on the Constitution 145, 163–64 (Neil L. York, ed., 1988); Sherry, *supra* note 1, at 1161–64 (seeing Federalist ratification arguments as relying upon inherent limits on constitutional powers of government); *cf. id.* at 1166 (claiming that most representatives in the first Congress "recognized that enumeration of rights made little or no difference to the legal efficacy of such rights").

5. Gerald Stourzh, *Fundamental Laws and Individual Rights in the 18th Century Constitution, in* The American Founding—Essays on the Formation of the Constitution 159 (J. Barlow, L. Levy, & K. Masugi, eds., 1988). For example, the right to habeas corpus was considered "fundamental" within the British constitutional system, and yet Parliament could by a simple majority change or suspend it and, moreover, had done so. *Id.*

6. Over the years, Parliament has continued to be viewed as obligated to preserve the rights and liberties of the English people, and the people are considered to be the ultimate judges of whether that duty is being fulfilled. The English people have thus continued to see the British constitution as embodying fixed principles of a fundamental nature despite the doctrine of legislative sovereignty and supremacy. J. W. Gough, Fundamental Law in English Constitutional History 174–91; Stourzh, *supra* note 1, at 336.

7. Stourzh, *supra* note 5, at 172.

8. Edward S. Corwin, *The "Higher Law" Background of American Constitutional Law*, in 1 Corwin on the Constitution, 79, 117 (R. Loss, ed., 1981).

9. Stourzh, *supra* note 5, at 170.

10. At the least, in failing to textually provide for the exercise of the power of judicial review, the state constitutions left serious doubt about precisely how fundamental law would function in the new era. As we will see, the federal Constitution thus marked an important development in the full-blown recognition of this separate category of distinctly legal norms.

11. *See supra* chapter 3, notes 73–75 and accompanying text (indicating one court's disapproval of a power of judicial review).

12. Sherry, *supra* note 1, at 1146.

13. *Id.*

14. For Madison's role in the failure to obtain a national power to veto state laws, see chapter 3 *supra,* especially note 41 and accompanying text.

15. Sherry, *supra* note 1, at 1147–50. The process of clarifying and making explicit governing assumptions carried well into the Convention. Thus Sherry observes that the supremacy of the Constitution itself, as opposed to federal legislation, was not added to the Supremacy Clause until John Rutledge proposed doing so on August 23, 1787. *Id.* at 1149. Four days later, the delegates also agreed without opposition to William Samuel Johnson's proposal to add cases arising under the Constitution to Article III's definition of federal jurisdiction. *See id.*

16. *See id.* at 1150–55.

17. *See, e.g., id.* at 1154–55.

18. *Id.* at 1155–56.

19. *Id.* at 1155–56.

20. *Id.* at 1156. For a skeptical treatment of Sherry's view of the state constitutions, see chapter 2 *supra,* notes 71–116 and accompanying text.

21. *Id.*

22. The typical instructor of courses on constitutional law would at least find this surprising. Those who have spent substantial amounts of time in thinking with the founding generation would not find this suprising at all. *See, e.g.,* Akhil Reed Amar, The Bill of Rights: Creation and Reconstruction 125–29 (1998).

23. *Id.* at 1157.

24. *See supra* chapter 2 notes 88–100 and accompanying text.

25. *See supra* chapter 2, notes 21–26 and accompanying text (on popular sovereignty), and notes 85–92 and accompanying text (on the general goal of permanent constitutional provisions).

26. As we have seen, Sherry takes the view that the tradition of unwritten individual rights embodied the idea of unchangeable norms that were not subject to legislative repeal or popular amendment. *See supra* Chapter 2, notes 58–117 and accompanying text. Sherry argued that the state constitutions themselves recognized this very distinction, but the federal Constitution clearly does not recognize any such distinction, either in its text or structural division.

27. Sherry, *supra* note 1, at 1157–58.

28. *Id.* at 1157 (finding that "[t]he innovation of the summer of 1787 was to explain why a written constitution was a part of fundamental law, not to redefine the whole of fundamental law").

29. *See, e.g.,* U.S Const. art. I, § 9.

30. Sherry, *supra* note 1, at 1157–58.

31. Sherry, for example, acknowledges that bills of attainder actually happened in America, so she perceives the Bill of Attainder Clause as the enactment of a "positive right." Sherry, *supra* note 1, at 1157. But Madison viewed bills of attainder in the same light as *ex post facto* laws, with both of them being "contrary to the first principles of the social compact, and to every principle of sound legislation." James Madison, The Federalist No. 44, at 301 (Jacob E. Cooke, ed., 1961). The written constitution does not purport to place these limitations on different constitutional grounds; nor does it suggest that one of these rights could be eliminated by amendment, but the other could not.

32. Moreover, if the state governments under those constitutions were "universally" regarded as "possessing all powers except those explicitly denied them in their constitutive documents," C. Massey, *supra* note 4, at 87, it follows that the whole idea of inherent and implied limitations on government was foreign to the state constitutional systems.

33. *Id.* at 1157.

34. Such a distinction between the two provisions seems implausible on its face and is contradicted by thoughtful spokesmen of the era. Both prohibitions appear to be designed to preserve an individual's rights to notice and a fair trial (including the right to be judged by a jury of one's peers) in which the judgment is based on preexisting standards, as well as to preserve the separation of functions between the judicial and legislative branches of government. *See, e.g.,* Madison's Notes, *quoted in* Sherry, *supra* note 1, at 1157 & n. 135 (James Wilson, Aug. 22, 1787) (suggesting that ex post facto laws violate "the first principles of Legislation"). Moreover, the provisions overlap considerably, inasmuch as many bills of attainder rested on ex post facto decision making and would thus amount to ex post facto laws. *See, e.g.,* 3 Debates in the Several State Conventions on the Adoption of the Federal Constitution 140 (J. Elliot 2d ed. 1866) [hereinafter Elliot's Debates] (Patrick Henry, Virginia Ratifying Convention, June 9, 1788, defending enactment of a bill of attainder in Virginia, which is described by him as an "*ex post facto* law," and which he acknowledges was viewed by many as "tyrannical legislation").

Sherry concludes that the framers drew this distinction because bills of attainder had been accepted in practice during this general period, and the prohibition was therefore not viewed as rooted in natural law. Sherry, *supra* note 1, at 1157–58. On Sherry's own theory, though, the founders' embrace of natural law methodology should have kept open the issue of the status of bills of attainder under natural law, and it is difficult to see the logic under which *ex post facto* laws would be seen as violative of natural law while bills of attainders would not. A more straightforward explanation as to why some viewed only the Bill of Attainder Clause as essential is that the recent experience with bills of attainder belied the contention that there was no need for such a safeguard; there presumably had not been a similar experience with broader examples of criminalizing what had been innocent conduct when performed.

35. *See* U.S. Const. preamble; *id.* art. III, sect. 2, cl. 1; *id.* art. V; *id.* art. VI, cl. 2. This reading is reinforced, moreover, by the text of the later adopted Ninth Amendment, which reads: "The enumeration in the Constitution, of certain rights, shall not be construed to deny or disparage others retained by the people." "The Constitution" here clearly refers to the document in which rights might be enumerated and does not include unwritten fundamental law.

36. On its face, Article III appears to state the exclusive bases for federal jurisdiction, and the Supremacy Clause limits the supreme authority of federal legislation only with the requirement that the laws are "made in pursuance [of this Constitution]." U.S. Const. art. VI, cl. 2.

37. James Wilson, 2 The Documentary History of the Ratification of the Constitution 383 (Merrill Jensen, ed., 1976) [hereinafter Ratification of the Constitution] (Pennsylvania Ratifying Convention, Nov. 28, 1787).

38. James Wilson, 2 Ratification of the Constitution, *supra* note 37, at 383.

39. *Id.* Samuel Chase argued that the people's sovereignty "is like the light of the sun, native, original, inherent, and unlimited by human authority" while governmental authority "is only borrowed, delegated and limited by the grant of the people." Baltimore Md. J., Feb. 13, 1787, *quoted in* Gordon S. Wood, The Creation of the American Republic 1776–1787, at 371 (1969).

40. *Id.* at 348 (Nov. 24, 1787). Wilson concluded that this sovereignty "is a power paramount to every constitution, inalienable in its nature, and indefinite in its extent." *Id.* at 349. A consequence is "that the people may change the constitutions whenever and however they please." *Id.* at 362 (Nov. 24, 1787). This is not only their right, but it is one of "which no positive institution can ever deprive them." *Id.*

41. *Id.* at 361–62. For a treatment of Wilson's recognition that the people are in charge of their constitutions and hold plenary power to alter them, see A. Amar, *supra* note 22, at 109–25.

42. Gordon S. Wood, *The Political Ideology of the Founders*, in Toward a More Perfect Union: Six Essays on the Constitution 7, 22 (Neil L. York, ed., 1988). *See also* G. Wood, *supra* note 39, at 530–32 (popular sovereignty became the key to answering objections to the Constitution based on the impossibility of having dual sovereigns).

43. 2 Ratification of the Constitution, *supra* note 37, at 449 (Dec. 1, 1787).

44. 2 Ratification of the Constitution, *supra* note 37, at 361–62 (Nov. 24, 1787); *see* G. Wood, *supra* note 39, at 535 (quoting Francis Hopkinson describing the Constitution as "[a] WHOLE PEOPLE exercising its first and greatest power—performing an act of SOVEREIGNTY, ORIGINAL, and UNLIMITED"). Notice that even if unwritten principles had been conceived as being a part of the Constitution, the above described arguments would place them within the reach of the

people's sovereign power to amend. Compare these views with those attributed to the founding generation by modern scholars who would place overwhelming weight on the concept of natural rights, giving that concept (or perhaps a judge's conception of its requirements) power to override the collective will of the people. *See supra* chapter 1, at n. 13 and accompanying text.

45. 4 Elliot's Debates, *supra* note 34, at 9 (James Iredell, July 24, 1788), *quoted in* G. Wood, *supra* note 39, at 542.

46. Even a modern advocate of unenumerated rights, Calvin Massey, has acknowledged that the Antifederalists asserted that "it was necessary to have 'an express stipulation for all such rights as are intended to be exempted from civil authority,'" because "the combination of the Constitution's supremacy clause and the lack of a bill of rights meant that natural rights secured by state constitutions were no longer safe." C. Massey, *supra* note 4, at 58. *See also id.* at 87. Although he fails to acknowledge it, such statements defy the concept of inherent, implied constitutional rights that are the premise of his reading of the Ninth Amendment.

47. Although Professor Sherry and others appear quite clearly to deny the priority given to popular sovereignty in American constitutional thought of this period, Thomas C. Grey acknowledges this priority in finding that under the Constitution "the sovereign people could grant the power to violate natural rights (as they did, for instance, in authorizing slavery)." Grey, *supra* note 4, at 164. For Grey the viable issue becomes whether they were nevertheless committed to implied rights wherever natural rights had not been rejected in the document itself. But Grey's distinction between the status of slavery and other implied natural rights is problematic. The protection offered slavery by the Constitution is oblique and indirect; we infer it from a host of provisions that basically presume the continuation of slavery's preexisting status within positive law. On its face, the Supremacy Clause appears to recognize Congress' plenary authority as to matters within the scope of the powers granted by the Constitution (read in light of the doctrine of implied powers recognized textually in the Necessary and Proper Clause) at least as directly as the Constitution as a whole recognizes slavery. It is not clear why a presumption in favor of natural rights strong enough to overcome the apparent thrust of the Supremacy Clause would not be strong enough to overcome provisions merely presuming the continuation of the reality of slavery.

More philosophically, although Grey describes the Federalist position as Cokean because it purports to place "implied limitations on legislative power," *id.* at 163, Coke's limitations were thought to rest in the very nature of law. But the Federalists, as Grey understands them, invoked principles that were in fact subject to the sovereign will (albeit of the people rather than of the crown). Grey sees the Federalists as invoking something like Blackstone's rule of construction in favor of common right and reason, rather than Coke's original dictum.

48. *See* Grey, *supra* note 4, at 164.

49. Even while acknowledging that they conceded "this vast implied power to government," Professor Massey insists that it would be a mistake to assume

that the "Antifederalists were simply unvarnished positivists" because, after all, they also made statements supporting recognition of inalienable natural rights. C. Massey, *supra* note 4, at 58. Yet even Massey acknowledges it was a standard view that, without the addition of a bill of rights, "individuals may be presumed to cede to governments the power to invade their natural rights." *Id. See supra* notes 32 and 46 for additional insight on Massey's views. Perhaps Massey sees the Antifederalists as "varnished" positivists, but there is little room for doubt that the views they expressed during the debate over a bill of rights were positivist in nature, notwithstanding their commitment to the concept of natural rights.

50. Patrick Henry, 3 Elliot's Debates, *supra* note 34, at 410, 446 (Virginia Ratifying Convention, June 14, 1788). *See Letters of Agrippa, in* 4 The Complete Anti-Federalist 106, 108 (Herbert Storing, ed., 1981) (Jan. 29, 1788) (claiming that "when people institute government, they of course delegate all rights not expressly reserved"); *Essays by the Impartial Examiner, in* 5 The Complete Anti-Federalist, *supra,* at 172, 177 (Virginia Independent Chronicle, Feb. 20, 1788) (contending that members of the social contract are "presumed" to give up to government their power to act freely unless they expressly reserve particular powers; without express reservations, the "universality of the grant" will "include every power of acting, and every claim of possessing or obtaining any thing"). Notice that this view of the sovereign power of the people directly contradicts Sherry's claim of unalterable fundamental law rights.

51. G. Wood, *supra* note 39, at 457–63, 536–47. As illustrated here, even people with every reason to want to believe in a nonpositivist reading of the history find themselves acknowledging the positivist nature of the arguments advanced in the bill of rights debate. *See supra* notes 32, 46, 49 for examples.

52. *Letters from a Federal Farmer, in* The Complete Anti-Federalist, *supra* note 50, at 247 (Oct. 12, 1787) ("[t]he truth is . . . it is mere matter of opinion and men usually adopt either side of the argument, as will best answer their purposes"); *id.* at 323 ("[t]he Supreme power is undoubtedly in the people, and . . . they reserve all powers not expressly delegated by them to those who govern"). Even so, the Federal Farmer acknowledged: "But the general presumption being, that men who govern, will in doubtful cases, construe laws and constitutions most favorably for encreasing [sic] their own powers; all wise and prudent people, in forming constitutions, have drawn the line, and carefully described the powers parted with the powers reserved." *Id.* at 248.

53. *Id.* at 323. The author was alluding to the pattern established by the Articles of Confederation, which, of course, included no bill of rights.

54. *An Old Whig II, in* 13 Ratification of the Constitution, *supra* note 37, at 399–400 (Philadelphia Independent Gazetteer, Oct. 17, 1787) (arguing that rights might be protected by delegation of limited powers "*unless* the powers which are *expressly given* to Congress are *too large*") (emphasis in original); *Denatus, in* 5 The Complete Anti-Federalist, *supra* note 50, at 260, 263 (Virginia Independent Chronicle, June 11, 1788) (if the Constitution had actually formed a confederation with carefully defined powers "[t]here would be no need of a bill of rights. . . .");

see also McAffee, *supra* note 2, at 1229 n. 52. Indeed, a few moderate Antifederalists even contended that a bill of rights would not have been essential under the proposed Constitution if it had included a provision expressly reserving all rights and powers not granted to the federal government. *E.g.,* Samuel Spencer, 4 Elliot's Debates, *supra* note 34, at 163 (North Carolina Ratifying Convention, July 29, 1788); McAffee, *supra* note 2, at 1244 n. 118.

55. Even those who conceded the theoretical possibility of the Articles of Confederation approach insisted on the need for a bill of rights by claiming that the powers granted the national government were not sufficiently narrow and specific to justify reliance on the enumerated powers scheme as the exclusive mechanism for securing freedom of the press and other fundamental rights that the Constitution did not specifically protect. *See, e.g., Letters from a Federal Farmer, in* 2 The Complete Anti-Federalist, *supra* note 50, at 346–47 (Oct. 12, 1787) (inferring extent of national power from broad language of grants of powers, the Necessary and Proper Clause, and the lack of limiting language as to the supremacy of national treaties); Samuel Spencer, 4 Elliot's Debates, *supra* note 34, at 163, 168 (North Carolina Ratifying Convention, July 29, 1788) (arguing for the necessity of a bill of rights and a declaration that all "not decreed to Congress" is reserved to the states so as to establish a clear "fence" or "boundary" by which to measure when the people's rights have been "trampled upon"); *An Old Whig II* (Oct. 17, 1787), *in* 13 Ratification of the Constitution, *supra* note 54, at 399–400 (although reliance on delegated powers could in principle work, the proposed Constitution fails to reserve powers not granted); *id.* at 402–03 (further contending that the Necessary and Proper Clause granted unlimited power to Congress).

56. The Federal Farmer, for example, observed that, in framing the state constitutions, "the people to adopt the shortest way often give general powers, indeed all powers, to the government, in some general words, and then, by a particular enumeration, take back, or rather they say however reserve certain rights as sacred, and which no laws shall be made to violate: hence the idea that all powers are given which are not reserved." *Letters from a Federal Farmer*, in 2 The Complete Anti-Federalist, *supra* note 50, at 324 (Jan. 20, 1788). In fact, as we will see, the Antifederalist objection to the proposed Constitution's omission of an express reservation of all rights and powers not granted to the national government was precisely that it made manifest a design to grant such general legislative power to a consolidated national government. *See infra* notes 96–102 and accompanying text. It is this Antifederalist insistence that a bill of rights was absolutely essential that Professor Sherry rejects in claiming that the framers of the Constitution believed in inherent, implied constitutional rights.

57. *See, e.g., id.* at 248–49 (Oct. 12, 1787) (contending that fundamental rights, especially procedural guarantees such as security against unreasonable searches and seizures and general warrants, the right to cross-examine witnesses, as well as the right to trial by jury in civil cases, are essential because of the powers clearly conceded to Congress).

58. *See* Warren M. Billings, *"That All Men are Born Equally Free and Independent": Virginians and the Origins of the Bill of Rights,* in The Bill of Rights and the States 335 (Patrick Conley & John P. Kaminski, eds., 1992).

59. George Mason, *Objections to the Constitution of Government Formed by the Convention, in* 13 Ratification of the Constitution, *supra* note 37, at 348 (Oct. 7, 1787). Moreover, Mason contended that the common law was subject to congressional abrogation because "it [the common law] stands here upon no other Foundation than it's having been adopted by the respective Acts forming the Constitutions of the several states." *Id.* Contrast Mason's approach with Alexander Hamilton's argument in *Rutgers v. Waddington* that rested on viewing the common law of nations as binding on the states. *See supra* chapter 3, notes 61–63 and accompanying text. *Compare* Alexander Hamilton, The Federalist No. 84, *supra* note 31, at 578 (observing that the New York constitution's adoption of the common law explicitly made the common law subject to legislative power; by contrast, declarations of rights "must be intended as limitations of the power of the government itself").

60. *See, e.g., Essays of Brutus, in* 2 The Complete Anti-Federalist, *supra* note 50, at 365 (Oct. 18, 1787) (with Supremacy Clause and broad national powers, "there is nothing valuable to human nature, nothing dear to freemen, but what is within [the new governent's] power," and neither "the constitution or laws of any state" can "prevent or impede the full and complete assertion of every power given"); *Essays by Cincinnatus, in* The Complete Anti-Federalist, *supra* note 50, at 13 (Nov. 8, 1787) (Supremacy Clause was "anxiously provided" so that state declarations of rights "may not shield [freedom] from the intended destruction in the new constitution"); *Letters of Centinel, in* 2 The Complete Anti-Federalist, *supra* note 50, at 168 (Nov. 30, 1787) (the convention drafted the Supremacy Clause "to level all obstacles to the supremacy of universal sway"); *Essays by a Farmer, in* 5 The Complete Anti-Federalist, *supra* note 50, at 14 (Feb. 15, 1788) (suggesting the people of Maryland would have no recourse to the state constitution's bill of rights in federal court and suggesting that they could not "take advantage of a natural right founded in reason" because under the written Constitution they could not plead "Locke, Sydney, or Montesquieu as authority," nor "the authority of the English judges"); *Aristocratis, in* The Complete Anti-Federalist, *supra* note 50, at 208 (1788) (Supremacy Clause reflects the framers' commitment to "the natural right of rulers 'to bind their subjects in all cases whatsoever'").

61. Chase complained that the Constitution "alters our [state] Constitution and annuls our Bill of Rights in many of its most essential parts." *Notes of Speeches Delivered to the Maryland Ratifying Convention, in* 5 The Complete Anti-Federalist, *supra* note 50, at 80. *See also id.* at 82 (Samuel Chase contrasting proposed Constitution to "our present form of government" in which "the legislature is not supreme but bound by the Constitution"). Some who have referred to the famous Chase/Iredell debate have commented that in 1787 it wasn't clear that Iredell was as yet an Iredellian; but if the ratification debates are taken seriously, it appears that in 1787 Chase was not yet a Chasean.

62. Alexander Hamilton, The Federalist No. 33, *supra* note 31, at 207.

63. *Id.*

64. If the Federalist answer were really based on inherent rights, they should have had a short and easy response to these arguments: the federal powers and the Supremacy Clause are subject to the same inherent and unalterable limits, rooted in natural law, that the state declarations of rights embody. But no such argument was made.

65. *See supra* chapter 4, *passim.*

66. After all, the idea of inherent rights would be equally applicable to constitutions of general or of specific powers; to the extent that the Federalist argument rested on inherent rights, the necessity for a bill of rights would hardly turn on whether it was a federal constitution or not. Yet this was the consistent position of the Federalist defenders of the Constitution. For an especially confusing (and therefore troubling) attempt to deny that the distinction between governments of general versus enumerated powers stood at the center of the debate over a bill of rights and eventuated in the Ninth Amendment, see Suzanna Sherry, *Natural Law in the States*, 61 Cinc. L. Rev. 171, 181–82 (1992).

67. Aristides, *Remarks on the Proposed Plan of Federal Government, in* 15 Ratification of the Constitution, *supra* note 37, at 517, 537 (Jan. 31–Mar. 27, 1788).

68. *Id.* at 537. *See also id.* (contending that if a compact authorizes the sovereign "to do all things it may think necessary and proper, then there is no limitation on its authority," as in a government of general powers, and liberty rests on sound policy, good faith and the virtue of leaders; but when the "compact ascertains and defines the power delegated," as in the case of the proposed Constitution, government cannot exert any power not conferred without "manifest usurpation").

69. Aristides, *Maryland Journal and Baltimore Advertiser,* Mar. 4, 1788, *cited in* Herbert A. Storing, *The Constitution and the Bill of Rights, in* How Does the Constitution Secure Rights? 15, 25 (1985).

70. Herbert A. Storing, *in* 5 The Complete Anti-Federalist, *supra* note 50, at 69 n. 3 (editorial notes).

71. Strangely, despite his accurate and insightful characterization of Aristides' argument in the terms quoted in text (accompanying note 70 *supra*), in a separate work Storing cites the same argument to support the suggestion that an individual rights jurisprudence would likely have developed even without a bill of rights. Storing, *supra* note 69, at 25. But if the argument is exceptional as well as dubious, it is difficult to see why it would foreshadow the development of an unwritten jurisprudence of rights in the absence of a bill of rights.

As additional support for this counter-factual speculation, Storing quotes another Federalist, Theophilus Parsons, as saying that "no power was given to Congress to infringe on any one of the natural rights of the people by this Constitution; and should they attempt it without constitutional authority, the act would be a nullity, and could not be enforced." 2 Elliot's Debates, *supra* note 34, at 162 (Massachusetts Ratifying Convention, Feb. 5, 1788), *quoted in* Storing, *su-*

pra note 69, at 25; *see also* Grey, *supra* note 4, at 163 (quoting Parsons). But Parsons is here taken out of context: in the language preceding the quoted passage, the convention reporter stated that "Mr. Parsons demonstrated the impracticability of a bill, *in a national constitution*, for securing rights, and showed the inutility of the measure" by making the described claims. 2 Elliott's Debates, *supra* note 5, at 162 (emphasis added). Read in context, Parsons' statement is best understood as a reiteration of the Federalist argument that individual rights are adequately protected by the Constitution's limited powers scheme. *See* McAffee, *supra* note 2, at 1269 n. 215 (arguing that "[i]f Parsons were referring to implied limitations, rather than rights reserved by limited grants of power, his argument need not have been limited, as it was, to the prospect, of including a bill of rights 'in a national constitution,' " and observing that Parsons was previously on record as opposing the ratification of a state constitution partly on the basis of its failure to include a bill of rights).

72. Aristides, *Remarks on the Proposed Plan of a Federal Government, in* 15 Ratification of the Constitution, *supra* note 37, at 517, 537.

73. Interestingly, Aristides, Alexander Contee Hanson, also relied upon a secondary defense of the omission of a bill of rights—the argument that a bill of rights was unnecessary under a republican government, given its system of checks and balances and the role of the people in controlling government through elected representatives. *Aristides, supra* note 24, at 4. His argument might have been based on the ability of the people to demand compliance with the natural law.

74. Sherry, *supra* note 1, at 1161–65 (treating ratification debate over omission of a bill of rights and Federalist concerns about the danger posed by inserting one without mentioning the nature of Antifederalist arguments as to the strict necessity for its inclusion); *id.* at 1161 n. 143 (justifying shortshrifting of ratification debates on ground that they "are essentially irrelevant" to the unwritten constitution debate inasmuch as the Antifederalists were "anti-nationalists" and the debate centered on "allocation of power between federal and state governments"; concluding that the "source of limitations on either government was not particularly at issue"). Professor Sherry shares this tendency to basically ignore the underpinnings of Antifederalist arguments in demanding a bill of rights with virtually all modern advocates of the inherent rights understanding of the Ninth Amendment.

75. For the view that inherent rights were a prominent feature of the state constitutions, see *supra* chapter 2; Sherry, *supra* note 66, at 172 (the "founding generation," which spanned the period from 1780 to 1820, "viewed the written constitution as only one of several sources of fundamental law"); accord Grey, *supra* note 4, at 159 (no one articulated the textualist position subsequently defended by Justice Iredell during the period of 1787); David N. Mayer, *The Natural Rights Basis of the Ninth Amendment: A Reply to Professor McAffee*, 16 S. Ill. U. L.J. 313, 326 (1992) (positing that "positivist" reading of the Constitution did not supplant the natural law reading until the nineteenth or twentieth centuries).

76. *See infra* notes 90–102 and accompanying text.

77. *Letters of Agrippa* (Jan. 9, 1788), *in* 4 The Complete Anti-Federalist, *supra* note 50, at 109. The author stated in so many words "that a constitution is not itself a bill of rights." *Id.* This is the opposite view from the one suggesting that rights were presumed to be inherent in constitutions, whether stipulated or not. Strangely enough, at least one modern advocate of the unenumerated rights reading of the Ninth Amendment has acknowledged that this was the Antifederalist position. C. Massey, *supra* note 4, at 58, 87. For the largely undefended position to the contrary, see Sherry, *supra* note 66, at 181–82.

78. *Letters from a Federal Farmer, in* 2 The Complete Anti-Federalist, *supra* note 50, at 246 (Oct. 12, 1787).

79. Saul Cornell, *The Changing Historical Fortunes of the Anti-Federalists*, 84 Nw. U. L. Rev. 39, 70–71 (1989) (suggesting that this Antifederalist natural rights commitment might justify "enlarging the sphere of liberty currently protected by the Ninth Amendment"—without confronting the *constitutional* views proffered by the same authors).

80. Grey, *supra* note 4, at 164 (acknowledging arguments reviewed above with the suggestion only that "*some of* the Antifederalists" adopted the view that legislative power "encompassed everything within the scope of the grant that was not explicitly withheld") (emphasis added). *But see* John P. Kaminski, *Restoring the Declaration of Independence: Natural Rights and the Ninth Amendment, in* The Bill of Rights: A Lively Heritage 141, 145 (Jon Kukla, ed., 1987) (confirming from review of ratification debate materials that "all Antifederalists agreed that natural rights had to be protected by a bill of rights").

81. *E.g.,* Sanford Levinson, *Constitutional Rhetoric and the Ninth Amendment*, 64 Chi.-Kent L. Rev. 131, 140 (1988) (suggesting that Antifederalists feared that failure to include a bill of rights might "serve as a future warrant for the aggrandizement of governmental power," as though concern might have been with a certain "forgetting," or perhaps with the potential for pretextual argument, rather than with the chance of the people in fact granting undue constitutional power—power to invade the fundamental natural rights).

82. *See generally* Mayer, *supra* note 75, at 319–23.

83. *Id.* at 320.

84. *Id.* at 320–21. Mayer's second argument directly referred to the posture of Federalists who acknowledged the Antifederalist position as to the necessity of bills of rights under the state constitutions. But it seems at least as plausible to think that Antifederalists articulated the same view for partisan reasons—so as to underscore the seriousness of the omission of a bill of rights from what they took to be a Constitution analogous with those in the states.

85. While Mason had been concerned at the convention about the reach of the Necessary and Proper Clause, shortly afterwards he presented a parade of horribles that could flow from the clause based on the construction suggested by some supporters of the Constitution at the convention. *George Mason's Objec-*

tions to the Constitution of Government Framed by the Convention, in 13 Ratification of the Constitution, *supra* note 37, at 350 (Oct. 7, 1787).

86. *Id.* at 348.

87. Similarly, the Federal Farmer offered both sorts of arguments on behalf of a bill of rights. A bill of rights did not "create new truths," but served to "establish in the minds of the people truths and principles which they might never otherwise thought of, or soon forgot." *Letters from a Federal Farmer, in* 2 The Complete Anti-Federalist, *supra* note 50, at 324 (Jan. 20, 1788). This appears as an argument that a bill of rights memorializes accepted limits on legitimate government authority; its purpose is to prevent a diminution of rights over time based on "forgetting" of fundamentals by the people—perhaps with the help of self-interested government leaders. Based on this rationale alone, one could conclude that a bill of rights is a useful prudential step, but not a logically or legally necessary one. The Federal Farmer might have stopped there, however, he did not; to the contrary, he contended that in the case of the federal Constitution "the people, by adopting the constitution, give many general undefined powers to congress, in the constitutional exercise of which, the rights in question may be effected." *Id.* at 325. And over the course of several pages of careful analysis he gave a detailed look at the real dangers presented by the Constitution and the absolute necessity for securing fundamental rights, including natural rights, in the positive law of the Constitution. *Id.* at 325–30.

88. Donald S. Lutz, Popular Consent and Popular Control 60 (1980); *accord* C. Massey, *supra* note 4, at 87; note 90 *infra* (views of Nathaniel Gorham); note 96 *infra* (views of Henry Lee and others show this as standard view). Similarly, Professor Philip Hamburger's review of the writing and speeches of the period led him to conclude that natural and customary rights were viewed as "imperfect" rights that did not become constitutional and legal rights until embodied in a written constitution. Philip A. Hamburger, *Natural Rights, Natural Law, and American Constitutions,* 102 Yale L.J. 907, 930–55 (1993).

89. *Cf.* Calder v. Bull, 3 U.S. (Dall.) 3, 394 (1798) ("[w]hen I say that a right is vested in a citizen, I mean that he has the power to do certain actions"). For insight on thinking about rights in the America of this period, see James H. Huston, *The Emergence of the Modern Concept of a Right in America: The Contributions of Michel Villey,* 39 Am. J. Juris. 185, 218–24 (1994).

90. Nathaniel Gorham, 1 Ratification of the Constitution, *supra* note 37, at 335 (Sept. 27, 1787).

91. *Id.* It is no wonder that one of the modern era's preeminent Bill of Rights scholars, Akhil Reed Amar, has concluded that "the federalism roots of the Ninth Amendment, and its links to the unique enumerated power strategy of Article I, help explain why no previous state constitution featured language precisely like the Ninth's—a fact conveniently ignored by most mainstream accounts." A. Amar, *supra* note 22, at 124.

92. *Letters from a Federal Farmer, in* 2 The Complete Anti-Federalist, *supra* note 50, at 231; *see id.* at 231–32, 247–50, 326–28. *Accord The Impartial Ex-*

aminer, 5 *id.* at 175–79. For a more complete summary of the social contract arguments, tracing their themes with conventional elements of social contract political theory, see Thomas B. McAffee, *Prolegomena to a Meaningful Debate of the "Unwritten Constitution" Thesis,* 61 U. Cinc. L. Rev. 107, 143–46 (1992).

93. *See* McAffee, *supra* note 2, at 1276 (suggesting that "[i]f the constitutional and legal status of unenumerated rights were so firmly established, surely the protection offered these rights by the background assumption of implied rights would have been a natural and straightforward response to the argument that a bill of rights was an absolute necessity").

94. The Federalist efforts to distinguish between the federal and state constitutions is developed below. *See infra* notes 96–101 and accompanying text. As to the British constitution, see 3 Elliot's Debates, *supra* note 34, at 246 (George Nicholas, Virginia Ratifying Convention, June 10, 1787) (contrasting British system's presumption that power is in the monarch's hands except as qualified by the enumerated rights of the people with the federal Constitution's proposition that Congress cannot meddle with any right unless the limited grants of authority empower them to do so); McAffee, *supra* note 2, at 1230–32 nn. 58–59; Russell L. Caplan, *The History and Meaning of the Ninth Amendment,* 69 Va. L. Rev. 223, 241 n. 71 (1983).

95. Whereas in the state constitutions, the people had "invested their representatives with every right and authority which they did not in explicit terms reserve," 2 Ratification of the Constitution, *supra* note 37, at 167 (James Wilson, *Speech in the State House Yard,* Oct. 6, 1787), under the federal Constitution "the reverse of the proposition prevails, and everything which is not given, is reserved." *Id.* at 167–68. It cannot be surprising that even advocates of the unenumerated rights reading of the Ninth Amendment accurately perceive that Wilson and other defenders of the Constitution saw the distinction between state constitutions of general powers and their federal constitution of enumerated powers as at the center of their defense. *See* C. Massey, *supra* note 4, at 87. Thus James Wilson complained that the Antifederalists were demanding a few rights to be reserved when, under the proposed Constitution, they held the fee simple. 2 Ratification of the Constitution, *supra* note 37, at 382, 389 (Pennsylvania Ratifying Convention, Nov. 28, 1787). This general premise undergirded the most direct response to the Antifederalist critique: the people had secured their rights by granting only a small portion of their sovereign power to the national government. This is also the standard Federalist argument treated above in text.

In addition, some Federalists also emphasized the theme that the people could curb any abuse of power by exercising their acknowledged right and power to alter and reform their government (including the Constitution itself). Framed this way, the argument from popular sovereignty became a variation on the broader theme of popular control and the dispensability of bills of rights under a republican form of government. On this view, the people can hold government in check by the power of their vote or other collective action. Notice that while these arguments might refer to the rights thought to be held inherently by the people, the allusion is to retained sovereign power and its implications for the possibilities for securing liberty rather than to implied constitutional limits on powers granted to government by the Constitution.

96. Henry Lee, 3 Elliot's Debates, *supra* note 34, at 186 (Virginia Ratifying Convention, June 9, 1788) (whereas under state governments, the people "reserved to themselves certain enumerated rights" and "the rest were vested in their rulers," under the federal Constitution, "the rulers of the people were vested with certain defined powers"); *supra* note 90 (statement by Nathaniel Gorham, before Congress referencing the "unlimited powers" of state governments in the absence of a bill of rights). The slogan that under the proposed Constitution all not granted was reserved thus became the central theme of the Federalist defense of the omission of a bill of rights. *See* McAffee, *supra* note 2, at 1230–32, 1246–47, 1232 n. 62 (citing statements by Washington, Madison, Hamilton, and James Iredell).

97. The debate centered on whether the federal Constitution adequately defined, and limited, the powers. Consider these words of James Wilson: "[W]hen general legislative powers are given, then the people part with their authority and, on the gentleman's principle, retain nothing. But in a government like the proposed one, there can be no necessity for a bill of rights. For, on my principle, the people never part with their power." 2 Ratification of the Constitution, *supra* note 37, at 470 (Dec. 4, 1787). While Wilson would have admitted that, even under the state constitutions, the people retained the sovereign power through constitutional amendment to take back what they had granted, he was equally clear that a grant of general legislative power amounts to at least a temporary grant of all power not expressly reserved in a bill of rights. For additional documentation that in general the Federalists agreed that the people granted all not expressly reserved to governments of general powers, see McAffee, *supra* note 2, at 1230–32, 1250–54, 1269–71 & n. 215. A question never addressed by advocates of the view that the framers of the federal Constitution believed the Constitution implicitly secured inherent constitutional rights is why they would hold such a view of a government of limited powers while opposing such a view with respect to state constitutions governing legislatures with general powers.

98. McAffee, *supra* note 2, at 1229 & n. 52, 1243–44 & n. 115 (collecting sources); Caplan, *supra* note 94, at 235–36 nn. 246–47. If nothing else had, the Antifederalist uniform contention that the omission of Article II was itself proof of the need for a bill of rights belies the modern claim by a noted constitutional law scholar that "the assertion that federalism was meant to protect . . . individual constitutional freedoms . . . has no solid historical or logical basis." A. Amar, *supra* note 22, at 129 (citing Jesse H. Choper, Judicial Review and the Political Process 244 (1980).

99. *See, e.g., Letters of Centinel, in* 2 The Complete Anti-Federalist, *supra* note 50, at 169 (Nov. 30, 1787) ("the omission of such a declaration *now*, when such great devolutions of power are proposed, manifests the design of consolidating the states"); *Essays by Cincinnatus, in* 6 *id.* at 8 (Nov. 1, 1787) (calling Wilson's distinction between the federal and state constitutions a "professional

figment" and arguing that the omission of a provision like Article II of the Articles of Confederation created a presumption "that the framers of the proposed constitution, did not mean to subject it to the same exception"); *Essays by a Farmer, in* 5 *id.* at 15 (Feb. 15, 1788) (notion that all not granted is reserved is "political nonsense" that is "untrue in theory and impossible in practice").

100. Wilson suggested, for example, that the demand for a bill of rights rested on the uncritical application of assumptions underlying other constitutional systems to the federal Constitution. This is why he said that "[a] proposition to adopt a measure that would have supposed that we were throwing into the general government every power not expressly reserved by the people would have been spurned at, in that house [the Philadelphia Convention], with the greatest indignation." 2 Ratification of the Constitution, *supra* note 37, at 387–88 (Pennsylvania Ratifying Convention, Nov. 28, 1787).

101. *E.g.,* 4 Elliot's Debates, *supra* note 34, at 139, 141 (Archibald Maclaine, North Carolina Ratifying Convention, July 28, 1788) ("[t]here is an express clause [the Necessary and Proper Clause] which . . . demonstrates that [Congress is] confined to those powers which are given"); Thomas B. McAffee, *The Bill of Rights, Social Contract Theory, and the Rights "Retained" by the People*, 16 S. Ill. U. L.J. 267, 317 n. 61 (1992).

102. The Federalist argument against the necessity of a bill of rights rested, then, on the efficacy of the limited powers scheme as a device for protecting the people's natural rights. Some commentators, however, have taken particular Federalist statements, such as James Iredell's allusion to the "rights which are not intended to be given up," as referring to implied limitations on the powers granted to the national government. Sherry, *supra* note 1, at 1162–63, *quoting* 4 Elliot's Debates, *supra* note 34, at 167 (James Iredell, July 29, 1788, North Carolina Ratifying Convention); *accord* Grey, *supra* note 4, at 1162–63. It has thus been suggested that the Federalists argued against the necessity of a bill of rights because they "expected these grants of power to be read against the background of accepted assumptions about natural rights." Daniel Farber & Suzanna Sherry, A History of the American Constitution 380–81 (1990). On this view, the scheme of enumerated powers would protect rights because the powers were conceived as "subject to inherent limitations." *Id.*

But this construction of the Federalist argument rests on speculation, fails to account for their emphasis on distinguishing the federal Constitution from the constitutions of the states, and ignores the content of the actual debate as to whether the Constitution adequately defined and limited the powers granted to the national government. *See, e.g.,* Madison, 1 Annals of Cong. col. 438 (J. Gales, ed., 1789) (June 8, 1789) (acknowledging before Congress that the enumerated powers could be construed to permit the invasion of basic rights—an argument resting on a straightforward treatment of the idea of enumerated powers and reserved rights). For additional criticism of the inherent limitations reading of the Federalist argument against the necessity of a bill of rights, see McAffee, *supra* note 2, at 1271 n. 218.

103. *From Roger Sherman,* 14 Ratification of the Constitution, *supra* note 37, at 386, 389.

104. 4 Elliot's Debates, *supra* note 34, at 171 (July 29, 1788); *accord From Roger Sherman,* 14 Ratification of the Constitution, *supra* note 37, at 386, 387 (contending that states have nothing to fear from the federal government because the "distinction between their jurisdictions will be so obvious, that there will be no danger of interference").

105. 2 Ratification of the Constitution, *supra* note 37, at 493, 496 (Pennsylvania Ratifying Convention, Dec. 4, 1787).

106. On natural rights generally, *see supra* notes 82–84 and accompanying text; Eugene Van Loan, *Natural Rights and the Ninth Amendment,* 48 B.U. L. Rev. 1, 10–16 (1968). As to the Necessary and Proper Clause argument, see Gary Lawson & Patricia B. Granger, *The "Proper" Scope of Federal Power: A Jurisdictional Interpretation of the Sweeping Clause,* 43 Duke L.J. 267 (1993); Randy Barnett, *Necessary and Proper,* 44 U.C.L.A. L. Rev. 745, 773–86 (1997). For a discussion of this novel and revisionist reading of the Sweeping Clause, see *supra* chapter 4, Fundamental Rights and the "Proper" Scope of the Necessary and Proper Clause.

107. These points are developed *supra* in chapter 4. *See also* Thomas B. McAffee, *The Federal System as Bill of Rights: Original Understandings, Modern Misreadings,* 43 Vill. L. Rev. 17, 82–92 (1998); Thomas B. McAffee, *A Critical Guide to the Ninth Amendment,* 69 Temple L. Rev. 61, 86–87 (1996).

108. 2 Elliot's Debates, *supra* note 34, at 455 (Dec. 4, 1787). *See also* Edmund Randolph, 3 Elliot's Debates, *supra* note 34, at 569 (Virginia Ratifying Convention, June 15, 1788) (asking as to freedom of the press: "Where is the page where it is restrained?. . . I again ask for the particular clause which gives liberty to destroy the freedom of the press").

109. *See, e.g.,* Lutz, *supra* note 88, at 99.

110. James Wilson, *Speech in the State House Yard* (Oct. 6, 1787), *in* 2 Ratification of the Constitution, *supra* note 37, at 168.

111. *Id.* Wilson proffered that "so popular a privilege" would not be neglected and offered that the citizens of the district should probably seek a fundamental law guarantee. *Id.* If the Federalist argument that the idea of limited powers guaranteed freedom of the press rested on its status as an inherent right, the same implied limitation would logically be read into Congress' legislative power as to the district as well. Wilson's course of reasoning clarifies that his argument from limited powers is to be understood straightforwardly.

112. Van Loan, *supra* note 106, at 10; Jeff Rosen, *Was the Flag Burning Amendment Unconstitutional?,* 100 Yale L.J. 1073, 1077 (1991) (contending that only the "failure to distinguish alienable and inalienable rights" prompted Professor McAffee to conclude that the "Federalists believed 'that even inalienable rights may be granted away'").

113. *See* Barnett, *supra* note 106, at 637.

114. That this argument has remained so popular is itself odd. If the omission of a bill of rights could not pose a threat to some rights because they were considered "inalienable" and therefore "could not, in principle, be surrendered to the state," Hearings Before the Senate Comm. on the Judiciary, 100th Cong., 1st Sess. 3053 (1987) [hereinafter Bork Hearings] (testimony of David A.J. Richards), it would seem curious that these rights might be endangered because they were omitted from an enumeration of rights. The inference that a written constitution lacking a bill of rights might cede up all such rights seems at least as plausible as the inference from an enumeration of rights that those not included are granted away. It is difficult to believe that the Constitution's proponents were arguing otherwise.

115. A number of commentators have placed special weight on the natural rights views of the founding generation as a key to understanding the role of the Ninth Amendment. *See, e.g.*, L. Levy, *supra* note 2, at 274–80; Grey, *supra* note 4, at 165; Sherry, *supra* note 1, at 1164–65; Jordon Paust, *Human Rights and the Ninth Amendment: A New Form of Guarantee*, 60 Cornell L. Rev. 231, 254–60 (1975).

116. *See* 2 Ratification of the Constitution, *supra* note 37, at 388–89, 391 (Pennsylvania Ratifying Convention, Nov. 28, 1787).

117. Elliot's Debates, *supra* note 34, at 445 (Virginia Ratifying Convention, June 14, 1788).

118. 2 Ratification of the Constitution, *supra* note 37, at 470 (Pennsylvania Ratifying Convention, Dec. 4, 1787).

119. *See* Bork Hearings, *supra* note 114, at 3047–48 (quoting 4 Elliot's Debates, *supra* note 34, at 149.)

120. *Id.*

121. Iredell engaged Samuel Spencer, one of the Constitution's opponents, as to how to secure the people's natural rights. Spencer had objected that "[t]here is no declaration of rights, to secure to every member of society those unalienable rights which ought not be given up to any government." 4 Elliot's Debates, *supra* note 34, at 137 (North Carolina Ratifying Convention, July 28, 1788).

122. *Id.* at 149.

123. *Id.* at 171 (North Carolina Ratifying Convention, July 29, 1788).

124. *Id.* at 172 (emphasis added).

125. *Id.* at 149.

126. Bork Hearings, *supra* note 114, at 3057.

127. As one example, the Federal Farmer clearly suggested that people in government would resolve all doubts in their own favor. *Letters from a Federal Farmer, in* 2 The Complete Anti-Federalist, *supra* note 50, at 248 (Oct. 12, 1787).

128. The Federal Farmer contended, for example, that the Supremacy Clause effectively abolished the authority of all "ancient customs, rights, the laws or the constitutions heretofore established." *Id.* at 246–47. He also believed that the supremacy of national treaties and the Necessary and Proper Clause meant that the

federal government was not limited in powers, as had been the federal government under the Articles of Confederation. *See id.*

129. *Id.* at 324 (Jan 20, 1788). While the author seems to contemplate a more explicit version of the Tenth Amendment, and does not necessarily refer to an equivalent of the Ninth Amendment, his formulation powerfully anticipates the shape of the compromise the contending parties eventually reached: a combination of specific limitations and a general reservation of rights as a comprehensive system for securing the rights of the people.

130. The Federal Farmer even appears to provide a critique of Wilson's insistence that the question presented was an either-or question: you must either enumerate powers and reserve rights, or enumerate rights and thereby imply general powers. Suggesting that this "danger" argument rested on "general indefinite propositions without much meaning," he goes on to assert that "the man who first advanced [the "danger" argument] . . . signed the federal constitution, which directly contradicts him." *Id.* at 323. If I understand his argument, it is that Wilson claimed that a bill of rights would be dangerous even though he embraced the Constitution that purported to limit government both by a system of enumerated powers and reserved rights as well as by a partial enumeration of rights.

131. As a voice that refuses to die, the claim that the founders sought to secure natural and inalienable rights in the Ninth Amendment is renewed in a new form with each generation of scholars. *See, e.g.,* Jeff Rosen, *supra* note 112, at 1073, 1074–81; A. Amar, *supra* note 22, at 348 n. 3. *But see* Thomas B. McAffee, *supra* note 101, at 267, 296–99. Even though he adopted a reading of the original meaning of the Ninth Amendment that directly contradicts the work of his former student, Professor Amar suggests that Rosen's treatment effectively underscored the "popular-sovereignty theory" underlying the Ninth Amendment's reference to rights "retained by the people." Considering that Rosen's interpretation would not recognize the power of the people to amend the Constitution in a way that contradicted the "true" understanding of an acknowledged inalienable right, Amar does not explain how his perception of the argument can be reconciled with his own view as to the plenary authority of the people to amend their constitutions.

132. *See, e.g.,* Alexander Hamilton, The Federalist No. 84, *supra* note 31, at 575, 580; 3 Elliot's Debates, *supra* note 34, at 190–91 (Edmund Randolph, Virginia Ratifying Convention, June 9, 1788); James Madison to Thomas Jefferson, *in* 1 Bernard Schwartz, The Bill of Rights: A Documentary History 614, 616 (1971) (specifically noting that "experience proves the inefficacy" of "parchment barriers" in a bill of rights).

133. Indeed, the Federalist argument was described by one Antifederalist as the "argument of danger." 2 Ratification of the Constitution, *supra* note 37, at 425, 427 (Pennsylvania Ratifying Convention, Nov. 30, 1787).

134. *See* McAffee, *supra* note 2, at 1233 (citing James Madison and James Iredell).

135. Ratification of the Constitution, *supra* note 37, at 168 (Oct. 6, 1787).

136. Samuel Holden Parsons to William Cushing, *in* 3 Ratification of the Constitution, *supra* note 37, at 569 (Jan. 11, 1788). One Federalist put the argument bluntly, contending that by a bill of rights "the people have lamented the sovereignty retained by them." *Reply to George Mason's Objections to the Constitution, in* 3 *id.* at 154 (Dec. 26, 1787).

137. James Wilson, 2 Ratification of the Constitution, *supra* note 37, at 391 (Pennsylvania Ratifying Convention, Nov. 28, 1787). Wilson also said that "[i]f we attempt an enumeration, everything that is not enumerated is presumed to be given," with the implication that we have thrown "all implied power into the scale of government." *Id.* at 388. Wilson's argument that the people had to choose between enumerated powers and reserved rights, on the one hand, or enumerated rights as limitations, on the other, is squarely opposed to any general presumption working in favor of inherent rights that would limit the power of government. For a complete analysis of Wilson's argument, see McAffee, *supra* note 2, at 1249–53.

138. James Iredell was especially clear on this point. He contended that a bill of rights under a state constitution "would not only have been proper, but necessary" because "it would have then operated as an exception to the legislative authority in such particulars." 4 Elliot's Debates, *supra* note 34, at 149 (North Carolina Ratifying Convention, July 29, 1788). But under a government of "expressly defined" powers, "a bill of rights is not only unnecessary, but would be absurd and dangerous." *Id.*

139. James Madison, 3 Elliot's Debates, *supra* note 34, at 620 (Virginia Ratifying Convention, June 24, 1788). For a complete treatment of this argument against a bill of rights, see McAffee, *supra* note 2, at 1249–59.

140. The argument of danger seems debatable for at least three reasons. First, it appears as an abstract and awkward theoretical limitation on the people's sovereignty—popular sovereignty that had been so eloquently defended by James Wilson, a major proponent of the danger argument and of the people's sovereignty. On this view, the people cannot choose to preserve their rights both by seeking to limit the delegated powers as well as by creating exceptions to them. Second, this theoretical view appears to rest on the assumption that inclusion of a bill of rights embraces Antifederalist constitutional theory and assumes that we are substituting a bill of rights for enumerated powers. *See* 2 Ratification of the Constitution, *supra* note 37, at 387–88 (Nov. 28, 1787) ("[a] proposition to adopt a measure that would have supposed that we were throwing into the general government every power not expressly reserved by the people would have been spurned at, in that house, with the greatest indignation"). But the Ninth Amendment itself is proof that one may adopt limitations to guard against the abuse of power given without intending to cede all power to the federal government. Third, Wilson's theory fails to take account of the proposed Constitution's stating exceptions to the exercise of power, as in Article I, Section 9, while also ignoring that the proponents of a bill of rights additionally advocated a provision generally reserving

to the people and the states all rights and powers not included among the enumerated powers.

141. 2 Ratification of the Constitution, *supra* note 37, at 387, 388 (Pennsylvania Ratifying Convention, Nov. 28, 1787).

142. For various commentators who make this assumption, see McAffee, *supra* note 2, at 1249 n. 137 (citing authorities).

143. *See supra* note 137 and accompanying text.

144. Ratification of the Constitution, *supra* note 37, at 167 (Oct. 6, 1787) (contending that the people in the states had "invested their representatives with every right and authority which they did not in explicit terms reserve").

145. *Letters from a Federal Farmer, in* 2 The Complete Anti-Federalist, *supra* note 50, at 326 (Jan. 20, 1788).

146. 3 Elliot's Debates, *supra* note 34, at 461 (Virginia Ratifying Convention, June 15, 1788).

147. 12 Ratification of the Constitution, *supra* note 37, at 510 (Oct. 29, 1787).

148. *A Federal Republican, in* 3 The Complete Anti-Federalist, *supra* note 50, at 86 (Oct. 27, 1787) (emphasis omitted).

149. *See supra* chapter 4, notes 96–102 and accompanying text, referring to Edmund Randolph's efforts to justify the inclusion of some exceptions to granted powers.

150. Virginia's first proposed amendment provided: "That each state in the Union shall respectively retain every power, jurisdiction, and right, which is not by this Constitution delegated to the Congress of the United States, or to the departments of the federal government." 2 B. Schwartz, *supra* note 132, at 842.

151. *Id.* at 844. In New York, the ratifiers were especially clear that they were combining the concern of the Antifederalists with having a clause that reserved what had not been granted and the concern of the Federalists that enumerating exceptions to powers granted might raise an inference of extended powers. The New York proposal declared:

[T]hat every Power, Jurisdiction and right, which is not by the said Constitution clearly delegated to the Congress of the United States, or the departments of the Government thereof, remains to the People of the several States, or to their respective State Governments to whom they may have granted the same; And that those Clauses in the said Constitution, which declare, that Congress shall not have or exercise certain Powers by the said Constitution; but such Clauses are to be construed either as exceptions to certain specified Powers, or as inserted merely for greater Caution. (2 B. Schwartz, *supra* note 132, at 911–12)

152. *See, e.g.,* Caplan, *supra* note 94, at 251–52; Leslie B. Dunbar, *James Madison and the Ninth Amendment*, 42 Va. L. Rev. 627, 631–32 (1956); Calvin Massey, *Federalism and Fundamental Rights: The Ninth Amendment*, 38 Hastings L.J. 305, 309–10 (1987).

153. Madison's original draft reads as follows: "The exceptions here or elsewhere in the Constitution, made in favor of particular rights, shall not be construed so to diminish the just importance of other rights retained by the people, or as to enlarge the powers delegated by the constitution; but either as actual limita-

tions of such powers, or as inserted merely for the greater caution." (1 Annals of Cong., *supra* note 102, at col. 452.)

154. Laurence Sager, *You Can Raise the First, Hide behind the Fourth, and Plead the Fifth. But What on Earth Can You Do with the Ninth Amendment?*, 64 Chi.-Kent L. Rev. 239, 246 & n. 14 (1988).

155. *Id.* at 246–47.

156. Virginia Ratifying Convention, *in* 2 B. Schwartz, *supra* note 132, at 844 (June 27, 1788).

157. 2 Ratification of the Constitution, *supra* note 37, at 387, 388 (Pennsylvania Ratifying Convention, Nov. 28, 1787).

158. The Federalist No. 84, *supra* note 31, at 579.

159. 2 B. Schwartz, *supra* note 132, at 844 (June 27, 1788).

160. *Id.*

161. 1 Annals of Cong., *supra* note 102, at col. 435.

162. *See, e.g.,* L. Levy, *supra* note 2, at 272 (suggesting that there was "[n]o precedent" for Madison's proposed Ninth Amendment, and that it "stamped the Bill of Rights with his creativity").

163. 1 Annals of Cong., *supra* note 102, at col. 435.

164. 1 Annals of Cong, *supra* note 102, at col. 439.

165. *See, e.g.,* John Hart Ely, Democracy and Distrust 36 (1980); Norman Redlich, *Are There "Certain Rights . . . Retained By the People"?*, 37 N.Y.U. 787, 805 (1962).

166. 2 B. Schwartz, *supra* note 132, at 825. This statement is important for two reasons. First, Madison here directly asserts that it is not just particular omitted rights of some indefinite number that could be seen as "given" to the national government, but "every thing omitted." Giving up the rights reserved by the enumeration of powers meant converting the national government to one of general powers, subject only to specified exceptions. Second, Madison directly associated this argument with the argument against the necessity for a bill of rights by stating that under the system already proposed "every thing not granted is reserved." *Id.* Little wonder that Madison favored a bill of rights "provided it be so framed as not to imply power not meant to be included in the enumeration." James Madison to Thomas Jefferson, *in* 1 B. Schwartz, *supra* note 132, at 614, 615 (Oct. 17, 1788).

167. *Id.* at 1188.

168. *Id.*

169. *Id.* Leonard Levy underscores that Madison "did not challenge Randolph's assertion that the amendments preceding the Ninth and Tenth did not exhaust the rights of the people that needed protection." L. Levy, *supra* note 2, at 281. But Randolph is at least as clear that these rights were all the powers not given by the Constitution to Congress. This is why Levy is not following the argument when he concludes that Randolph "concluded, illogically, that the course of safety lay not in retaining unenumerated rights but in providing against an extension of the powers of Congress." *Id.*

170. 2 B. Schwartz, *supra* note 132, at 1188.

171. *Id.*

172. *Id.* at 1189, 1190 (letter from Madison to President Washington, Dec. 5, 1789).

173. *Id.* Here, as elsewhere, the common ground between the parties is evident. In *Letters from the Federal Farmer*, the line-drawing metaphor is relied on as it is in Madison's statement: "When we particularly enumerate the powers given, we ought either carefully to enumerate the rights reserved, or be totally silent about them; we must either particularly enumerate both, or else suppose the particular enumeration of the powers given adequately draws the line between them and the rights reserved, particularly to enumerate the former and not the latter. . . . " (2 The Complete Anti-Federalist, *supra* note 50, at 324.) *See generally* McAffee, *supra* note 2, at 1287–93.

6

The Ninth Amendment and Modern Constitutional Theory

It has become popular to think that the Ninth Amendment might contribute to the resolution of fundamental issues concerning the nature of our consitutional order.[1] At one time, the standard reading of the Ninth Amendment saw it as closely related to the concerns of federalism. But those days are far from us. Once defended by a majority of the Supreme Court,[2] the federalism based reading of the amendment was held by only two members of the Supreme Court in dissenting opinions in *Griswold v. Connecticut*.[3] It now seems accurate to say that a majority of commentators have endorsed the reading offered by Justice Goldberg's concurring opinion in *Griswold*.[4] It is now a standard refrain that the Ninth Amendment is "a uniquely central text in any attempt to take seriously the process of *construing* the Constitution."[5]

This book is an attempt to call this new seeming consensus into doubt. I have attempted to show that the Ninth Amendment can only be understood as part of our system of federalism. To understand this, one must see that federalism was viewed as a rights-protective system by those who drafted the federal Constitution.[6] They believed that the scheme of enumerated, and limited, powers that was a key feature of the proposed Constitution would suffice to protect many of the rights cherished by the people. This is why the Articles of Confederation played a central role in the ratification debates; those who brought us the new Constitution believed that it would similarly limit the powers of the national government and protect many of the rights of the people. This is also why the enumerated powers scheme figured so prominently in their debating points: they believed that they had secured most of the rights cherished so dearly by the people by limiting the powers granted to the Congress, and they believed that a review of the proposed Constitution would bear them out.[7]

THE NINTH AND TENTH AMENDMENTS

It is crucial to understanding the Ninth Amendment that one sees its relationship to the Tenth Amendment. Perhaps the most common objection to a federalism based reading of the Ninth Amendment is that it makes it redundant of the Tenth.[8] If this argument ever had any merit, it did not move the committee that drafted Virginia's proposed amendments. That committee, which included James Madison, Patrick Henry, and George Mason, provided that all powers not granted are reserved (our Tenth Amendment), and that the enumeration of limits on government does not imply extended powers (our Ninth Amendment, though worded differently). Why could these distinguished gentlemen have thought both these provisions were necessary?

The Tenth Amendment grew out of fears that the omission of such an explicit guarantee of reserved powers might raise an inference that general legislative powers were intended.[9] It is equivalent, as we have seen, to Article II of the Articles of Confederation.[10] The Ninth Amendment, by contrast, addresses the altogether different threat to the rights protective enumerated powers scheme, a threat which might arise from the enumeration of specific limitations on government powers.[11] In contrast, the Tenth Amendment does not by its terms address any inference which flows, or arguably could flow, from the enumeration of rights in the Constitution.

One loose suggestion is that the Ninth Amendment should be analogized to the Tenth Amendment, into which we have read "tacit postulates of states' rights."[12] Although the words of the Tenth Amendment do not appear to offer anything tangible to the states, some Supreme Court justices have insisted "that the constitutional plan as a whole" contemplates that some exercises of delegated powers "would so erode the meaningful existence of the states as separate polities that such exercises should be deemed unconstitutional."[13] Laurence Tribe appeals for "the same generous spirit of attention to text and structure" on behalf of the Ninth Amendment.[14]

The analogy is intriguing. The Ninth Amendment has become a symbol, whatever the intended meaning of the language, of a constitutional philosophy of inherent and inalienable rights. To the extent that an "unwritten" Constitution is the best interpretation of our "Constitutional plan as a whole,"[15] the Ninth Amendment's reference to the people's retained rights seems on its face like a reasonable textual home for this general view. But the historical evidence shows that the text of the Ninth Amendment was inserted to accomplish a much more restricted purpose—to prevent the evisceration of the enumerated powers scheme. There is no reason to think that the Ninth Amendment's language was intended to strengthen the argument for unwritten affirmative rights derived from constitutional structure.

Why do so many rely upon a text that was not written to address their views? The real case for these modes of interpretation must be made apart from the text and history of the particular provisions relied upon. The Ninth Amendment is a hostage in a broader debate about the relative strengths of various ways of reading the Constitution. It is no more a "central text"[16] in the battle over inherent rights than the text of Tenth Amendment is a proper one for defending a broad structural interpretation in favor of a states' rights reading of the Constitution.

A LIMITED NATIONAL GOVERNMENT AND UNENUMERATED RIGHTS

More recently, it has been suggested that the Tenth Amendment by itself should have been sufficient to foreclose a construction undercutting enumerated powers, even if the logical grounding of such a proposed construction was the enumeration of rights rather than the mere omission of an explicit statement of reserved powers.[17] The suggestion is that the Ninth Amendment remains superfluous if we accept the traditional understanding of its terms. One should remember, however, that proposals for a general reserved powers provision, virtually identical to our Tenth Amendment, were on the table during the entire period of time when the proponents of the Ninth Amendment charged that the enumeration of rights would pose a danger to the enumerated powers scheme. That members of the Virginia delegation still thought there was a need for a provision spelling out the appropriate inferences to be drawn from provisions recognizing limits on powers tells us something important—and it is one key to understanding the Ninth Amendment.

About eighty years after the adoption of the Bill of Rights, the Supreme Court in the *Legal Tender Cases*[18] actually asserted that the provisions in the Bill of Rights showed "[t]hat, in the judgment of those who adopted the Constitution, there were powers created by it, neither expressly specified nor deducible from any one specified power, or ancillary to it alone, but which grew out of the aggregate of powers conferred upon the government, or out of the sovereignty instituted."[19] This is almost exactly the argument that Wilson and others stated might grow out of the inclusion of rights limitations in the Constitution.

Apart from illustrating the role that the Ninth Amendment could have played, this decision is of interest for two reasons. First, it is difficult to see how the language of the Tenth Amendment would foreclose this sort of argument about how to derive granted powers. Second, this argument clearly violates the Virginia proposal that would have prohibited an inference of a new or extended power from the enumeration of limits on the powers granted. If anything, that this argument was made is a kind of vindication of Edmund Randolph's concern that the amendment, after it had been altered in Congress, did not adequately state that limiting provisions raised an inference "against extending the powers of Congress by their own authority."[20] It also stands as a quiet testimony to how little we have learned about the framers' system of enumerated powers and the original meaning of the Ninth Amendment.

THE NINTH AMENDMENT AND NATURAL RIGHTS

It has recently been contended that the Ninth Amendment refers to rights "retained" by the people as a matter of social contract theory. They are natural rights that the people keep as they enter into society.[21] But this ignores the text of the Ninth Amendment, as well as what we know of its history. The Ninth Amendment as a text provides that there are "other" rights, in addition to those "retained" elsewhere in the Bill of Rights. This reference to enumerated rights ties the amendment to the rights already "retained" by the people, and Madison made it clear that bills of rights often "specify positive rights" that are "essential to secure the liberty of the people," even if they are not among the natural and inalienable rights.[22] This tells us that, when referring to rights in the Ninth Amendment as well as the Bill of Rights, Madison was at least referring to more than natural and inalienable rights. More fundamentally, though, the word "retained" permeated the discussions of enumerated powers and reserved rights that were central to the debate over ratification of the Constitution. For example, note that Madison stated the view that "because the powers are enumerated," it followed that "all that are not granted by the constitution are *retained*."[23]

It is now a familiar claim that the Ninth Amendment is the textual embodiment of a view that looks for rights that go beyond the text. This sort of rights foundationalist account of the Constitution has potentially profound implications for our legal order, as well as for the practice of judicial review. The traditional understanding of our constitutional system is the one articulated by Chief Justice Marshall in *Marbury v. Madison*.[24] On this view, the Constitution constitutes the supreme law adopted by the sovereign people—law that controls, and prevails above, the lower-level decisions of their agents.[25] On this view, courts are empowered to override decisions of the legislature precisely because they owe a greater fidelity to the decisions of the true sovereign than to the people's representatives.

A rights foundationalist theory of the Constitution, by contrast, carries the potential to privilege judicial views of natural law or political morality over the views of the people who are the source of judicial office. The Ninth Amendment, in this view, has come to symbolize seeing the Consititution as "a sustained project to define and maintain the proper relationship between government and its citizens,"[26] rather than a binding text adopted by a sovereign people.[27] The goal of this book has been to show that a sovereign people has spoken to these issues and that their purposes did not include giving unrestrained power to the judiciary.

NOTES

1. *E.g.,* Lawrence Sager, *You Can Raise the First, Hide behind the Fourth, and Plead the Fifth. But What on Earth Can You Do with the Ninth Amendment?,* 64 Chi.-Kent L. Rev. 239, 254–61 (1988); Douglas Laycock, *Taking Constitutions Seriously: A Theory of Judicial Review* (Book Review), 59 Tex. L. Rev. 343, 344–56 (1981). The sources cited in chapter 1 raise this issue.

2. United Pub. Workers v. Mitchell, 330 U.S. 75, 95–96 (1947).

3. 381 U.S. 479, 519 (1965) (Black, J., dissenting); *id.* at 529 (Stewart, J., dissenting).

4. *Id.* at 486 (Goldberg, J., concurring). Works endorsing his reading are cited throughout this work. *See also* Thomas B. McAffee, *Prolegomena to a Meaningful Debate of the "Unwritten Constitution" Thesis,* 61 U. Cin. L. Rev. 107, 107 n. 4 (1992); Thomas B. McAffee, *A Critical Guide to the Ninth Amendment,* 69 Temple L. Rev. 61, 63 n. 11 (1996).

5. Laurence H. Tribe, *Contrasting Constitutional Visions: Of Real and Unreal Differences,* 22 Harv. C.R.-C.L. L. Rev. 95, 100 (1987).

6. Professor Akhil Amar concludes, quite correctly, that, in the minds of the framers, "populism and federalism—liberty and localism—work together." Akhil Reed Amar, The Bill of Rights: Creation and Reconstruction 123 (1998).

7. This is why Professor Amar determined that "[t]he Ninth Amendment also sounds in part in federalism," but concluded wistfully that "many constitutional scholars have missed the beat" in failing to see this connection. *Id.*

8. Professor Amar calls this "[t]he obvious counterargument," which he says is "chanted like a mantra by most mainstream scholars." *Id.* The only problem is that "this obvious counterargument is obviously wrong, and no amount of chanting can save it." *Id.*

9. Thomas B. McAffee, *The Original Meaning of the Ninth Amendment,* 90 Colum. L. Rev. 1215, 1307 (1990).

10. *See supra* Chapter 4, at notes 30–35 and accompanying text.

11. Thus Richard Kay correctly observes that "redundancy in legal documents is not particularly odd." Richard S. Kay, *Adherence to the Original Intentions in Constitutional Adjudication: Three Objections and Responses,* 82 Nw. U. L. Rev. 226, 271. Kay goes on to say that "the drafting history of the Bill of Rights explains the presence of both provisions." *Id.*

12. Tribe, *supra* note 5, at 99.

13. *Id.*

14. *Id.* at 100.

15. *See generally* Charles Black, Structure and Relationship in Constitutional Law (1969).

16. Tribe, *supra* note 5, at 100.

17. *See* Michael J. Perry, The Constitution in the Courts 65 (1993).

18. 79 U.S. (12 Wall.) 457 (1870).

19. *Id.* at 535.

20. 2 Bernard Schwartz, The Bill of Rights: A Documentary History 1188 (1971) (letter from Burnley to James Madison, Nov. 28, 1789).

21. *See, e.g.,* David Richards, Foundations of American Constitutionalism 220 (1989); Jeff Rosen, *Was the Flag Burning Amendment Unconstitutional?* 100 Yale L.J. 1073 (1991).

22. 1 Annals of Cong. col. 454 (Joseph Gales ed., 1789).

23. *Id.* at col. 455 (emphasis added).

24. 5 U.S. (1 Cranch) 137 (1803).

25. *Id.* at 177–78. For Alexander Hamilton's classic defense of judicial review, which also emphasizes the Court's role in implementing the people's superior law, see The Federalist No. 78, at 521 (Jacob E. Cooke, ed., 1961).

26. Sager, *supra* note 1, at 263. One can get at least a sense of what is at stake in this sometimes arcane debate by thinking through the implication that a validly adopted, timely constitutional amendment could potentially be held to be unconstitutional under the rights foundationalist account of the Ninth Amendment. *See* Rosen, *supra* note 21. For a critique of the view that the Ninth Amendment enables courts to avoid giving effect to a duly adopted constitutional amendment, see Thomas B. McAffee, *The Bill of Rights, Social Contract Theory, and the Rights "Retained" by the People,* 16 So. Ill. U. L.J. 267, 296–299 (1992).

27. For a critique of this sort of vision of our constitutional order, see Thomas B. McAffee, *Substance above All: The Utopian Vision of Modern Natural Law Constitutionalists,* 4 S. Cal. Interdisc. L.J. 501 (1996).

Bibliography

MONOGRAPHS

Adams, John. *The Works of John Adams*. 10 vols., Charles Adams, ed., Freeport, New York: Books for Libraries Press, 1850–56.

Adams, Wili Paul. *The First Constitutions: Republican Ideology and the Making of the State Constitutions in the Revolutionary Era*. Chapel Hill: University of North Carolina Press, 1980.

Amar, Akhil Reed. *The Bill of Rights: Creation and Reconstruction*. New Haven: Yale University Press, 1998.

The American Constitution: For and Against, J. R. Pole, ed., New York: Hill and Wang, 1987.

American Political Writing During the Founding Era, 1760–1805. Charles Hyneman, and Donald Lutz, eds., Indianapolis: Liberty Press, 1983.

Barnett, Randy E., ed. *The Rights Retained by the People: The History and Meaning of the Ninth Amendment*. Fairfax, Virginia: George Mason University Press, 1989.

Berger, Raoul, *Congress v. The Supreme Court*. Cambridge, Massachusetts: Harvard University Press, 1969.

Berns, Walter, *Taking the Constitution Seriously*. New York: Simon and Schuster, 1987.

The Bill of Rights: A Documentary History. Bernard Schwartz, ed., New York: Chelsea House Publishers, 1971

The Bill of Rights: A Lively Heritage. Jon Kukla, ed., Richmond: Virginia State Library and Archives, 1987.

Black, Charles, *Structure and Relationship in Constitutional Law*. Baton Rouge, Louisiana: Louisiana State University Press, 1969.

Blackstone, William, *Commentaries on the Laws of England*. 4 vols., Chicago: University of Chicago Press, 1979, reprint of 1765–69 ed.

The Complete Anti-Federalist. 7 vols., Herbert J. Storing, ed., Chicago: University of Chicago Press, 1981.

Contexts of the Bill of Rights. Stephen L. Schechter, and Richard Bernstein, eds., Albany, New York: New York State Commission on the Bicentennial of the United States Constitution, 1990.

Corwin, Edward S. *Liberty Against Government*. Baton Rouge, Louisiana State University Press, 1948.

Corwin, Edward S. *Corwin on the Constitution*. Richard Loss, ed., Ithaca: Cornell University Press, 1981.

Creating the Bill of Rights. Helen E. Veit, Kenneth R. Bowling, and Charlene Bangs Bickford, eds., Baltimore: Johns Hopkins University Press, 1991.

Currie, David P. *The Constitution in the Supreme Court: The First Hundred Years* 1789–1888. Chicago: University of Chicago Press, 1985.

The Debates in the Several State Conventions on the Adoption of the Federal Constitution. Jonathan Elliot, ed., Philadelphia: J. B. Lippincott & co., 2d ed., 1836–59.

The Documentary History of the Ratification of the Constitution. Merrill Jensen, ed., Madison, Wisconsin: The State Historical Society of Wisconsin, 1976 .

Dworkin, Ronald. *Freedom's Law: The Moral Reading of the American Constitution*. Cambridge, Mass: Harvard University Press, 1996.

Eidelberg, Paul. *The Philosophy of the American Constitution: A Reinterpretation of the Intentions of the Founding Fathers*. New York: Free Press, 1968.

Ely, John Hart. *Democracy and Distrust*. Cambridge: Harvard University Press, 1980.

Essays on the Constitution of the United States. Paul Leicester Ford, ed., Brooklyn, N.Y., Historical Priting Club, 1892.

Farber, Daniel A. and Sherry, Suzanna. *A History of the American Constitution*. Saint Paul, Minn.: West Publishing Co., 1990.

Farrand, Max. *The Framing of the Constitution of the United* States. New Haven: Yale University Press, 1913.

The Federalist. Jacob Cooke, ed., Middletown, Conn.: Wesleyan University Press, 1961.

The Framing and Ratification of the Constitution. Dennis J. Mahoney, and Leonard W. Levy, eds., New York: Macmillan, 1987.

Goebel, Julius, Jr. *History of the Supreme Court of the United States: Antecedents and Beginnings to 1801*. New York: The Macmillan Company, 1971.

Goldstein, Leslie Friedman. *In Defense of the Text: Democracy and Constitutional Theory*. Savage, Maryland: Rowman & Littlefield Publishers, Inc., 1991.

Gough, J.W. *Fundamental Law in English Constitutional History.* Oxford: Clarendon Press, 1961.

Gunther, Gerald and Kathleen Sullivan, *Constitutional Law.* Westbury, N.Y.: The Foundation Press, 13th ed., 1991.

Hamilton, Alexander. *The Papers of Alexander Hamilton.* 27 vols, New York: Columbia University Press, vols., 1961.

Jaffa, Harry V. *Original Intent and the Framers of the Constitution: A Disputed Question.* Washington, D.C.: Regenery Gateway, 1994.

Jefferson, Thomas. *Notes on the State of Virginia.* William Peden, ed., Chapel Hill: University of North Carolina Press, 1955.

Jefferson, Thomas. *The Writings of Thomas Jefferson.* 20 vols., Washington, D.C.: Library ed., Issued under the auspices of the Thomas Jefferson Memorial Association of the United States, 1903.

John Marshall's Defense of McCulloch v. Maryland. Gerald Gunther, ed., Stanford, Calif.: Stanford University Press, 1969.

Kamman, Michael, *Sovereignty and Liberty.* Madison: University of Wisconsin Press, 1988.

Kelly, Alfred H., Winfred A. Harbison, and Herman Belz, *The American Constitution: Its Origins and Development.* New York: Norton, 1983.

Kmiec, Douglas W. and Stephen B. Presser. *The American Constitutional Order: History, Cases, and Philosophy.* Cincinnati, Ohio: Anderson Publishing Co., 1998.

The Law Practice of Alexander Hamilton. Julius Goebel, ed., New York: Published under the auspices of the William Nelson Cromwell Foundation by Columbia University Press, 1964.

Leder, Lawrence J. *Liberty and Authority: Early American Political Ideology, 1689–1763.* Chicago: Quadrangle Books, 1968.

The Letters and Papers of Edmund Pendleton 1734–1803. Charlottesville, Virginia: Published for the Virginia Historical Society by University Press of Virginia, 1967.

Levy, Leonard, *Original Intent and the Framers' Constitution.* New York: Macmillan, 1988.

Life and Correspondence of James Iredell. 2 vols., Griffth John McRee, ed., New York: P. Smith, 1949.

Lutz, Donald S. *The Origins of American Constitutionalism.* Baton Rouge: Louisiana State University Press, 1988.

Lutz, Donald S. *Popular Consent and Popular Control.* Baton Rouge: Louisiana State University Press, 1980.

Madison, James, *The Writings of James Madison.* 9 vols., Galliard Hunt, ed., New York: G.P. Putnam's Sons, 1900.

Malcolm, Joyce Lee, *To Keep and Bear Arms: The Origins of an Anglo-American Right.* Cambridge, Mass.: Harvard University Press, 1994.

Massey, Calvin R. *Silent Rights: The Ninth Amendment and the Constitution's Unenumerated Rights.* Philadelphia: Temple University Press, 1995.

McDonald, Forrest. *Norvus Ordo Seclorum: The Intellectual Origins of the Constitution.* Lawrence, Kansas: University Press of Kansas, 1985.

McLaughlin, Andrew Cunningham, *The Courts, the Constitution, and Parties: Studies in Constitutional History and Politics.* New York: De Capo Press, 1912.

Morgan, Robert J. *James Madison on the Constitution and the Bill of Rights.* New York: Greenwood Press, 1988.

Paine, Thomas. *The Selected Work of Tom Paine.* Howard Fast, ed., New York: Carlton House, 1945.

Perry, Michael J. *The Constitution in the Courts: Law or Politics?* New York: Oxford University Press, 1994.

Reid, John Philip. *The Concept of Liberty in the Age of the American Revolution.* Chicago: University of Chicago Press, 1988.

Reid, John Philip. *Constitutional History of the American Revolution: The Authority of Rights.* Madison, Wis.: University of Wisconsin Press, 1986.

Richards, David A. J. *Foundations of American Constitutionalism.* New York: Oxford University Press, 1989.

Stoner, James R. *Common Law and Liberal Theory: Coke, Hobbes, and the Origins of American Constitutionalism.* Lawrence, Kan.: University Press of Kansas, 1992.

Thorpe, Francis N. *The Federal and State Constitutions, Colonial Charters, and Other Organic Laws of the State, Territories, and Colonies Now or Heretofore Forming the United States of America.* Washington: Gov't. Print. Off., 1909.

Varnum, James. *The Case, Trevett v. Weeden: On Information and Complaint,* Providence: Printed by John Carter, 1787.

Wood, Gordon S., *The Creation of the American Republic, 1776–87.* Chapel Hill: The University of North Carolina Press, 1969.

Wright, Benjamin F., *American Interpretations of Natural Law: A Study in the History of Political Thought.* New York: Russell & Russell, 1931.

ARTICLES AND BOOK SECTIONS

Adler, Mortimer, *Robert Bork: The Lessons to Be Learned,* 84 Nw. U.L.Rev. 1121 (1990).

Aristocratis, *The Government of Nature Delineated* (1788), in 3 The Complete Anti-Federalist. Herbert J. Storing, ed., 7 vols., Chicago: Univ. of Chicago Press, 1981, p. 196.

Aristides, *Remarks on the Proposed Plan of Federal Government, in* 15 Documentary History of the Ratification of the Constitution. Merrill Jensen, ed., 1976– , p. 517.

Barber, Benajamin, *The Rights of We the People Are All the Rights There Are*, in
    To Secure the Blessings of Liberty. Sarah Baumgartner Thurow, ed.,
    Lanham, Md.: University Press of America, 1988, p. 189.

Barber, Sotirious A., *The Ninth Amendment: Inkblot or Another Hard Nut to
    Crack?* 64 Chi.-Kent L. Rev. 67 (1988).

Barnett, Randy E., *Reconceiving the Ninth Amendment*, 74 Cornell L. Rev. 1
    (1988).

Barnett, Randy E., *Introduction: James Madison's Ninth Amendment*, in The
    Rights Retained by the People: The History and Meaning of the Ninth
    Amendment, Randy E. Barnett, ed., Fairfax, Virginia: George Mason
    University Press, 1989.

Barnett, Randy E., *Unenumerated Constitutional Rights and the Rule of Law*, 14
    Harv. J.L.&Pub. Pol'y 615 (1991).

Barnett, Randy E., *Necessary and Proper*, 44 U.C.L.A. L. Rev. 745 (1997).

Belz, Herman, *Constitutionalism and the American Founding*, in The Framing
    and Ratification of the Constitution. Levy, Leonard W. and Mahoney,
    Dennis T., eds., New York: Macmillan, 1987, p. 333.

Berns, Walter, *The Constitution as Bill of Rights*, in How Does the Constitution
    Secure Rights? Robert A. Goldwin and William A. Schambra, eds.,
    Washington: American Enterprise Institute, 1985, p. 50.

Billings, Warren M., *"That All Men are Born Equally Free and Independent"*:
    Virginians and the Origins of the Bill of Rights, in The Bill of Rights and
    the States. Patrick J. Conley and John P. Kaminski, eds., Madison, Wis.:
    Madison House, 1992, p. 335.

Black, Charles, Jr., *"One Nation Indivisible": Unnamed Human Rights in the
    States,* 66 St. John's L. Rev. 17 (1991).

Brennan, Terry, *Natural Rights and the Constitution: The Original "Original In-
    tent,"* 15 Harv. J.L. & Pub. Pol'y 965 (1992).

Caplan, Russell, *The History and Meaning of the Ninth Amendment*, 69 Va. L.
    Rev. 223, 262 (1983).

Chase, Samuel, *Notes of Speeches Delivered to the Maryland Ratifying Conven-
    tion*, in 5 The Complete Anti-Federalist. Herbert Storing, ed., 7 vols.,
    Chicago: Univ. of Chicago Press, 1981, p. 80.

Cornell, Saul, *The Changing Historical Fortunes of the Anti-Federalists*, 84 Nw.
    U. L. Rev. 39 (1989).

Essays of Brutus, in 2 The Complete Anti-Federalist. 7 vols., Herbert Storing, ed.,
    Chicago: University of Chicago Press, 1981, p. 365.

Essays by Cincinnatus, in 6 The Complete Anti-Federalist. 7 vols., Herbert Stor-
    ing, ed., Chicago: University of Chicago Press, 1981, p. 5.

The Essex Result, in American Political Writing During the Founding Era,
    1760–1805. Hyneman, Charles and Lutz, Donald, eds., Indianapolis:
    Liberty Press, 1983.

Finkelman, Paul, *The First Ten Amendments as a Declaration of Rights*, 16 S.I.U.
    L.J. 351 (1992).

Flaherty, Martin S., *The Most Dangerous Branch*, 105 Yale L.J. 1725 (1996).

Garson, Robert, *The Intellectual Reference of the American Constitution*, in Reflections on the Constitution: The American Constitution After Two Hundred Years. Manchester, New York: Manchester University Press, Maidment, R.A., and Zvesper, John, eds., 1989, p. 1.

Grey, Thomas C., *The Original Understanding and the Unwritten Constitution*, in Toward a More Perfect Union: Six Essays on the Constitution. Neil L. York, ed., Provo, Utah: Brigham Young University, 1988, p. 145.

Hamburger, Philip A., *The Constitution's Accomodation of Social Change*, 88 Mich. L. Rev. 239 (1989).

Hamburger, Philip A., *Natural Rights, Natural Law, and American Constitutions*, 102 Yale L.J. 907 (1993).

Hemmenway, M., *A Sermon, Preached Before His Excellency John Hancock*, in Wood, Gordon S., *The Creation of the American Republic, 1776–87*, at 375. Chapel Hill: The University of North Carolina Press, 1969.

Heyman, Steven J., *Natural Rights, Positivism and the Ninth Amendment: A Response to Professor McAffee*, 16 S. Ill. L.J. 327 (1992).

Huston, James H., *The Emergence of the Modern Concept of a Right in America: The Contributions of Michel Villey*, 39 Am. J. Juris. 185 (1994).

Kaminski, John P., *Restoring the Declaration of Independence: Natural Rights and the Ninth Amendment*, in The Bill of Rights: A Lively Heritage. Jon Kukla, ed., Richmond: Virginia State Library, and Archives, 1987, p. 141.

Katz, Stanley, *The American Constitution: A Revolutionary Interpretation*, in Beyond Confederation: Origins of the Constitution and American National Identity. R. Beeman, S. Botein, and E. Carter, eds., Chapel Hill: Published for the Institute of Early American History and Culture, Williamsburg, Virginia, by the University of North Carolina Press, 1987.

Kramnick, Isaac, *The Discourse of Politics in 1787: The Constitution and Its Critics on Individualism, Community, and the States*, in To Form a More Perfect Union: The Critical Ideas of the Constitution. Herman Belz, Ronald Hoffman and Peter J. Albert, eds., Charlottesville: Published for the United States Capitol Historical Society by the University Press of Virginia, 1992, p. 166.

Laycock, Douglas, *Taking Constitutions Seriously: A Theory of Judicial Review*, 59 Tex. L. Rev. 343 (1981).

Lawson, Gary and Patricia B. Granger, *The "Proper" Scope of Federal Power: A Jurisdictional Reading of the Sweeping Clause*, 43 Duke L.J. 267 (1993).

Lerner, Ralph, *The Constitution of the Thinking Revolutionary*, in Beyond Confederation: Origins of the Constitution and American National Identity. Richard Beeman, Stephen Botein, and Edward C. Carter II, eds. Chapel Hill: Published for the Institute of Early American History and Culture,

Williamsburg, Virginia, by the University of North Carolina Press, 1987.

Letters of Agrippa, in 4 The Complete Anti-Federalist. 7 vols., Herbert Storing, ed., Chicago: Univ. of Chicago Press, 1981, p. 68.

Letters of Centinel, in 2 The Complete Anti-Federalist. 7 vols., Herbert Storing, ed., Chicago: Univ. of Chicagao Press, 1981, p. 168.

Levinson, Sanford, *Constitutional Rhetoric and the Ninth Amendment*, 64 Chi.-Kent L. Rev. 131 (1988).

Levison, Mark and Charles Kramer, *The Bill of Rights as Adjunct to Natural Law*, Det. C.L. Rev. 1267 (1991).

Lofgren, Charles, *The Origins of the Tenth Amendment: History, Sovereignty, and the Problem of Constitutional Intention*, in Government from Reflection and Choice: Constitutional Essays on War, Foreign Relations and Federalism. New York: Oxford University Press, 1986, p. 108.

Macedo, Stephen, *Morality and the Constitution: Toward a Synthesis for "Earthbound" Interpreters*, 61 U. Cin. L. Rev. 29 (1992).

Mason, George, *Objections to the Constitution of Government Formed by the Convention*, in 2 The Complete Anti-Federalist. Herbert J. Storing, ed., Chicago: Univ. of Chicago Press, 1981, p. 11.

Mason, George, *Objections to the Constitution of Government Formed by the Convention*, in 13 The Documentary History of the Ratification of the Constitution. John P. Kaminski and Gaspare J. Saladino, eds., Madison: State Historical Society of Wisconsin, 1981.

Massey, Calvin R., *The Anti-Federalist Ninth Amendment and its Implications for State Constitutional Law*, 1990 Wis. L. Rev. 1229.

Mayer, David N., *The Natural Rights Basis of the Ninth Amendment: A Reply to Professor McAffee*, 16 S. Ill. U.L.J. 313 (1992).

Mayer, David N., *Justice Clarence Thomas and the Supreme Court*'s *Rediscovery of the Tenth Amendment*, 25 Cap. U.L. Rev. 339 (1996).

McAffee, Thomas B., *The Bill of Rights, Social Contract Theory, and the Rights "Retained" by the People*, 16 S. Ill. U.L.J. 267 (1992).

McAffee, Thomas B., *A Critical Guide to the Ninth Amendment*, 69 Temple L. Rev. 61 (1996).

McAffee, Thomas B., *The Federal System as Bill of Rights: Original Understandings, Modern Misreadings*, 43 Vill. L. Rev. 17 (1998).

McAffee, Thomas B., *The Original Meaning of the Ninth Amendment*, 90 Col. L. Rev. 1215 (1990).

McAffee, Thomas B., *Prolegomena to a Meaningful Debate of the Unwritten Constitution Thesis*, 61 U. Cinc. L. Rev. 107 (1993).

McAffee, Thomas B., *The Role of Legal Scholars in the Confirmation Hearings for Supreme Court Nominees—Some Reflections*, 1 St. John's Legal Comm. 211 (1991).

McAffee, Thomas B., *Substance Above All: The Utopian Vision of Modern Natural Law Constitutionalists*, 4 So. Cal. Interdisciplinary L.J. 501 (1996).

Michael, Helen K., *The Role of Natural Law in Early American Constitutionalism: Did the Founders Contemplate Judicial Enforcement of "Unwritten" Individual Rights?* 69 N.C.L. Rev. 421 (1991).

Moore, Michael S., *Do We Have an Unwritten Constitution?* 63 S. Cal. L. Rev. 107 (1989).

Palmer, Robert C., *Liberties as Constitutional Provisions 1776–1791*, in Constitution and Rights in the Early American Republic. Williamsburg, Va.: Institute of Bill of Rights Law, Marshall-Wythe School of Law, 1987.

Paust, Jordan, *Human Rights and the Ninth Amendment: A New Form of Guarantee*, 60 Cornell L. Rev. 231 (1975).

Peterson, Merrill, *Thomas Jefferson, the Founders, and Constitutional Change*, in The American Founding: Essays on the Formation of the Constitution. J. Barlow, L. Levy, and K. Masugi, eds. 1988, p. 276.

Philodemus [Thomas Tucker], *Conciliatory Hints, Attempting, by a Fair State of Matters, to Remove Party Prejudice*, in American Political Writing During the Founding Era 1760–1805. 2 vols., Charles Hyneman, and Donald Lutz, Indianapolis: Liberty Press, 1983, p. 606.

Randolph, Edmund, *Essay on the Revolutionary History of Virginia*, in Schwartz, Bernard, The Bill of Rights: A Documentary History. New York: Chelsea House Publishers, 1971, p. 249.

Redlich, Norman G., *Are There "Certain Rights . . . Retained by the People?"* 37 N.Y.U. L. Rev. 787(1962).

Rosen, Jeff, *Was the Flag Burning Amendment Unconstitutional?* 100 Yale L.J. 1073 (1991).

Rush, Benjamin, *Defense of the Confederation*, in Wood, Gordon S., *The Creation of the American Republic, 1776–87*. Chapel Hill: The University of North Carolina Press, 1969, p. 174.

Sager, Lawrence G., *You Can Raise the First, Hide Behind the Fourth, and Plead the Fifth. But What on Earth Can You Do with the Ninth Amendment?* 64 Chi.-Kent L. Rev. 239 (1988).

Sherman, Robert, *The Letters of a Countryman*, in Essays on the Constitution, Paul Ford, ed., Brooklyn, N.Y.: Historical Printing Club, 1892, p. 222.

Sherry, Suzanna, *The Founders' Unwritten Constitution*, 54 U. Chi. L. Rev. 1127 (1987).

Sherry, Suzanna, *Natural Law in the States*, 61 U. Cin. L. Rev. 171 (1992).

Stourzh, Gerald, *Fundamental Laws and Individual Rights in the 18th Century Constitution*, in The American Founding: Essays on the Formation of the Constitution. J. Barlow, L. Levy, and K. Masugi, eds., New York: Greenwood Press, 1988, p. 159.

Tribe, Laurence H., *Contrasting Constitutional Visions: Of Real and Unreal Differences*, 22 Harv. C.R.-C.L. L. Rev. 95 (1987).

Van Alstyne, William, *Notes on a Bicentennial Constitution: Antinomial Choices and the Role of the Supreme Court (Part 2)*, 72 Iowa L. Rev. 1281 (1987).

Van Loan, Eugene, *Natural Rights and the Ninth Amendment*, 48 B.U.L. Rev. 1 (1968).

Vieira, Edwin, Jr., *Rights and the United States Constitution: The Declension from Natural Law to Legal Positivism*, 12 Geo. L. Rev. 1447 (1979).

West, Thomas G., *The Rule of Law in the Federalist*, in Saving the Revolution: The Federalist Papers and the American Founding. Charles Kesler, ed., New York: Free Press, 1987, p. 150.

West, Thomas G., *The Classical Spirit of the Founding*, in The American Founding: Essays on the Formation of the Constitution. J. Barlow, L. Levy & K. Masugi, eds., New York: Greenwood Press, 1988, p. 30.

Wilmarth, Arthur E., *The Original Purpose of the Bill of Rights: James Madison and the Founders' Search for a Workable Balance Between Federal and State Power*, 26 Am. Crim. L. Rev. 1261 (1989).

Wood, Gordon S., *Democracy and the Constitution,* in How Democratic Is the Constitution? Robert A. Goldwin and William A. Schambra, eds., Washington, D.C.: American Enterprise Institute for Public Policy Research, 1980, p. 1.

Wood, Gordon S., *Interests and Disinteredness*, in Beyond Confederation: Origins of the Constitution and American National Identity. Richard Beeman, Stephen Botein, and Edward C. Carter II, eds. Chapel Hill: Published for the Institute of Early American History and Culture, Williamsburg, Virginia, by the University of North Carolina Press, 1987.

Wood, Gordon S., *The Political Ideology of the Founders*, in Toward a More Perfect Union. Neil York, ed., Provo, Utah: Brigham Young Univ., 1988, at p. 7.

Index

Adams, John, 35 n.71
Adams, Willi Paul, 29 n.18, 30
  nn.27–28, 33 n.48
Address by Sydney, 44 nn.140,
  142–45
Amar, Akhil Reed, 5 n.13, 31 n.34, 36
  n.74, 148 nn.22–23, 158 n.91, 164
  n.131, 173 nn.6–8
Anti-monopoly guarantee, proposal
  for, 99–100
Aristides, 130–31, 155–56 nn.67–73
Articles of Confederation, 88

Barber, Sotirious A., 5 n.6
Barnett, Randy E., 5 nn.5, 14, 103–04
  nn.9, 14–16, Ninth Amendment,
  84–85, 102 n.3, 103–04 nn.9,
  14–15
Bayard v. Singleton, 58, 77 n.115
Belz, Herman, 7 n.29, 28 nn.2, 5–6,
  29 n.14, 30 nn.19, 21–22, 42
  nn.117–118, 44 n.146
Berns, Walter, 6 n.23

Billings, Warren, 18, 34 nn.56, 58,
  154 n.58
bills of attainder, 18, 34 n.54, 46
Bills of Rights, 9, 11–13, 15–24,
  26–27, 119–20; argued to be a
  threat to rights, 94–96, 140–42;
  debate over omission from proposed constitution, 119–20; federal system conceived of as
  equivalent to, 83–85; omission
  from early state constitutions,
  26–27, ratification context as a
  factor in debate, 120; skeptics of
  the value of, 120. *See also* Declarations of rights
Black, Charles, 174 n.15
Blackstone, William, 3–4, 7 n.27, 23,
  40 n.103, 62
Bork, Robert, 2, 5 nn.8–10
Brennan, Terry, 5 n.13
Burnley, Hardin: Ninth and Tenth
  Amendments as equivalents, 88;
  and Virginia debate on Ninth

Amendment, 88, 145–47, 167–68
nn.167–73

Caplan, Russell L., 116–17
nn.146–48, 154, 159–60 nn.94, 98,
166 n.152
Cautionary provisions, 101–02
Chase/Iredell debate, 1, 4 n.3
Checks and balances, 47–48, 50, 66
n.5, 69 n.24
Civil Juries, 46, 97–98, 113–14
nn.112–21
Coke, Edward, 3–4, 6 nn.24, 26,
50–56, 61–66, 151n.47
Collective rights, 14–15, 19–20,
23–24, 27, 31 n.29, 35 n.69, 40
nn.102–04, 42 nn.112–14, 44
n.146, 83–84, 86–88, 102 n.2,
105–06 nn.22, 29, 34–35
Commonwealth v. Caton, 58–60
Confederation period, 45–81
Conscientious objectors, 99
Consent of the governed, 12–15
Constitutions, state, 9–44; conceived
during confederation period,
46–50; written, 10–12
Corwin, Edward S., 4 n.1, 25, 43
nn.122–23, 148 n.8; two theories
of judicial review, 61–62, 79
nn.137–38, 140–41, 81 n.166
Currie, David P., 4 n.3

Declarations of rights, 15–24, peo-
ple's power to amend, 19–23
Declaratory provisions, 84–85, 88,
103 n.9, 105 nn.18–19, 107 n.44
Delaware constitution, people's
power to amend, 21
Dr. Bonham's Case, 4, 6 n.24, 50–56
Dworkin, Ronald, 4 n.2

Efficiency: competed with need to
protect rights, 96–97; omission of

prohibition on standing armies,
98–99. *See also* Energy
Ely, John Hart, 145, 167 n.165
Energy: competed with need to pro-
tect rights, 96–97
Essential principles, original Bill of
Rights to include only, 97–100
Essex Result, The, 28 n.4, 40 nn.101,
103–04
Executive power, distrust of 14, 25
Ex post facto laws, 18, 34 n.53, 46

Farber, Daniel & Sherry, Suzanna, 27
n.1
Federal powers, limited as a key to
lack of need for a bill of rights,
83–85, 92–94
Frames of government, "form" of 9,
14–15, 19, 21–22
Fundamental law, 4, 6 n.26, 19, 35
n.67

General legislative powers: states as
governments of, 64, 84, 89–90,
94–95, 104 n.11, 109 n.57
Goebel, Julius, Jr., 6, nn.24–26, 28
nn.2, 3, 36 n.73, 42–44 nn.116,
127, 129, 131–35
Goldstein, Leslie Friedman, 29–30
nn.18–19, 36 n.74, 66 n.5, 68–69
nn.22, 24
Grey, Thomas C., 3, 5–7 nn.7, 14,
19–21, 27, 68–69 nn.21, 27, 72
nn.51, 54–55, 75–76 nn.83, 93,
79–80 nn.145, 157
Griswold v. Connecticut, 84, 103
nn.7–9, 169, 173 nn.3–4

Hamburger, Philip, 6 n. 22, 39
nn.96–99, 40 n. 67, 41 nn.105–06
Hamilton, Alexander, 31 n.29, 52–54,
73–74 nn.58–74, 79 n.143, 115
n.134, 117 n.156, 130, 155
nn.62–63, 174 n.25, equates liberty

with freedom to choose representatives, 31 n.29
Henry, Patrick, 18, 33 n.52, 87, 96
Holmes v. Walton, 57–58, 76–77 nn.104–14
Hyneman, Charles, & Lutz, Donald S., 28 n.4, 31–32 nn.36, 43, 40 nn.101, 103–04

Inalienable rights, 23–24, 28 n.4, 33 n.45, 137–40; subject to qualification, 23
Inherent rights, 3–4, 15–16, 19, 51–58, 61–65, 73–75 nn.67–70, 74, 82, 78–81 nn.133, 143, 145, 157, 163, 119
Iredell, James, 63–65, 79–80 nn.146–59, 138, 163 nn.121–25

Jaffa, Harry V., 4 n.5, 5 n.13
Jay, John, 47, 68 n.15
Jefferson, Thomas, 33 n.45, 47, 68 n.19; anti-monopoly guarantee, 99, 116 nn.141, 143
Judges: people's right between order and liberty, 13–15, 23, 30–31 nn.23, 36
Judicial independence, 25, legislative interference in early republic, 25–26
Judicial review: during confederation period, 51; need for power recognized, 50–51, perception as oligarchy, 50, and republican government, 61–62
Jury trial, right to 18, 34 nn.53–54, 54–56, 74–76 nn.75–98, 113–14 nn.115–21

Katz, Stanely, 28 n.3
Kay, Richard S., 174 n.11
King, as a threat to rights, 17
Kmiec, Douglas W. & Presser, Stephen B., 5 n.7, 7 nn.26–27

Lawson, Gary & Granger, Patricia B., 103 n.5, 109–13 nn.52–56, 58–62, 64, 66, 68, 70, 77–78, 87, 92, 104, 113
Law, unwritten, 11, 50–58, 62–66, 68 n.21, 74–75 nn.74, 82, 79 nn.143, 145
Laycock, Douglas: Ninth Amendment, 84, 104 n.13, 173 n.1
Legislative discretion: invoked to justify omission of rights, 99
Legislative supremacy: doctrine of opposed judicial review, 50; lack of safeguard against abuse, 26
Legislatures: boundaries to legislative power, 47, lack of safeguards, 26; legislative excesses, 46–48; and popular right to control and to govern, 14–15; power to control other branches, 13–14; sovereignty, 14–15; in states, 14–15, 17; tension between their power and popular rights, 10, 13–14, 17–18; virtually unlimited power, 25
Letters of Agrippa, 38 n.91
Letters from a Federal Farmer, 29 n.10, 35 n.67, 38 n.91
Levinson, Sanford, 5 n.9, 102 n.3
Levison, Mark & Kramer, Charles, 6 n.18
Levy, Leonard, 98, 102 n.5, 114 n.126, 147 n.2, 163 n.115, 167 nn.162, 169
Liberty, political liberty equated with self-government, 17, 31 n.29; popular control as key to obtaining, 14–15, 17–18; trust in representative government, 26–27
Locke, John, 3–4, 11, 19
Lofgren, Charles, 107 n.44
Lutz, Donald S., 21–22, 27 n.1, 33, n.49, 36–38, nn.75, 84–86, 88–89, 40, n.100, 42–43 nn.112, 124–26, 128, 66 nn.2–4, 158 n.88

Macedo, Stephen, 5 n.6, 6 n.21
Madison, James, 29 n.13, 32 n.43, 35 n.67, 38 n.92, 143–47; and Congress' draft of Ninth Amendment, 146–47, 168 nn.172–73; and "moderate" revision of constitution, 99, 115 n.136; and national veto of state laws, 49; and Necessary and Proper Clause, 93–94; and stronger federal government, 47–50; and Tenth Amendment, 88
Mason, George, 61, 79 n.139; and natural law as basis for judicial review, 61, 79 n.139; supremacy clause as basis for need of bill of rights, 129–30
Massachusetts' constitution: provided for separation of powers 35 n.70; provision for amendment, 38 n.90; property rights under, 40 n.102
Massey, Calvin R., 6–7 nn.15, 26, 147 n.4, 149 nn.32–33, 151 nn.46, 49, 157 n.77; and state power to create rights, 100–02, 116–17 nn.144–45, 149–52
McDonald, Forrest, 31 nn.29, 31, 40–41, nn.102, 105; account of reaction to *Rutgers v. Waddington* decision, 60–61, 78 nn.132–34
McLaughlin, Andrew, 36 n.76
Monopolies, provisions against, 99–100, 116 nn.140–43
Moore, Michael S., 4 n.2
Morris, Gouverneur, 47, on impact of *Holmes* case, 58, 77 nn.112–14

Natural law, 2–3, 11–12
Natural rights, 9, 15–19, 119–20
Necessary and Proper Clause, 89–100, 108–16 nn.49–143
Ninth Amendment, 1, 4–5 nn.5–7, 84–85, 92–96, 101–02, 102 n.3, 169–73, and natural law, 2–3, 84–85, 103–05 nn.6–16

North Carolina Constitution, 36 n.77, 39 n.95

Omission of bills or declarations of rights early state constitutions, 26–27

Palmer, Robert C., 14, 30 n 26, 31 n. 32, 35 nn.68–69, 72, 40–42 nn.102–03, 108–09, 112–17
People: as all-powerful, 14–15, as committed to freedom, 14; and power to alter and reform government, 13–14, 21; and power to establish rights, 17
Pendleton, Edmund, 3, 6 n.17; and *Commonwealth v. Caton*, 58–60
Pennsylvania constitution, 14–15, 30 nn.24–25, 34–39 nn.64, 72, 77, 82, 90, 95
Perry, Michael J., 174 n.17
Popular control, 15, 26–27, tendency to assume that it was enough, 15, 17
Popular conventions, 13–14, 50–51, 62
Popular rights, 83, 102 nn.1–2
Popular sovereignty, 2, 4, 12–15, 23, 107 nn.38–40, 120–21; and assumption that people were committed to freedom, 14–15, 34 n.59, 45, 49; and debate over omission of a Bill of Rights, 127–37; as key to effectively limiting government, 34 n.59
Popular tyranny, 48
Powers enlarged, Ninth Amendment to prevent, 101–02, 117 nn.155–58
Powers reserved, as means of securing rights, 84–86, 88, 104 nn.12–15, 106–08 nn.28–29, 45–48

Randolph, Edmund, 33 n.52, 95–96, 112 nn.97–99, 145–47, 167–68 nn.167–73
Reform: need for constitutional reform, 26, 47–49
Reid, John Philip, 28 n.9, 114 n.122
Republican theory, 17
Reverse preemption, 100–01
Richards, David A. J., 138–39, 163–64 nn.119–31, 174 n.21
Rights, individual, 19–23, 51; and retained powers as closely related, 102 nn.3–4
Rosen, Jeff, 162 n.112, 164 n.131, 174 n.21
Rutgers v. Waddington, 52–54, 73–74 nn.58–74

Sager, Lawrence G., 6 n.16, 173–74 nn.1, 26
Schwartz, Bernard, 33 n.52, 42 n.117, 106 n.36, 117 n.157, 174 n.20
Scott, Austin, 57
Separation of powers, 25–26, 46
Sherry, Suzanna, 5–6 nn.7, 14, 21, 19–23, 32 n.40, 34 nn.53–54, 60–63, 65, 37 n.83, 44 nn.136–37, 51–54, 57–60, 63, 71–79 nn.40, 42, 54–57, 62–64, 66, 70–71, 74, 77–78, 81–82, 89, 93, 103, 106–08, 111, 118, 120–25, 133, 145, 150, 147–49 nn.1, 12–13, 15–21, 26–28, 30–31, 34, 155–56 nn.66, 74–75
Slavery, 3, 6 n.19
Snowiss, Sylvia, 7 n.27
Social Contract, 1, 18–19
Sovereignty, parliamentary (*see also* Popular sovereignty): 11
Standing armies, 98–99, 114–15 nn.127–35
State-created rights: Ninth Amendment as arguable source of, 100–02, 116–17 nn.144–58

Stoner, James R., 6 n.26
Stourzh, Gerald, 35 n.67, 65–66, 66 n.5, 80 nn.161–63, 164–65, 120–21, 147–48 nn.5–7, 9
Sweeping clause: as a source of rights, 89–94, 96–100,108–09 nn.49–57
Symsbury Case, 56–57, 76 nn.99–102

Tenth Amendment, 85–88, 170–71, 174 n.11
Trevett v. Weeden, 54–56, 74 n.75
Tribe, Laurence H., 173–74 nn.5, 12–14, 16
Tucker, Thomas (Philodemus), 32 n.43

Unenumerated rights, 1, 4 n.2, 87, 95, 98, 101–02
Uniformity, lack of: right to civil juries, 97–98

Van Alstyne, William, 29 n.12
Varnum, James, 54–56, 74–76 nn.75–76, 79–80, 84, 86, 88–89, 91–92, 94–96
Veto, executive power, 48
Vieira, Jr., Edwin, 5 n.6
Virginia bill (or declaration) of rights, 30 nn.23–24, 39 n.57, 51–52 nn.106, 110–11
Virginia state constitution: asserted all power is derived from people, 30 n.23, magistrates as people's servants, 30 n.24; provided for separation of powers, 25

Washington, George, 47
West, Thomas B., 7 n.29
Wilson, James, 107 n.38, 109 n.57, 111–14 nn.80, 82, 93, 95, 105, 119–20, 126–27, 150 nn.37–41, 160–63 nn.97, 100, 110–111, 116, 118, 165–66 nn.137, 140–42, 144;

argument for a provision like the
  Ninth Amendment, 94
Wood, Gordon S., 4, 7 nn.28–29, 29
  n.17, 31–32, nn.33, 35, 38, 43, 34
  n.66, 40 n.104, 42–43 nn.116, 122,
45, 66–72 nn.1, 5–7, 11–12, 14,
  17–18, 22–23, 25, 27, 29–30,
  36–38, 40, 43–46, 48–50, 74
  nn.70, 73, 81 n.163, 126
Written constitution, 4, 9–12

About the Author

THOMAS B. MCAFFEE is Professor of Law at the University of Nevada, Las Vegas. He has also taught at the Southern Illinois University Law School and at the University of Utah College of Law. He has published widely on topics related to American constitutional law, theory, and history.

CPSIA information can be obtained at www.ICGtesting.com
Printed in the USA
LVOW100500151112

307432LV00005B/224/P

9 780313 315077